GW00361714

Valerie Swane's
ROSE

BOOK

Valerie Swane's

ROSE
BOOK

Angus&Robertson
An imprint of HarperCollins*Publishers*

An Angus & Robertson Publication

Angus&Robertson, an imprint of
HarperCollins*Publishers*
25 Ryde Road, Pymble, Sydney NSW 2073, Australia
31 View Road, Glenfield, Auckland 10, New Zealand
77–85 Fulham Palace Road, London W6 8JB, United Kingdom
10 East 53rd Street, New York NY 10022, USA

First published in Australia in 1994

Copyright © The Estate of Valerie Swane 1994

This book is copyright.
Apart from any fair dealing for the purposes of private study,
research, criticism or review, as permitted under the Copyright Act,
no part may be reproduced by any process without written
permission. Inquiries should be addressed to the publishers.

National Library of Australia
Cataloguing-in-Publication data:
Swane, Valerie, 1926–92.
    Valerie Swane's rose book.

    Rev. ed.
    Includes index.
    ISBN 0 207 17916 6.

    1. Roses. I. Swane, Valerie, 1926–92. Australian rose book. II. Title.
    III. Title : Rose book. IV. Title : Australian rose book.
635.933372

Cover photograph by Valerie Swane
Typeset by Midland Typesetters, Maryborough, Vic.
Printed by Griffin Press, Adelaide

9 8 7 6 5 4 3 2 1
97 96 95 94

CONTENTS

INTRODUCTION

Modern roses are truly international. Since Plant Patents were introduced in the United States in 1930 and similar legislation followed in other countries, plant hybridists — the creators of new roses — have been assured of protection for their 'inventions' in much the same way as an author receives a return on his or her books. Roses are created for the *world* market and sold worldwide which means they are adaptable to a wide range of climatic conditions, not just those of their country of origin. They may be hybridised in the United States, United Kingdom, France, Germany, Holland, Denmark and New Zealand but they are grown and sold under licence in every country where the climate is suitable. Indeed, before being marketed to the world they are tested for at least three years in a range of climates to determine their adaptability and performance.

Breeding roses is a highly specialised business and perfecting a new variety can take up to ten years, including time spent testing the new variety in a variety of climates. Many of the world's rose breeders are the third and fourth generation of their family to follow this profession.

Their search for the perfect rose is neverending. Of course a beautiful bloom, especially a scented one is an important aim. Other aims are new and different colours, novel flower forms, longer flowering periods, greater resistance to fungal diseases, improved cut flower life, tidier bushes that retain their leaves longer and the creation of roses which are suitable for even more purposes in the garden, from ground covers to shrubs.

Every year roses *do* improve. My father's roses were much less healthy than those my brother Geoff now grows. Improved vigour, larger and more numerous blooms, more roses with scent, richer colours, longer flowering periods, better stem length and greater disease resistance are attributes of modern roses which rescue gardeners from the stringent maintenance roses used to need.

My nurserymen family has been growing roses for seventy four years, registering the changes by introducing new roses with unfamiliar names and allowing old, well-loved roses to disappear because they did not measure up to the new ones.

Roses deserve to be widely grown on the grounds of their beauty, utility and climatic adaptability. They have changed for the better in the last fifty years, particularly the past ten, making gardening with roses much easier.

I am indebted to Jennifer Rowe, formerly of Angus & Robertson Publishers, who planned this book. I am also grateful to my brother Geoff, Mrs Bette Lloyd, John Teulon, my brother Ben, my niece Elizabeth Swane and Jack Christensen, formerly of Armstrong's Nurseries, California, for their advice; to Dr Peter Valder for advice on species groups; and to Greg Lamont for advice on cut flower varieties.

Facts were checked in the following absorbing books: *The Book of the Rose*, by Michael Gibson, Macdonald and Jane's Publishing Group Limited, London, 1981; *The Complete Book of Roses* by Gerd Krussmann, Timber Press, Portland, Oregon, USA, 1981; *The Rose*, consultants Janet Browne and Stuart Mechlin, Marshall Cavendish, London, 1979; *Look to the Rose* by Sam McGredy, Dent, Melbourne and Sydney, 1981; *Modern Roses 9*, compiled and published by the American Rose Society, Shreveport, Louisiana, 1986; *Roses* by Roger Phillips and Martyn Rix, Random House, New York, 1988.

Roses are now being used differently. Some replace shrubs, others are ground covers, colour makers, etc. They are individuals and must be seen and treated as such if they are to be grown for pleasure and without fuss.

The object of this book is to provide a guide to roses for a variety of climates and uses so that the joy of growing roses can be shared by even more people.

VALERIE SWANE

THE STORY OF THE ROSE

Roses have a high reputation as dependable garden plants. But they have a greater meaning than that. They have captivated us from the earliest times and are our most enduring symbol for both divine and human attributes.

The innumerable legends from classical to medieval times that involve the rose and the loveliness of the flower itself, have established the mystique which surrounds this much-loved flower.

Hybridisation has created today's handsome roses which are more free-flowering, vigorous and less disease-prone than their forebears. Twentieth-century colour printing has communicated these developments to the world, recruiting new devotees of the rose at an unprecedented pace. Proof is seen in the quantity produced annually. One American company alone grows over 8 million bushes a year!

Acquiring a rose is a complex and often emotional experience. Beauty is, of course, important, but the questions of choice and what constitutes good value are often entangled with the rose's association with some historical or mythical event. There is usually an association between ourselves, the rose, and a person, place or time, which stirs our memories.

History

Roses are entwined throughout history in myth, religion, art and medicine. The flower is the most popular decorative motif in history.

Roses are thought to have originated 12 to 15 million years ago and were first cultivated by the Chinese from 1737 to 2697 BC. Confucius records that many roses were planted in the Imperial Garden in Peking. The Peking library at that time contained over 600 works on horticulture. The beautiful China and tea roses were cultivated in China for at least 2000 years before they reached the West in the nineteenth century.

Roses were known to the Sumerians. A clay tablet, dated 2250 BC, mentions rosewater and 'attar of roses'.

The oldest-known picture usually regarded as being a rose is a fresco in the Palace of Knossos on Crete and was probably painted 3500 years ago. It is light pink with five petals and three leaflets and is thought to be *Rosa richardii* (= *R. sancta*) or a form of *Rosa gallica*, the Holy Rose of the Egyptians.

Stylised roses were used as decorations on the floor and mouldings of banquet halls in Nineveh around 1700 BC, and in 1200 BC the Medes and the Persians were using the rose as a religious symbol.

Delivery notes preserved through being fused together in a fire in the twelfth century BC show that the Mycenaeans in Greece used rose-scented oil for anointment.

In the ninth century BC the blind Greek poet, Homer, recorded that Hector, who was killed by Achilles during the siege of Troy (1206 BC), was rubbed with oil of roses after his death and then embalmed by Aphrodite in the Greek camp during the night. He describes Achilles' shield as being decorated with roses.

According to legend roses grew in the Hanging Gardens of Babylon, built for Queen Semiramis (Sammur-amat), who ruled for three years from 809–806 BC. Biblical references to the rose are numerous but whether they refer to rose species or other plants is still debated by scholars and rosarians.

The poet Sappho, who lived on Lesbos in the eighth century BC, wrote the first poem to the rose describing it as the queen of flowers. Further testimony to the high esteem in which ancient Greece held the rose is given by a lawyer, Solon, who stated that 'fallen women' were forbidden to wear the rose wreath. Herodotus (490–420 BC) described a strongly scented 'rose with sixty petals' which King Midas of Phrygia brought with him when he went into exile in Greece.

The father of botany, Theophrastus (372–287 BC), details two rose types — the double and the single, or wild rose. He stated that the inhabitants of Phillippi (later a Christian community) had collected wild roses for their gardens. He noted rose propagation techniques, the practice of burning prunings and the fact that in Egypt roses bloomed two months earlier than those in Greece. Pliny wrote of the hundred-petalled *Rosa centifolia* — not the same rose as the rose of that name we grow today.

To ensure a constant supply of fresh rose blooms Epicurus of Athens (371-341 BC) created the finest private rose garden of the time. Alexander the Great (356-323 BC) is thought to have brought eastern roses to Egypt from where they were eventually exported to Rome. In Egypt the rose soon eclipsed the lotus flower in popularity. Many centuries later Napoleon's scientific mission to Egypt noted extensive rose nurseries in one small area there together with about thirty ovens used to distil rosewater for wealthy locals. For export the ancient Egyptians produced artificial roses from coloured wood shavings scented with rose balm. Egyptian tombs show that 2000 years ago *Rosa x richardii* (*R. sancta*) the Holy Rose, which was perhaps a form of *R. gallica*, was used in their religious and funeral ceremonies.

In the first century AD Dioscorides wrote *Materia Medica — The Basic Description of the Medicinal Drugs in 6 Books*, and included the use of roses for healing and beauty treatment. Also in that century the Greek historian Plutarch declared that garlic grown near roses increased their perfume!

That the Greeks loved their roses is evident from many records. They were the first to grow roses in pots and called these collections 'Gardens of Adonis', attaching so much importance to the bushes that their pots were made of silver. It was believed that the scent of the flowers would keep the household healthy, so Greek gardens could be seen and smelled from the living room and were usually at the back of the house. They were filled with violets, lilies and roses. Outside the cities large areas were also devoted to the commercial production of roses.

In the third century BC the Greeks introduced roses to the Romans, beginning an obsession that lasted until the fall of the Roman Empire. Wearing garlands and wreaths of roses was reserved by the Romans for the winners of great victories or the recipients of the nation's highest honours. Wearing roses in wartime was forbidden and infringement was punished with imprisonment.

The Romans' attitude was both poetic and practical. They have left a legacy of both poetry and treatises on rose culture. Their dedication was excessive and within fifty years they had changed the status of the rose from a near luxury to an everyday necessity, indoors and out.

Nero epitomised this excess, spending huge amounts on blooms for one banquet and on another occasion covering an entire beach with rose flowers. At his banquets roses were rained down on the guests from the ceiling and on one occasion two guests were stifled under the weight of the petals. Vast rose nurseries, mostly at Paestum, 100 kilometres (62 miles) south of Naples, partly supplied the demand. The balance were imported from the thriving nurseries in Egypt.

Virgil, Ovid and Horace expressed wonder at the Roman practice of using glasshouses and watering with warm water to force roses to bloom in winter. Horace was critical of the extent to which grain fields and orchards were given over to the more rewarding production of roses. Even so there were not enough roses to meet demand and the Romans had to rely on shiploads of cut blooms which took six days to come from Egypt.

Chaplets of roses were worn by the Romans to keep the head cool and sober and to overcome the stale smell of wine in their hair. Desserts, jellies, wine and honey were flavoured with roses.

Never before or since the Roman Empire has devotion to roses reached such extravagant heights. Some historians maintain that lavish spending on roses contributed to Rome's economic decline. The rose cult declined with the Empire and roses actually fell into disrepute. They had been dedicated to the Goddess of Love and the God of Wine so that after the decline several centuries passed before the Christian Church enthusiastically embraced the rose as a religious symbol. The Virgin Mary is referred to as 'The Mystical Rose' and 'The Rose of Heaven'. Red roses symbolise her sorrow, white her joy and gold her glory. They also stand for the crown of thorns, Christ's wounds and the blood of martyrs. The rosary and many Christian saints are connected with the rose. Pope Leo IX created the Order of the Golden Rose in 1049, first to honour virtuous women and later as a reward to cities and organisations who had served him well. King Henry VIII received it twice. The Golden Rose is still blessed on Rose Sunday, the Fourth Sunday of Lent.

Others to play a conspicuous part in the rose story were the Persians who produced huge quantities of 'attar of roses' and, together with the Arabians and the Moors, created magnificent rose gardens. The Moguls transported roses to the lands they conquered.

Roses were grown for scent, ornament, medicinal purposes and food flavouring in England and what are now France and Germany, and in China and Japan. Frequently the rose has been a symbol of power and a faction sign — the Tudor Rose, and the Roses of York and Lancaster are examples.

Roses have always attracted rich and powerful friends. The most devoted and influential was the French Empress Josephine. Her love for roses increased as she grew older, and after Napoleon divorced her she spent all her time with flowers, endeavouring among other things to collect all the roses known at that time for her garden. Even while France and England were at war a free exchange of roses and rose knowledge took place between Josephine and English scientists, including Sir Joseph Banks. Through her, Pierre Joseph Redoute (The Raphael of the Rose) was engaged to paint her flowers in a national collection called the 'Vellums'. His beautiful life-like paintings became sought-after prints, which, just as our colour catalogues do today, inspired people to grow roses. They are still the world's best-selling prints of roses and are found on everything from wastepaper baskets to china plates.

Josephine's influence led to the fashionable world using hybridisation to produce new and different roses. The creation of new roses through hybridisation has become the basis of the rose industry and is highlighted by annual awards for the year's new roses.

Josephine's desire to collect every known rose was feasible in her day but would be impossible now since there are over 40 000 different roses from which to choose.

Tamora

PHOTOGRAPH: DENSEY CLYNE

HISTORY OF MODERN ROSES

Until the sixteenth century people simply collected roses from the wild and transplanted them into their gardens. Then between 1790 and 1800, Koelreuter, a German Park Superintendent at Karlsruhe, described the parts of the flower, the process of fertilisation and the role of insects in pollination.

To a large extent this finding was disregarded. Most growers simply sowed seeds and awaited the results which were not always true to the parent. This was due to the fertilisation process being cross-pollinated at random by insects.

Between 1790 and 1800 the value of budding (a form of grafting) a desired rose onto the strong root system of *Rosa canina* was practised to produce roses on stems (standards and half standards). The fact that budding ensured reproduction of a rose identical to the parent led to the method being applied to bush roses as well as standards.

Even so budding was mainly reserved for roses which could not be reproduced satisfactorily from cuttings, seeds or divisions. In time it became standard practice because trueness-to-type could be guaranteed and strong growth resulted from the better root system.

The possibilities of hybridisation were realised and new varieties were developed by interested amateurs as well as professional growers. New varieties were kept true-to-type by budding. Several of the early hybrids are still grown, eg, Kaiserin Auguste Viktoria, Violacee, and Tour de Malakoff.

The bush and climbing roses had their antecedents in Asia. They were brought to Europe by intrepid plant collectors who included Robert Fortune, George Forrest, J. J. Booth, J. Dalton Hooker, Max Ernest, Wichura (after whom wichuraiana roses are named), Francis Kingdon Ward, Ernest H. Wilson (who returned with more roses than anyone else), William Kerr, Philip Franz von Siebold, Nathaniel Wallich, Père J. A. Soulie, Joseph Rock, W. Purdo and Augustine Henry. There were many others.

Among the roses they introduced were the China or Bengal rose *Rosa chinensis* which contributed the feature of repeat blooming to modern hybrids; *Rosa bracteata* — the Macartney Rose; *Rosa banksiae* (named after the wife of Sir Joseph Banks), Hume's Blush, Tea-Scented China, Park's Yellow Tea and Scented China. The latter no longer exists. Park's Yellow Tea and Scented China were important ancestors of all tea roses. Fortune's Double Yellow, which is still grown, and numerous others were also introduced.

Hybridisation or 'crossing' of species and their progeny began in earnest in the eighteenth century. In Italy, Holland, Luxembourg, England, France and North America, rose hybridisation took place on a large scale. By 1870, in France alone the numbers of varieties in cultivation had reached 6000. The results of hybridisation produced a variety of plant and flower forms not known before. They included climbers, miniatures, floribundas, shrubs, grandifloras and polyanthas. The most important hybrid was the cross of the hybrid perpetuals with the tea roses. This resulted in the hybrid tea class that is the mainstay of the rose industry today.

Roses are classified from the date 1867 because what is regarded as the first hybrid tea, La France, was introduced at that time. Roses before that date are classified as old garden roses, even if an individual rose carrying the characteristic features of its class appeared later. Though La France is usually recorded as being the first hybrid tea this is uncertain. Old roses are Moss roses, *Rosa alba* (prior to 1800), China (prior to 1819), Noisette (1819), Bourbon and Portland (1817), tea roses (1833), Boursault (1892), foetida hybrids (1837), hybrid perpetuals (1837), *R. pimpinellifolia* (=*spinosissima*), the Kordes hybrids (1932) and the species roses. Roses not included among old roses are hybrid teas (since 1867), floribunda, grandiflora, polyantha, hybrid musks, rubiginosa hybrids (1894), rugosa hybrids, multiflora hybrids, wichuraiana hybrids, kordesii varieties and shrub roses.

The main groups of roses in Western Europe at the beginning of the nineteenth century were gallicas, centifolias, albas, musk and damasks. These were difficult to separate because they were very similar to one another.

The hybrid teas were welcomed not only for their handsome flowers but for their other very important advantages — smaller, tidier bushes, continuous flowering habit (many old roses tend to flower only in autumn or spring), a unique colour range, longer stems, more robust growth habit and fragrance. Scent in the hybrid teas comes from their tea parentage. Contrary to popular opinion it is lacking in the hybrid perpetuals.

The range of hybrid teas was extended in 1897 by crossing the progeny of *R. foetida* (Austrian Yellow) and *R. foetida bicolor* (Austrian Copper). The bicolours and bright yellows are a result.

Peace, raised by Meilland of France, and introduced in 1946, brought to roses vigour and an abundance of exceptional, beautifully formed flowers with gentle gradations of colour. It began a new era in rose hybridising.

In 1950, Kordes of West Germany introduced the brilliant vermilion roses. The first was Super Star which is mildew prone in some climates. The best are the wonderfully scented Alexander and Fragrant Cloud.

In 1954, the hybrid tea Charlotte Armstrong was crossed with the floribunda Floradora and produced Queen Elizabeth. This was seen as an advance in hybridising roses because of the hybrid's very strong growth and masses of blooms up to 10 cm (4 in) across, carried in clusters. In the United States a new class called grandiflora was formed to accommodate it. In England another much more cumbersome term was chosen — floribunda–hybrid tea type.

An earlier similar problem arose after 1870 with the hybridisation of the Japanese *Rosa multiflora* (then called *Rosa polyantha*). The varieties obtained were called polyantha hybrids and later on polyanthas. They were crossed with the hybrid teas as well as all other roses of interest and another group of larger, more brightly coloured roses resulted. The name polyanthas was applied to the small-flowered varieties and the term hybrid polyanthas to those with large flowers. How to name the hybrids of hybrid polyanthas was a problem! The American rose breeder Lammerts used floribunda — a term which describes perfectly their profuse flowering habit — in place of hybrid polyantha or polyanthas. The term floribunda is now used in the United States and the southern hemisphere. In the United Kingdom they are usually termed 'cluster-flowered'.

Rose Protection

The propagation and distribution of new roses and other plants may be protected (as authors' rights are) by legislation in various countries. This ensures that the raiser of the new variety is able to realise on his or her investment and is able to control the quality of the plants sold by licensing the grower/distributor and retaining the right to revoke the licence if necessary. The raiser receives a royalty on each plant sold over a variable period of time. Once a rose is protected the holder of the right or grant may take civil action against anyone infringing his or her right.

The first rose to be protected was New Dawn which received United States Plant Patent Number 1 in 1930. Subsequently France, Germany, Denmark, Switzerland, Great Britain and other countries introduced legislation. The first rose registered in Australia under The Plant Varieties Rights Act 1987 was Young-at-Heart introduced in 1989 by Swane's Nursery for the National Heart Foundation.

To obtain protection it must be shown that: the plant is new and different from any other; that it is not already in commerce; that it may be reproduced true-to-type by asexual propagation and; that it has not already been protected.

The effect of plant protection has been to stimulate rose breeding worldwide. Until 1930 Europe was the centre of rose breeding but this changed with the introduction of Plant Patents in 1930 and the United States became the principal source of new roses. For gardeners the fact that a rose (or any plant) has been protected by legislation is an indication of its quality since registration costs are high (about $3500) and are expended only on the most worthy varieties.

CLASSIFICATION OF ROSES

Hybridisation is responsible for the hybrid teas, floribundas, miniatures and climbers illustrated in this book. The breeding lines are bewildering, the direction they take depends on the hybridiser's aim — form, colour, vigour, scent or any other characteristic.

Hybridisation is a complex, time-consuming process — it takes ten years to produce, test and launch a new rose — and it has created the absorbing and difficult problem of rose classification which occupies many rosarians today. Rose classification attempts to put order into a fascinating and often confused story and indicates the dedication of those who fall under the spell of roses.

At the World Federation of Rose Societies meeting in Pretoria in 1979 the following classification of modern roses was adopted. It is based on the work of the Classification Sub-Committee of the Royal National Rose Society, Great Britain, and is taken verbatim from *The Complete Book of Roses* by Gerd Krussmann.

Modern Garden Roses

Roses of hybrid origin not bearing any strong resemblance to wild roses (species) and not included in classifications in general use before the introduction of hybrid tea roses.

NON-CLIMBING
Plants with self-supporting stems.

Non-Recurrent Flowering Flowering season limited, in summer (or spring) with at best only occasional blooms in the autumn.

Non-Recurrent Flowering Shrub Plants usually taller and/or possibly wider than bush roses and particularly suitable for use as specimen plants.

Recurrent Flowering Flowering season long or with a marked resurgence later.

Recurrent Flowering Shrub Plants usually taller and/or possibly wider than bush roses and particularly suitable for use as specimen plants.

Bush Varieties of moderate height particularly suitable for cultivation in groups. Hybrid teas and floribundas are 'bush' roses.

Large Flowered (Hybrid Tea) Roses having double flowers, of medium to large size, of the traditional hybrid tea form (eg, petals overlapped to form a conical, ovoid or other symmetrical centre) and usually capable of being cut as a single flower (with or without side buds) on a long stem.

Clustered Flowered (Floribunda) Roses distinguished primarily by a mass of flowers produced in trusses, clusters or on many stems. The flowers may be single, semi-double or double.

Polyantha Roses with small flowers, usually of rosette form, borne in large clusters. Distinctive foliage, the leaflets smaller than those of cluster flowered roses.

Miniature Roses with miniature flowers, foliage and growth.

Old Garden Roses

The old garden roses were already well established in classifications in common use before the introduction of hybrid tea roses. (These old classes were based largely on presumed genetical and botanical affinities and in general do not fit easily into a modern classification based mainly on functional garden qualities.)

NON-CLIMBING
Plants with self-supporting stems.

PHOTOGRAPH: DENSEY CLYNE

The Yeoman

Alba   Roses displaying the influence of *Rosa alba*.

Bourbon   Roses displaying the influence of *Rosa* x *borboniana*, supposedly a hybrid between the China rose and Autumn Damask.

Boursault   Roses supposedly displaying the influence of *Rosa chinensis* and *Rosa pendulina*.

China   Roses displaying the influence of *Rosa chinensis*.

Damask   Roses displaying the influence of *Rosa damascena*.

Gallica   Roses displaying the influence of *Rosa gallica*.

Hybrid Perpetual   Roses usually obtained by interbreeding Bourbon roses with China and/or Damask roses.

Moss   Roses with mossy outgrowth on sepals and/or pedicels.

Portland   Roses allied to Duchess of Portland, a hybrid suggesting the influence of China and Damask roses.

Provence (Centifolia)   Roses displaying the influence of *Rosa centifolia*.

Sweet Briar   Roses displaying the influence of *Rosa rubiginosa*, the Sweet Brier or Eglantine.

Tea   Roses displaying the influence of *Rosa* x *odorata*, supposedly a hybrid between *Rosa chinensis* and *Rosa gigantea*.

CLIMBING
Plants climbing or rambling with long, sprawling or arching stems normally requiring support.

Ayrshire   Roses displaying the influence of *Rosa arvensis*.

Boursault   Climbing roses supposedly displaying the influence of *Rosa chinensis* and *Rosa pendulina*.

Climbing Tea   Climbing roses with flowers similar to those of tea roses.

Noisette   Roses displaying the influence of *Rosa* x *noisettiana*, supposedly a hybrid between *Rosa chinensis* and *Rosa moschata*.

Sempervirens   Roses displaying the influence of *Rosa sempervirens*.

Wild Roses

Species and varieties or hybrids (single or double flowered) which bear a strong resemblance to species.

NON-CLIMBING
Plants with self-supporting stems.

CLIMBING
Plants climbing or rambling with long, sprawling or arching stems normally requiring support.

ROSE MUTATION, HYBRIDISATION AND PROPAGATION

It is interesting and also useful to understand a little of the techniques involved in the hybridisation and propagation of roses: both because as an amateur you may wish to try your hand at these techniques; and because it is helpful, when growing roses, to be aware of the complexities involved in the creation of these plants.

Rose Mutations or 'Sports'

It is quite common for bud mutations to occur in many plants, particularly roses and especially those roses like the hybrid teas which have a complicated ancestry. In 1960 S. G. Saakov showed that in a sixty eight year period to 1935, of 3,270 hybrid teas, 127 developed mutations. Exactly what causes mutations or 'sports' has not been established though it is generally thought to be the result of a complicated hybridogene formation. Whatever the cause, some of the loveliest roses are mutations.

One of the best known examples is the Moss Rose which came about as a sport of *R. centifolia* and was known in 1696. It was one of sixty sports in a 230 year span and no new sports of this species have appeared since.

The most common mutation of all is the development of a climbing rose form from a bush or shrub rose. This is indicated by the appearance of long flexible growths. Well-known mutations are the climbing forms of Avon, Peace, Mister Lincoln, Sutter's Gold and Pascali.

Hybridisation

This book is concerned mainly with modern garden roses — the ever-increasing range of hybrids which produce colourful flowers for six to nine months of the year depending on climate.

Why do we need more roses and what are the hybridisers looking for?

Beautiful as they are all roses have faults. Hybridists aim to eliminate these and to introduce improved forms. They want roses which will be vigorous and covered in large, disease-resistant shining foliage with long stems suitable for cutting. Flowers must be long lasting, sun resistant and rain tolerant, with high-pointed or globose buds opening to many petalled (at least thirty to thirty five) fragrant flowers which retain their form even when fully open. They are also searching for particular colours.

Single flowers tend to open and fall too quickly for areas with long hot summers. Very full blooms may fail to open after rainy weather. Some roses are more disease prone than others and the lasting qualities of most could be improved. Blue roses are not truly blue, many red roses become purplish with age and some yellows fade. The possibility of black and truly blue roses continues to intrigue raisers.

Rose hybridisation is a business but for many amateurs it is also an interest, one that can be followed at home in the garden without the cost incurred by the commercial raisers.

Modern roses are the product of the discoveries of the sexuality of plants, the potential of artificial pollination, the laws of heredity and the process of selection.

Hybridisation occurs in nature too but much more slowly. It is for this reason that species (as distinct from hybrid) roses have comparatively simple and unmixed ancestry. Seedlings of species roses are therefore almost identical to their parents. Of the 250 or more species roses, only half a dozen or so were needed to give rise to the modern hybrids. But the seeds of hybrids do not reproduce their parents. Their progeny will be distinct. A study of genetics shows that, leaving aside the section Caninae, a rose inherits its qualities equally from its seed and its pollen parent. This and the hybridiser's objectives determine the selection of parents.

Ideally a seed parent (mother) is chosen because it is known to produce heavy crops of hips, the vessels containing the seeds. Though the pollen parent will influence the ability to set hips, heredity is also very important. A large crop of viable seed is a basic requirement for the hybridiser's work. The selected parents should both be fertile.

Hybridising begins with the first spring flowers and continues until mid-summer which allows the hips time to ripen. A day before the cross is made and just as the flower is beginning to unfold, the petals are removed. The stamens are also removed but can be kept for use in other, later crosses.

The pollen is taken from the male parent two days before the petals unfold. Using fine tweezers and scissors the anthers are cut away as the flower unfolds. They are stored in paper or in a clean glass container for two days until they dry out, at which time they will burst and discharge their yellow dust-like pollen. The container should be labelled for the sake of accuracy.

Once removed the anthers should not be exposed to bright light or sunlight. (The pollen can be stored in tightly closed glass or plastic containers in a refrigerator at 1°–3°C (34°–38°F) and about 45 per cent humidity.)

The germinative qualities of pollen should be tested to avoid disappointment. The ingredients needed for testing are distilled water and cooking sugar. To 50 ml (1½ fl oz) of distilled water in a small clean bottle add 10 g (½ oz) of sugar. Only a few drops are needed for each experiment but the solution does not last longer than a week.

Cut a head of bloom the day before from the rose to be tested and put it indoors in a vase without water. Shake a little pollen onto a glass slide and place a drop of sugar solution on the pollen using a sterile glass rod. Press on the top half of the slide. Or use another glass slide as a cover, first surrounding the pollen with a thin ring of lanolin then applying the sugar solution and finally pressing the glass over all, allowing the lanolin to hold both together.

At 20°C (68°F) the oval pollen grains which look like ears of wheat will begin to swell, become spherical and commence germination. Four hours later the germination tubes in the pollen sac will be thirty to fifty times the original diameter of the pollen grains. The germination result will be visible under a magnifying glass and counting will be unnecessary.

Pollen is transferred by a fine brush (use a separate clean one for each cross) or by dipping the bloom in the pollen which must be dry. (To clean brushes, use alcohol, paint thinner or mineral spirits.) The stigma should not be dampened by dew, rain or spray. The initial pollination usually achieves fertilisation but a second one can be applied if there is any doubt about the variety's ability to set seed.

When the cross is made outdoors the blooms are covered with a paper bag or plastic cup to protect them from unwanted forms of fertilisation. Indoors, in an insect-free glasshouse, covering the blooms is unnecessary. The parentage of every pollinated bloom is recorded.

A day before pollination, on properly prepared blooms, a secretion will form on the stigma and the pollen grains will adhere to this. The secretion helps the rapid development of the pollen tube and in a few days it passes through the stigma and enters the ovary, completing the fertilisation process. Two weeks later hips should be recognisable and will be beginning to swell. The covering can be removed. (In unsuccessful pollination the hips soften and become black or greenish yellow. They should be cut off. Other unaffected hips can be allowed to remain.)

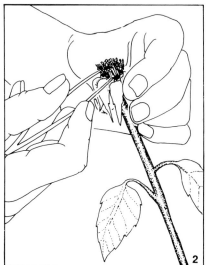

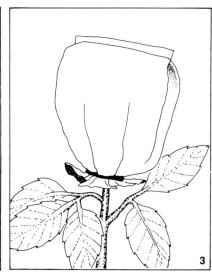

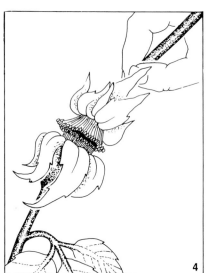

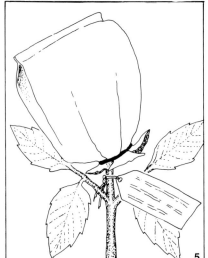

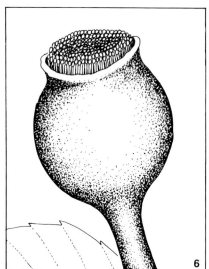

1 *Select a fertile pollen parent.*

2 *Remove petals as flower unfolds; pull off stamens to prevent self-pollination.*

3 *Cover flower with paper bag to prevent unwanted forms of fertilisation.*

4 *When sticky secretion forms on stigma, either apply pollen grains from a pollen-laden cut flower or brush on specially prepared pollen.*

5 *Replace bag and label flower with names of both parents.*

6 *The hip containing the seeds will begin to swell.*

7 *Sow seeds in a steam-cleaned seed-raising mix.*

When the seeds are ripe they become orange or yellow. Before the worst frosts appear the stem bearing the hips is cut off and put in a vase of water until the hips are completely ripe. They can remain until fully ripe. Colour is the guide to ripeness. The hips need to be cut open, the seeds scooped out, cleaned and allowed to dry two weeks before being stored in a cool moist place. Seeds are variable in size and quantity and their adherence to the hip. Roses with red or orange hips have white or pale yellow seeds; black or brown hips produce pinkish seeds.

Before sowing, clean and test seeds by immersing them in water, rinsing off hairs and discarding seeds which float as these are probably empty.

In early winter sow the seeds in seedling boxes under a pane of glass or in a glasshouse. Use a commercial steam-cleaned seed raising mix and sow the seeds on rows of sand 5 cm (2 in) apart, pressing the seeds until they are just resting on the top of the soil.

Germination depends on cool temperatures. For two months keep the seed boxes at 6°C (43°F). About three months later germination will commence and daytime temperatures can be allowed to reach 15°C (59°F). By late spring germination will be complete.

The seed leaves (cotyledons) of healthy seedlings are dark green or sometimes reddish. Pale yellow or albino seedlings should be discarded as should seedlings with misshapen leaves. (Early true leaves are smooth.)

The seedlings usually flower in their first spring. Those with more than thirty petals may be kept and looked at more closely next year. Generally only one or two seedlings in every thousand is worth a second look.

In commercial breeding programmes prospective new roses are planted into the field and observed for two or three years. Then the raiser may send them to various trial grounds in the United States and Europe for observation over another two to three years. Success comes if the rose receives an award from one of the national rose authorities.

The raiser may patent or protect the rose under legislation and license nurserymen to grow it, which takes another two or three years. He or she then receives a royalty for a given period on each one sold as a reward for these efforts over ten years.

Before a new rose reaches the market the raiser must spend time building up sufficient stocks of the new clone to be able to supply the 'budwood' (nucleus material of the clone) to those who will grow and distribute it. They keep the rose true-to-type by budding it on to a root system suitable for the area in which it will be sold.

Propagation

Though many roses can be grown easily from cuttings, in commercial practice few are, budding being the preferred means.

Budding is a form of grafting which allows a desirable cultivar to be grown on the stronger root system of a closely related plant. It is used for many plants which do not have a strong root system when grown from cuttings or which are subject to root-rot diseases or fail to come true-to-type from seed. Budding saves propagation material to the extent that six to ten roses can be produced from the material needed for one cutting-grown rose. Micro-propagation is used for many miniature roses.

Budding commences in late spring and finishes in early autumn in hot dry areas. In subtropical parts it commences earlier and in cold climates a little later. Budwood may be cut in autumn and stored at –1°C (30°F) over winter enabling an early start to be made as soon as the rootstocks are ready.

Without refrigerated budwood the grower must wait on his or her stock bed of roses to bloom before being able to cut budwood. This takes several weeks and when there is a large crop time this becomes important, particularly as the wood must be at a certain stage of maturity and the stocks must be 'running' (sap flowing freely) for budding to be a success. (Refrigerated budwood would not be essential on home garden projects unless stocks or budwood were unavailable at the selected time.)

In 'shield' or 'T' budding, a T-shaped incision is made in the rootstock about 6 cm (2½ in) above ground. From the budwood stick, which is the 21 cm (8¼ in) of stem below a finished flower head, a leaf bud taken from the axil of a leaf is cut and its pithy centre removed leaving the green cambium — a layer just below the bark — exposed. The sides of the T incision are kept apart at the top with a budding knife. The bud is slid in behind these two flaps so that the cambium layers of stock and bud meet. The knife is removed leaving the bud visible in the slit between the two sides of the cut. Excess wood from the bud is cut away at the top of the T and the bud is carefully tied in place with a rubber, plastic or raffia tie which leaves the bud itself exposed.

The leafy part of the rootstock is kept intact to feed the bud when the union of bud and understock has taken place. The bud tie is then removed.

In winter the rootstock foliage is cut away completely which directs all food to the bud. This, combined with warm spring days, induces growth and by mid or late spring the new plant should be flowering. If it is a field-grown plant it is usually not sold until the following winter when it will be dug and marketed. Container plants are treated in the same way except that they can be sold at least six months earlier because the container keeps the roots intact, eliminating the need to wait for winter to dig.

The most popular rootstocks are forms of *Rosa multiflora*. *R. multiflora fortuniana* is favoured for some sandy soils. Another form, Dr Huey, is a California selection grown for its vigorous root system and quick uniform growth. All three are raised from cuttings.

The oldest and quickest method of producing large numbers of rootstocks is to raise seedlings of *Rosa multiflora* and bud these or take cuttings from them.

Other rootstocks include forms of *Rosa canina* and *Rosa manetti*. Climate, soil and nursery practice dictate which stock is used. Selection of a suitable stock is essential for satisfactory growth.

All stocks are capable of 'suckering' (sending up shoots from below the bud union). Suckers can be distinguished from the rose bush itself by their distinct foliage which has smaller leaflets. They should be cut off cleanly, level with the stem to allow the bark to heal over the cut. Suckers are a nuisance but are not harmful if kept removed. They may occur on the stems of standard roses and should be rubbed off.

Some roses can be grown from cuttings, though commercially they seldom are, because budded roses produce better performing, more uniform crops which is not the case with roses on their own roots.

The cuttings are made in autumn from pencil-thick, current season's growth which has already flowered. Cut out the soft, thin growth near the top. Make cuttings 23 cm (9 in) long — one from each shoot. Remove all but the top two leaves. Make slanting cuts to just above the dormant buds at the top and base of the cutting. Dip the base in hardwood hormone powder. Plant cuttings 15 cm (6 in) deep — several together in a pot. Place in a semi-shaded position. Water well and follow with daily waterings (or twice daily in hot weather). Once the cuttings shoot, remove the pot, shake or wash the soil away and either pot or plant out the rooted cutting. Only the strongest plants are worth trying to propagate this way.

PLANNING A ROSE GARDEN

Roses can be used for almost all landscape purposes except for providing shade, and even that can nearly be achieved by some of the old shrub roses which reach small tree height.

Some gardens are planted exclusively with roses. In these, climbers and shrub forms screen the boundaries, floribunda hedges define areas, miniatures edge paths, bush and standards, arranged according to size, provide mass colour, shade comes from climbers on pergolas or frames, and high weeping standards are tall accents. Ground-covering roses spread across soil between bushes, spill over walls joining garden levels and cascade from hanging baskets. Patios, terraces and stairs are bright with potted miniatures and standards in tubs add a formal note. The shapely combination of a tall-trunked rose and a large tub filled with annuals and small bulbs brings proportion to the garden. Lawn, paving or pebble paths give direction to the design, link various areas and are a viewing platform from which to enjoy the roses.

Management of the all-rose garden depends on its pathways which must be wide enough to allow prunings to be gathered up and carried away easily. Spacing of the bushes is also dictated by pruning. If bushes are closely planted and beds are wide it will be difficult to reach roses in the centre. Narrow beds of say four roses or less across, with a path on either side, are easy to care for. Alternatively, in very wide beds inconspicuous work paths can be left at suitable intervals by widening planting distances. Walking on the beds in a well-mulched rose garden is soon camouflaged by raking or mulch.

Paths make setting sprinklers easier, although permanent do-it-yourself on- or in-ground watering systems are much better because they eliminate the handling of hoses and reduce contact with thorny bushes. Water can also be kept off the foliage which is an aid to controlling fungal diseases.

The long flowering period and the almost evergreen habit of many modern roses means that, depending on the varieties used, a rose-dominated garden is colourful and scented for six to nine months. This very lovely garden depends for its success on careful consideration of maintenance needs and available gardening time. Early winter (or later in some climates) will be busy with pruning and from spring to autumn spraying will be needed to control pests and diseases. Success will rest on adequate maintenance.

All-rose gardens in the past have been restricted because of disease-prone roses and labour-intensive maintenance methods. This no longer applies if robust modern roses are planted and effective sprays and equipment are used. These facts are recognised in Europe where public rose gardens maintained by local government authorities are returning to favour because of their low upkeep cost. An example is the Scottish city of Aberdeen which annually plants thousands of roses beside its roadways.

The all-rose garden is rare now. Most gardens these days consist of shrubs. Where there are roses they are either set apart in individual beds as hedges or borders along driveways, climbing around pillars or against walls, or are mixed with shrubs and/or perennials. The separation of roses and shrubs was practised by early rose exhibitors to simplify maintenance and to produce their magnificent exhibition-quality blooms. The gardens of many modern exhibitors retain this business-like approach which almost negates the rose's ornamental value as a plant. It is a poor example for new gardeners too, as they assume separation to be the only way to grow roses.

Before exhibiting became popular, roses were grown beside shrubs and appreciated as plants and for their blooms. They flowered annually and reached shrub proportions. Then hybridisation created repeat-flowering bushes. Rose societies sprang up with competitive members dedicated to winning first prize for the perfect rose which had been carefully 'prepared' by pelleting the petals. 'Showing' dominated rose growing except in large gardens. There, the beauty and diversity of roses was demonstrated by mass planting a single variety to a 'bed'. This produced generous splashes of colour. Beds were joined by lawn or paving and became known as 'formal' rose gardens.

Between exhibition growing and formal rose gardens, now in decline, the potential of modern roses as shrubs was neglected and is only now being realised. What other shrub flowers so prolifically and for so long?

Shrubs, perennials, annuals and roses with similar aspect and cultural needs can be chosen carefully to grow together in happy mixes or gentle blends of colour, form and foliage that are charming all year. Plants can be arranged to compensate for one another during 'off' periods — for example, bulbs could surround leafless roses in winter. This approach is delightful in small gardens where space is precious. In large gardens it allows roses to be used without adding to the already high maintenance costs.

When planning a garden with roses consider their possibilities and adapt these to your situation. Plan flowers for the house by growing roses among shrubs which need the same aspect and care. Hide ugly fences with climbers or ramblers. Use roses to define paths, entrances and driveways — in some cases separate beds, each with a standard rose and annuals around it, are effective. Gain privacy and create a barrier to annuals and people with a thick hedge of floribundas. Camouflage buildings, garbage cans and compost areas with bush or climbing roses. Roses as an edging add colour to a lawn. Line both sides of a path, or fill corners, define areas, frame windows, accent a feature or create a focal point with roses. Cover banks and fill tubs and hanging baskets with ground cover roses. Add height, colour and shade to the garden with climbing roses on a sturdy old-fashioned pergola that doubles as a summerhouse. Tripods 5 m (yd) high on which rambling roses grow also add height and win attention. A climbing rose rambling through old trees and large shrubs creates a mellow effect. Plant scented roses under windows, especially dining room windows. The possibilities are unlimited.

Colour is a consideration too. Clashes can occur, especially with the scarlet roses. Placing 'blues' seems to be a problem for some people and a joy to others. A monochromatic colour scheme using either a single variety or different varieties of the one shade is a solution. Another way is to mix colours. Whichever method is used the overall effect is more colourful (at least in hedges and mass plantings) if at least two and preferably three roses of the one variety are placed side by side.

Bright, warm colours make spaces smaller and cool shades lend depth and length to an area. White roses separate and define all other colours though true scarlet is often too obvious near white. A background of dark-green foliage is a handsome foil for most roses though there are a few deep rose tones which look better with a light backdrop.

GENERAL PLANTING INSTRUCTIONS

Roses like the good life: a position in sun or a minimum of five hours sun daily (although some roses tolerate light to filtered shade); ample water especially in dry times; cool, moist, friable soil, free from the competition of grass and tree roots and enriched with humus; a 10–12 cm (4–5 in) deep mulch of old organic matter; freedom from too many pests and diseases and removal of old or excess growth. Fulfilling these basic requirements will keep roses alive and blooming for over thirty years. Eighty-year-old bushes are not uncommon in old gardens.

Climate

Roses can be found which will exist in every temperate climate but this does not mean they will flourish. Roses enjoy warm temperate, cool temperate, Mediterranean and highland climates including their frosts and cold winters. As with other plants which are deciduous, for the best growth, roses require a period of dormancy in winter.

Tropical areas are the least suitable, whereas roses in subtropical climates grow well if there is an adequate disease-control programme. Humidity in both areas encourages fungal diseases and the lack of a winter dormancy period in tropical climates forces year-round growth which shortens the life span. In these climates only the most vigorous varieties should be planted.

Most roses thrive under well-watered conditions in hot dry climates, because such climates inhibit fungal leaf spot diseases. However they need protection from hot drying winds.

Cold climates like the North Central States of America and Canada, Northern Europe and the coldest parts of the United Kingdom are suitable for roses when the plants are sheltered from cold biting winds. Where daily temperatures are below 20°C (68°F) for extended periods the plants will need to be covered with mounds of soil, purpose-made protective cones, straw or hessian, anything that keeps out frost and snow. See diagram, p. 20.

DEFINITIONS OF CLIMATIC TERMS
Below are definitions of climatic terms used in this book:
Tropical: Summer temperatures and atmospheric humidity are very high. Average temperature 20–30°C (68–86°F).
Subtropical: Fairly high and reliable rainfall throughout the year. Average temperature 15–20°C (59–68°F).
Temperate: Reliable rainfall all year round. Warm summers and cool winters. Average temperature 10–15°C (50–59°F).
Mediterranean: Hot dry summers and mild wet winters with fairly reliable and effective rainfall.
Frost/Snow Affected: Climates where the temperature is below 20°C (68°F) for extended periods throughout the year.

The Soil

Roses are gross feeders and open, free-draining, humus-rich soils allow their roots free access to food and water. They will grow on most soils except those that are wet and poorly drained. Clay soils (those that are sticky after wet weather and shrink forming large cracks in dry weather) can be improved by adding organic matter. Lime can be applied to break down heavy soils further but it may increase alkalinity. This can be detrimental as roses like a slightly acid soil with a pH of 6–7.

An alternative to liming is gypsum applied at the rate of one cup per square metre (yard), or, additions of coarse sand, peat or ash in conjunction with organic matter incorporated into the soil and applied to the surface as a mulch, can be used to improve texture.

Sandy soils pose other problems. In very sandy soil, water and nutrients drain (leach) away too freely. The addition of plenty of organic matter helps to retain them. In pure sand a floor of plastic or tin may be laid 45 cm (18 in) below the surface to prevent leaching. This does not overcome the need for soil amendment but it does prevent water and nutrient loss.

Above all, avoid digging into heavy clay subsoils. The fallacy that roses like clay stems from the fact that they grow very well on loams which have a clay subsoil. But roses will grow in any slightly acid, well-watered soil which drains freely. The higher its humus content, the richer rose growth will be.

Whether roses are to be planted in a bed of their own or as part of a mixed garden, soil preparation is the same except that among other plants avoid shrub roots interfering with rose roots by placing so that the outer edge of the square metre (yard) allowed for the rose just meets the outer edge of the shrub foliage.

Maintaining a compost heap to supply well-rotted organic matter to roses will pay off in terms of more blooms, healthier growth and less maintenance.

HOW TO TELL SOIL TYPES

Soil type depends on the type of rock beneath the soil, how steep the land is, and the time over which the climate has been acting on that rock to form the soil. Soil varies with depth, so dig a good, deep pit (profile) and have a look at the depth of the soil. Some soils are so shallow that you hit rock in one spadeful. Dig at least 1 m (yd) before deciding it is 'deep'.

Soil varies in texture with depth. Generally more clay is present in the deeper layers (horizons). Soils can be divided into four main groups.

Sandy Throughout Light sand to loamy sand at the surface, sandier, or clayey sand deeper in the profile. Such soils develop on recent (or old) beach sands, or on steep sandstone slopes, where they may also be very rocky and shallow.

Loam to Light Clay Throughout Crumbly well-drained loam on the surface becoming increas-ingly clayey with depth, but still crumbly. Such soils develop on some shales (specially thin beds with sandstone intermixed), volcanic rocks such as basalt and dacite, some mudstones, limestone, and young alluvium.

Loam to Heavy Clay at Depth A loamy surface soil, somewhat crumbly, gives way to massive blocky clay at depth. This sets hard in dry weather and turns into glug in wet. Many mudstones and shales develop soil like this.

Soil with a Sharp Change from Sand to Clay An upper layer of sand or loamy sand changing very quickly to heavy clay or sandy clay. Old mudstone, shale, sandstone and granite, form soil like this which is known as duplex soil.

Colour and acidity also vary with depth. Colour is fairly unimportant, except that you should aim to darken the surface soil with humus. If it becomes lighter in time, you are not looking after it properly. Lime decreases acidity.

SOIL PREPARATION FOR A NEW ROSE GARDEN

Each rose needs a square metre (yard) of space around it as a minimum. This should be dug over to at least 45 cm (18 in) deep. Plants with a long life, like roses, need stability. Deep digging encourages this and protects the roots from some of the effects of heat during summer. The easy way to prepare the soil is to rotary hoe the garden bed. An old fashioned way is to use the trenching method (see diagram opposite).

Trenching A trench 25 cm (10 in) wide is dug at one end of the area and the soil turned very thoroughly to a depth of 25 cm (10 in). The soil from this trench is placed at the other end of the area to be dug. This soil is then used to fill the last trench to be dug. The remainder of the area is dug systematically turning the soil from one trench into the previous one. The object is to break the soil up to improve drainage. Old organic matter (animal manure, grass clippings, mushroom compost etc) can be added at the same time. Ideally, this should be done at least a month and preferably two months before planting. Complete fertiliser can be added at the rate of three-quarters of a cup per square metre (yard). (If digging is done only at planting time or very close to it, do not add the fertiliser.)

SOIL PREPARATION FOR THE OLD ROSE GARDEN

Rose-Sick Soils New roses may fail in old gardens in which old rose plants have been productive for years.

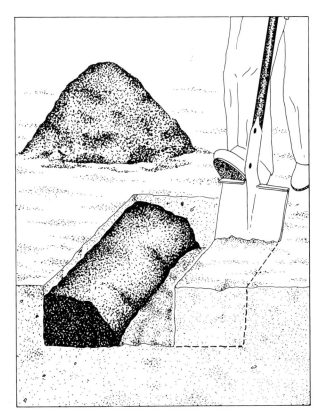

1 *Trenching breaks up the soil to improve drainage; a trench is dug 25 cm (10 in) wide and 25 cm deep.*
2 *Soil is then turned over from trench to trench.*

The old rose and its worn-out soil have adjusted to one another to some extent. The new rose will fail to flourish because it is unused to the deficiencies and disadvantages of the site. If planting into a site formerly occupied by roses, it is wise to remove as much soil as possible down to a spade or a spade-and-a-half depth and as wide as a metre (yard) square. Replace with new compost-enriched soil and then plant. The old soil's deficiencies of trace elements which earlier roses have used up, the problem of nematodes (root-knotting eelworms) and the accumulation of toxic substances produced by earlier roses which are often present in such circumstances, are avoided.

Buying Roses

Most roses are sold in autumn/winter when they are dug up from the fields and retailed either as packaged or bare root plants. They are also sold as potted plants from spring to autumn and in winter in warm climates. Autumn/winter is the principal rose-planting season,

although potted plants can be transplanted in any season, climate and conditions permitting. The advantage of field-grown roses is their size and quality. In the field both root system and top have developed without the restriction of a container. In some nurseries, after lifting from the field, they are planted back into a 'trench' to hold them for sales during the dormant period.

In warm temperate climates, roses are best planted during early winter. In subtropical and tropical climates, mid-winter is preferable. In Mediterranean-style and highland climates late winter and spring (in the coldest areas) are the appropriate times.

It pays to avoid buying packaged or bare-root roses very early in autumn. These have been dug at least a fortnight and probably three weeks before they reach the shop or nursery. This means that they were lifted in flower, or leaf, or both, and stripped of foliage and bloom to allow handling. While many roses will stand this, others do not and though purchased alive, they will exist on stored food until spring and will then fail to make ample new growth.

Roses need a period of dormancy (rest). Leaf fall is a sign that this has begun and that food storage is complete. The risk in early autumn planting is that food storage is prevented from fully taking place. The retailer makes an early sale but often the gardener loses in spring when, due to a lack of stored food, the bushes fail to grow satisfactorily.

This does not apply to roses that are *raised* in containers but it does apply to those *held* in them. Many roses are raised in containers. Others are field-grown, lifted and root pruned very severely to be jammed into containers for immediate sale. Their success rate is dubious because too much root has been removed and they have usually been dug too early. First-grade container roses have a well-established root system composed of both major and minor roots running throughout the soil, around the soil ball and usually through the drainage holes. They are sold in containers with a diameter of 20 cm (8 in) or more. Smaller sizes denote a lower grade of rose. Presentation is an infallible guide to quality. Poorly packaged or underpotted roses are a sign that costs have been saved on the handling with consequent adverse results on future growth. Often, they are field-grown plants which have had almost all their roots pruned off in order to fit them in the pot. They can be slow to develop because they lack a sound root system. The main advantage of potted roses is convenience. They may be purchased in flower which saves confusion over colour and variety.

The best grade of field-grown roses available packaged or bare-root will have been pruned most, from a metre (yard) high to one, two or three stems about 36 to 45 cm (14 to 17½ in) long and as thick as a man's little finger. Not all varieties produce three stems and stem number is therefore not the most reliable guide to quality since some roses only produce one main stem while young. Furthermore, with mechanical digging and packaging, nurserymen are tending to reduce the number of stems to facilitate handling. Cuts at the base will indicate that this has happened. Some browning of pruned limbs is normal but it should not extend down the stem. Insistence on two or three stems is impractical with many varieties.

The best guide to quality is stem thickness and the viability of the rose. It should *look* fresh with no sign of shrivelling on the wood or dying back on the tips. The stem should be green, reddish or brownish green. Colour varies with variety. For example, Peace has very green wood, Anne Marie Trechslin is bronze. If in doubt, press a fingernail into the wood about 8 cm or 10 cm (3 or 4 in) from the tip of the limb. It should go in easily and a green sappy layer should be visible. (This practice will not endear you to nurserymen and should only be followed in dubious cases since it's very like squeezing fruit in the greengrocer's.)

The best way to buy roses is to order them early, between summer and mid-autumn, and arrange to have them sent or collect them at the best time for planting for your climate. Whether you order or not this period is the time to visit rose shows and gardens and note the names of those roses you like because they are not in bloom during the autumn/winter planting period. Taking home packaged or bare-root rose bushes is not a problem though many people, used to heavy shrubs, imagine it will be and hire a trailer or have the plants delivered believing they will not fit in their car. Dozens can be fitted in easily in the car boot (trunk).

Standards are about 1.5 m (yd) long overall but up to a hundred can be packed to travel lying down in the car boot. Bush roses in containers will fit in the boot, each taking up 20 cm (8 in) in width because of the container. Potted standards may have to travel inside because of their height. Weeping standards go inside the car with their heads out the window. If purchasing weeping or standard roses, be sure to arrange for suitable stakes and a rose ring (for weepers only).

Bare-root roses packed for delivery will last seven to ten days without any trouble provided they are kept indoors in a cool, draught-free position.

Packaged roses will last three weeks in transit. Ideally though, all roses, including potted roses, should be planted within a few days of receipt to avoid drying out.

When to Plant

Potted roses can be planted all year round, climate permitting (see Buying Roses). Bare-root and packaged roses are planted in autumn/winter in warm areas, mid winter for subtropical and tropical areas and late winter/early spring for cool temperate and frost/snow affected areas. Bare-root and packaged plants are tied to these times because the roses are dormant and able to stand transplanting in a soil-less state. Also, from a cost viewpoint, a greater number can be handled in a smaller space without the disadvantages of the weight of soil. For these practical reasons autumn/winter is the prime rose time, the period when the widest selection of varieties is available. By comparison, potted roses are very limited both in number offered and varieties available. Also, they are more expensive because of the soil and container needed.

If planting must be delayed for periods up to a month, 'heel in' the bushes by digging one large hole with a slanting side, then bundle the roses tightly together at their stems and place in the hole as one plant using the method outlined for planting a single bush. Transfer to individual permanent positions before leaf growth develops in size to more than 8 to 10 cm (3 or 4 in), otherwise new root growth will be lost in the move. In climates with temperatures under 20°C (68°F) for prolonged periods, plant after frosts have finished or heel in the plants with a protective covering of straw etc. to avoid frost damage.

Planting

FROM CONTAINERS

Make a wide, shallow hole 5–8 cm (2–3 in) deeper than the plant's container and avoid disturbing the subsoil unduly. Avoid very deep holes. Like wells, these collect water and become a harbour for root-rot diseases because they are frequently dug into the subsoil where the clay base prevents drainage. Plant death may occur months or even years later, but this will be the cause. Narrow holes should also be avoided, especially in lawn areas. In lawns the hole should be at least a metre (yard) wide as grass roots are too competitive to permit quick growth.

Remove the plant from the container, taking care not to cut the roots. Fill the first 5–8 cm (2–3 in) of the hole with a mixture of peat and rich soil and place the plant on this. Fill the hole in and tap the soil gently down with the hands (feet are often too heavy). Finish with a saucer-shaped depression to allow water to soak in

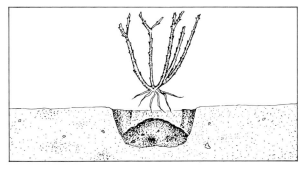

1 *Place the plant in a hole wide enough to take the roots.*

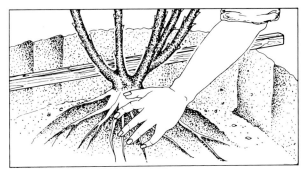

2 *Build a mound in the hole and spread the root system over it, using a stick to determine the soil level.*

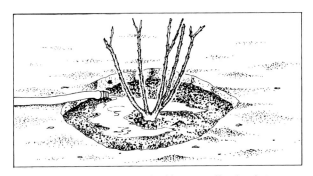

3 *Fill half way with soil and add water, allowing it to drain.*

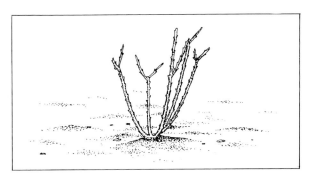

4 *Add more soil until it is 4 cm (1½ in) below the bud union.*

to the centre of the plant. Water the plant and allow it to drain. Add more soil if necessary to create a hilly surround to the saucer-shaped depression.

FIELD-GROWN, PACKAGED OR BARE-ROOT, BUSH-TYPE ROSES

Remove package and dispense with it and any root ties which may be present inside the package. Soak roots in a bucket of water for an hour, then place the plant in a hole wide and deep enough to accommodate the roots. Build a mound in the hole and sit the base of the root system on this with the roots trained down the side. Fill in half way with soil. Cover with water. Let this drain away, then fill in to 4 cm (1½ in) below the bud union with soil, finishing with a saucer-shaped depression 45 cm (17½ in) across, curved to drain water to the stem. Water again. Avoid fertiliser at planting time or place it in the base of the hole and cover with 5 cm (2 in) of soil to avoid root contact with the fertiliser. Or better still use rose planting foods and rose soils (not to be confused with rose fertilisers) to give roses a good start. A good rose soil mixed with existing garden soil is an ideal fill-in material.

STANDARD AND WEEPING STANDARD ROSES

With potted weepers or standards the stake is driven into the ground as close as possible to the stem after planting. With field-grown bar-root or packaged roses the stake is positioned first and driven 30 cm (12 in) into the ground. The rose is placed as close as possible to it and tied in position. Stakes are needed with these rose types to prevent displacement by wind and to keep the stem straight. Avoid planting any rose types deeper than they were in the nursery; the former soil level can be clearly seen on the stem.

Rose Losses

Losses among newly planted roses generally show up in spring though existence may be prolonged till summer when death may occur. Losses are due to mishandling; leaving the roses in their box (or package) for too long before planting (or in a room or position outdoors where sun causes drying out or builds up excessive heat within the pack), or leaving them in the garden in a bare-root state allowing wind or sun to dry the plants out. Nothing fails like a dry-rooted rose in a dry hole. Over-feeding, over-fertilising, too deep planting, poor drainage and fertilising while soil is dry are other causes. Sometimes failure to water or the presence of cock-chafer grubs will cause death. The grubs may attack the roots. They are greyish crescent-shaped grubs with orange markings and can be deterred by watering the ground with Endosulphan or Carbaryl.

Once planted, new roses should be kept damp, not wet and they should not be fertilised until summer growth has commenced; the last month of spring is early enough for first year roses to be fed. Even then fertilisers should be applied sparingly, say half a cup per plant sprinkled around the outermost edge only of the foliage, not in close to the stem.

Protection from Frost

Roses tolerate the frosts of warm temperate climates. In severely frosty areas they should be planted when frost danger is either nearly or completely over. Under these circumstances *in highland areas* and in frost/snow affected climates, some frost protection immediately after planting will be needed. After that in most areas roses will fend for themselves as, once conditioned, they tolerate frosts. However, frost protection will still be necessary in frost/snow affected climates. Surround the plant with four stakes and stretch hessian round to encircle them. Nightly, place a separate piece of hessian over the top and remove it each morning. Failure to remove it will reduce light and inhibit growth. Other methods of protection are illustrated opposite.

Wind Protection

Planting in a windy area is inadvisable since rose blooms will be affected. However, wind protection can be afforded by a screen of plants or shade cloth.

Maintenance

In order of importance rose maintenance consists of watering, building-up the soil, mulching, fertilising, keeping weeds and grass away from the root system, pest and disease control and pruning. Well-watered roses in a friable soil that is kept mulched will be less susceptible to disease and fewer pest and disease-control measures will be necessary.

The following are alternative methods of protecting bush, standard and climbing roses.

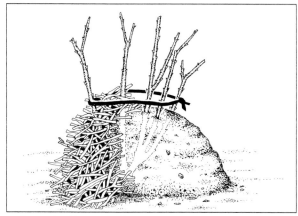

1 Mound soil over the bud union to a depth of 30 cm (12 in). Leave it exposed until the soil freezes. Cover the mound with straw to keep it frozen. Use wire mesh to keep it in place during wind or rain.

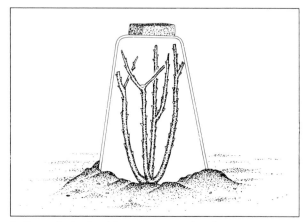

2 Cover the bush with a purpose-made polystyrene cone weighted down with a rock or brick. Mound soil around the base of the cone to keep it in place.

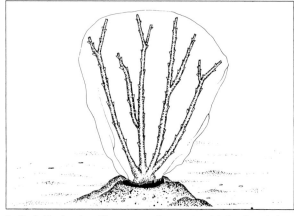

3 Pack the bush with straw and wrap it with burlap tied securely in place. Mound soil around the base.

Watering

Roses love water but it must be able to get away. Provided drainage is effective water can be applied generously. To encourage deep rooting it is preferable to water two or three times a week with long soakings, rather than to water daily. Prolonged, thorough soakings long enough to allow water to reach down to the base of the root system (a spade or spade and-a-half depth), is preferable to light sprinkling. Deep watering encourages deep rooting which affords protection for the roots during summer. Roses are perfect candidates for an inexpensive do-it-yourself 'drip' or 'spaghetti' watering system. Ground water is drip-fed or sprayed to each bush from a polythene pipe laid on (or in) the ground. Drip-feeding suits low pressure yet is very thorough. It helps control disease because it does not wet foliage. Roses planted on a slope should be built up on the lower side with stones or other material to ensure that water does not run off and that mulch can be retained. If drainage is dubious, raising the beds above the surrounding soil level can help. However, this should be avoided unless there is a drainage problem because it is possible to make the bed too dry by raising it.

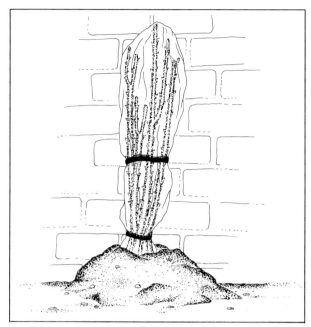

4 *Climbing roses: untie and bunch the canes. Wrap them in straw and burlap, and mound soil around the base.*

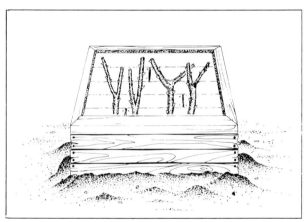

5 *Place a portable cold frame over small rose bushes. Mound soil around the base. Ventilate on cold days.*

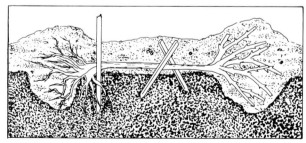

6 *Dig a trench to one side of the rose. Dig up the roots on the other side and bend the plant over into the trench. Use crossed stakes to hold the stem of standards and climbers in place. Cover the canes and roots with soil at least 10 cm (4 in) deep.*

Building Up the Soil

As explained under planting instructions, roses appreciate plenty of humus. Humus is old decayed animal or vegetable matter. Any organic matter can be allowed to rot down to form humus. Garden refuse, so long as it is not diseased, is ideal. The incorporation of this into the rose soil at least once a year will prove beneficial. Autumn or spring is a good time to add it. It can be dug in or spread down and then the mulch placed on top of it. Humus helps to keep the soil aerated and open so that the roots can run freely seeking the moisture and nutrients needed to support the plant. Humus, although it contains nutrients, is primarily designed to improve the texture of the soil. It does not eliminate the need to add fertiliser.

Fertilising

Fertilising keeps plants healthy and makes them less susceptible to disease and insect attack. In common with most other plants, fertilise roses about every six weeks from spring to early autumn. Some growers do not fertilise newly planted roses until early summer. Choose a complete fertiliser or a rose fertiliser as this will have the balanced nutrients needed by roses and other plants.

Plants require many chemical elements to make satisfactory growth. Twelve of these are taken up by the roots from the soil. The major elements are those needed in the greatest quantity and include nitrogen, phosphorus, potassium, calcium, magnesium and sulphur. Trace elements are also required, but in much smaller quantities. These include iron, manganese, boron, zinc, copper and molybdenum. Again, these are usually present in sufficient quantities in most soils although there have been many interesting cases where the absence of just one trace element has prevented a crop from reaching fruition. Soil is often unable to supply sufficient nitrogen, phosphorus and potassium for growth and these are the basic ingredients of most fertilisers.

Plants use nitrogen to produce leaves, stems and roots and phosphorus to promote flowers and fruit. Potassium strengthens their support tissues and increases their resistance to disease.

Quick-acting, water-soluble fertilisers are not so beneficial to roses in the garden situation as long-lasting, slow-acting complete foods. Old animal manure and blood and bone may also be used either on their own or, more effectively, in combination with the fertiliser programme.

FERTILISER TYPES

Fertilisers may be organic (animal or vegetable in origin) or inorganic (chemical). Both types have distinct advantages and disadvantages.

Organic Fertilisers These are animal or vegetable in origin, eg, cow manure or compost. They act as soil conditioners as well as fertilising the soil. They add material which improves aeration and drainage, and, therefore, plant health. However, the fertilising qualities of organic fertilisers are variable, being affected by age and many other factors.

Inorganic Fertilisers These contain fixed amounts of various chemicals, so that their quality is known. They can be formulated to suit particular types of plants with special needs, such as roses, azaleas and camellias, or to provide an all-purpose fertiliser to suit a wide range of plants. They are available in coated pellets, powdered, granular or liquid form as slow or fast-acting fertilisers. Unlike organic fertilisers, they add nothing to the soil-texture, supplying only food.

Compost

Under suitable conditions any organic materials, such as food scraps, prunings, grass clippings, paper, natural-fibre cloths (wool, cotton, etc) or animal dung, can be rotted down to a rich crumbly mulch or compost, which may be used to fertilise roses and other plants and enrich garden soil. Food scraps, garden waste and dung are generally used in home compost heaps, though paper and large branches can be used if they are first torn up or cut up finely. Compost needs to be kept moist and warm and it breaks down faster in warm seasons and climates.

More than one place should be provided for accumulating waste so that a cycle of filling, decaying and use can be established. In tropical, subtropical and warm temperate climates at least two heaps should be built; in Mediterranean, cool temperate and frost/snow affected climates the minimum is three heaps. In a small garden a single heap is untidy and space consuming but a simple pair of compost boxes is easy to build and provides the best results.

Compost is best made with a mixture of materials, though special leaf mulches can be made for special purposes, eg, lime-free for camellias and azaleas. A good mixture for making compost is as follows:

10 cm (4 in) household refuse
10 cm (4 in) prunings cut small, grass clippings
2 cm (¾ in) chicken manure
10 cm (4 in) household refuse
10 cm (4 in) prunings, clippings
thin dusting (4 mm (⅛ in)) of agricultural lime (helps to control odour)
10 cm (4 in) household refuse
10 cm (4 in) prunings, clippings
10 cm (4 in) torn-up paper (moistened)
thin dusting (4 mm (⅛ in)) of blood and bone, or ash

Repeat the layering until the box is full. Finish off with lime and cover with a layer of soil and soak thoroughly. A little slow-release fertiliser, eg, superphosphate, added just under the soil will increase the nutritional value of the compost by percolating through the heap as it is kept moist. Large prunings which would break down too slowly can be burnt and the ash added. Compost is ready when material just below the surface is unrecognisable, ie, crumbly and brown. Use as a fertiliser, either dug in or mulched, or mixed with soil to make potting mixes.

Note: DO NOT add perennial weeds such as oxalis or onion weed, which have bulbs, corms, etc. Often domestic heaps are not hot enough to kill them.
DO NOT put a bottom in the boxes. Earthworms must be able to come up into the heap.
DO NOT use a limed compost on azaleas or camellias.

Mulching

Mulching is the application of old animal manure or vegetable matter such as grass clippings, compost, lucerne hay or field crop residues around the base of plants in order to conserve soil moisture and to prevent the root system drying out, especially on shallow-rooted plants. It also insulates the roots from extreme heat and cold. The depth of mulch used varies according to the plants but is usually 8–10 cm (3–4 in) when first applied, and it is spread like a carpet throughout the garden, covering all the soil, or at least from the stem to the drip line (the outer edge of the plant's leaves). This covering inhibits weed growth unless the mulch itself contains weed seeds. The content of the mulching material should be considered before it is used. For example, manure from cows fed on perennial weeds will contain the seeds of those weeds many of which are almost ineradicable.

Fertiliser should be applied first. Mulching can cause a temporary yellowing of foliage if it is not thoroughly decayed material. As the mulch decomposes it absorbs the nitrogen and food from the soil and deprives the rose or shrub. This can be counteracted by applying fertiliser before mulching or by using very old dry, decayed, animal or vegetable matter.

A new mulch can be spread over an old one or the area may be dug up before a new one is spread.

Weed Control

Where mulching is employed, very little weed control will be necessary. However, if it becomes necessary, roses are fairly easy to weed. Apart from hand weeding, they are tolerant of many chemical weedicides. If these are applied either with a trickle bar or a weeding wand or watered on, weeding will be considerably easier. Avoid going near the green wood of roses with weedicides. The green wood is more susceptible to damage from weedicides than the brown wood.

Pest and Disease Control

Roses are susceptible to many diseases and several pests. Hot humid areas are more prone to black spot than dry inland areas. Humid weather encourages powdery mildew. To grow roses successfully, disease and pest control is essential and must be correctly timed and carried out regularly. See Appendix 1.

Equipment

Correct tools make rose growing enjoyable. Use a sharp spade to dig the soil initially and to keep garden edges free of grass. Use a fork to lightly turn in old mulch before adding the new. A wheelbarrow and shovel are useful, first for collecting mulch and materials for compost, and later for distributing it to the garden as mulch. A lightweight sharp chipping hoe is a useful tool for controlling weeds while they are young. Spraying equipment is very important. It pays to buy the best as spare parts are easily available.

PRUNING

For many, pruning is the biggest problem in rose growing. The physical difficulties posed by thorns and the confusing number of approaches to pruning, can be daunting, however, when the reasoning behind it is understood, pruning becomes enjoyable and constructive.

Shrubs and trees form a trunk and branches which become longer or taller as they grow older. Height and branching patterns are designed by nature to allow these plants to compete for the light and air needed for healthy growth. Woody plants grow through others to reach the light.

Roses grow quite differently from this, renewing themselves from their base instead of developing the thick, heavy wood of trees and shrubs. They send up a succession of short-lived, basal shoots to replace earlier ones which have atrophied. In the wild their relatively lax canes lean or climb on or through other plants to reach the light. Canes flower for a number of years and the quantity and quality of bloom deteriorates with time until they finally become unproductive. Hybridising has curbed the leaning and climbing tendencies of roses without changing their basal growth habit.

In modern roses pruning hastens the renewal cycle (the wave or 'flush' of flowering) by removing ageing wood and forcing strong new replacement shoots to grow. Another factor — bush size — is relevant to pruning. The larger a bush grows, the more flowers it will bear, though when unpruned it may be at the expense of their size.

Pruning is based on these facts. It maximises flower production and/or improves quality by forcing new basal shoots and maintains bushes in a size and shape in harmony with the garden's area.

Young wood is the most flower-productive. Ideally only wood three years old or less remains on the plant after pruning and the centre of the bush is left open. From above it looks like a vase with well-spaced branches outlining its sides. This shape allows air movement which aids control of black spot and other fungal diseases and it lets light into the bush for food-making and flower production.

The timing of pruning is important. Ideally it should be done just before spring growth commences. Earlier pruning, especially in cold climates with warm winter days, stimulates growth which, because it is unripe, is vulnerable and easily frost damaged, causing infection to spread down the stems into the firm wood, which looks like 'dieback' at first glance. Although new growth follows late pruning, it matures later so a flowering period is delayed or missed.

In warm temperate climates mid-winter is the best pruning time. In cold climates where spring comes late pruning is held back until just before spring growth commences.

After timing, the next pruning essentials are tools in first-class cutting order. Blunt tools make ragged cuts which become entry points for disease, which is made worse by the water resting in the cuts and cracks. Clean cuts avoid this by shedding water. Cuts are effective at an angle of approximately 45° to the stem with the top of the cut about 5 mm (¼ in) above an outward-facing bud and the base away from a bud to avoid stimulating inward-facing shoots.

When bark is damaged by pruning, it is better to lose some stem length by making a new, clean cut. This also applies if brown wood is present inside the stem. It may be dieback and cutting into clean wood well below it will be essential.

Guillotine-type secateurs are easier to manage and less damaging than the anvil style. Testing secateurs before buying is advisable. In use they become heavy to handle and their action is painful to the hands at first. Cut with the thick side of the secateurs under the cut to avoid squashing the stem. The best and most long-lasting secateurs are 'Felco'. Several different styles are available but the most popular is Grade 2. Spare parts are easily obtained.

Sharp secateurs will cut through most three-year-and-under growth. Use a pruning saw for heavier growth in old bushes. In large bushes where it is difficult to reach the centre, long-handled pruners will be helpful. Thick pruning gloves and a leather pruning apron are an investment which protects the hands and improves pruning by enabling close handling.

Cane does not last forever in roses and it is natural for it to wither and die. Removal of old wood or twigs

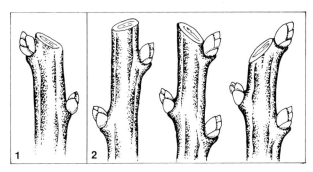

1 Pruning cuts should be made 5 mm (¼ in) above an outward-facing bud at a 45° angle and slope downwards away from the bud.

2 These stems have been cut incorrectly.

weakened from lack of light or some other cultural requirement is the first step in winter pruning and is also a form of plant hygiene which should be carried out all the year round.

The next stage is to make a balanced bush by cutting out all growths inside the 'vase' which may be crossing or be too close to each other.

This form of pruning can be done in any season. Autumn is preferable as it makes winter pruning easier — a consideration in large rose collections. Also there is no need to wait for winter to remove heavy wood past its prime if it is destined for winter sawing-off at ground level (as opposed to shortening canes).

Summer pruning is carried out in the last month of summer (mid summer in subtropical climates). It amounts to cutting each stem, whether flowered or not, as though picking flowers. The usual slanting cut is made with the bud facing the direction in which growth is to be developed. Eight to nine weeks later the bushes will be laden with blooms.

The third and last stage of pruning is governed by personal taste, plant habit and the use to which roses are being put. Some people like their bushes to be tall, others prefer short, rounded plants, and they are pruned accordingly. Tall bushes are produced from 'light' pruning, medium height from 'medium' cutting back, and short plants from severe or 'heavy' pruning. Sometimes a combination of these degrees of pruning is employed. A very tall rose may be severely pruned to keep its height uniform with a medium grower which is only lightly trimmed in order to add height.

Various landscape uses demand different degrees of pruning. Floribundas are planted for their mass display of colour. Each stem carries many flowers that are smaller than those of the hybrid tea but as a hedge or in a bed their colourful mass dominates. Bloom quantity, not size, is all important with the generous

free-flowering floribundas, so they are lightly pruned because longer canes mean more flower heads.

Hybrid teas do not have the quantity of bloom that floribundas carry but they are valued for their large size and lovely forms. Hybrid teas are often pruned hard (especially for exhibition) so that more food will be available to grow fewer, though larger and more perfect, blooms. Light, medium or heavy pruning is applicable to bush and floribunda roses.

The tendency in Australia is to prune main canes to heights between 36 and 45 cm (14–17½ in). In Europe 20 cm (8 in) is typical although taller heights are also used.

These variations illustrate both the near impossibility of damaging modern roses by pruning and their dependence on it. This is evident in neglected gardens.

Modern climbing roses are more difficult to prune due to their vigorous growth. They are not pruned in the first year after planting and often do not flower that year. Climbers should be trained horizontally in espalier fashion rather than allowed to follow their tendency to grow upwards. They are pruned immediately after flowering, followed as they age by a major pruning in winter to remove old canes at ground level.

The ends (terminals), where the nodes run close together, should be cut off about 20 cm (8 in) from the end. This is done at the end of autumn. It promotes flower-bearing auxiliary buds which will shoot vertically.

As with bush roses, wood should be restricted to canes no more than three years old. Old canes are removed at the base. New shoots and their growths are trained horizontally to form a framework from which laterals rise.

There are two kinds of laterals — those that have flowered and those with long climbing shoots without a terminal bud. Flowered laterals are cut back to two or three buds at their base. The non-flowered lateral is pinned horizontally into position, espalier fashion. New basal canes should be shortened back to hard wood and a plump growth bud.

Pillar or rambler roses are pruned in the same way. They are trained by twining them lightly around their supports. Cutting their flowers as soon as they fade will keep most ramblers flowering throughout the year.

Weeping standard roses are pruned at the end of autumn after flowering (not during winter) in the same way as outlined for climbers. Flowered stems are cut back by a third of their length reducing their lateral growths to three or four buds. Pruning the terminals of new canes allows auxiliary buds to develop. Their flower-bearing shoots bloom in spring. Since most weeping roses are spring flowering there is no point in summer pruning. In winter, old canes (three years and over) are removed. Miniature roses are lightly pruned as outlined for bush and floribunda.

The Removal of Hips

If roses are not picked, seed heads (hips) will form. All flowering plants strive to reproduce themselves by setting seed but then are slow to produce more blooms and the intevals lengthen between flowering 'flushes'. Picking the flowers (fresh or spent) stimulates roses to carry more blooms more quickly.

Disbudding

Disbudding is a form of pruning. It is applied more often to hybrid teas than to other roses. Hybrid teas with three, four or more roses per stem often have them in a bunch close together. All of these will flower, not necessarily together. Multiple blooms are excellent for garden and household colour but for exhibition purposes their size can be enlarged by disbudding or nipping out all or some of the side flower buds.

In floribundas there is a central flower which opens first in each truss. If this is removed one or two weeks before the truss is to be cut, it will accelerate the opening of the other flowers.

Watershoots

Watershoots are succulent growths arising from the graft. They carry a candelabra of flower-laden stems. Stake these if they are not strong enough to withstand wind and do not prune until they have flowered. Then remove the centre and several side shoots, leaving only three or four stems.

ROSES—AN ILLUSTRATED GUIDE

How to Use This Section

All the roses illustrated are easily maintained if given basic care. Each has been included because it is robust, fast-growing, highly resistant to disease, free flowering and in almost every instance, repeat flowering. Each rose has also been chosen for its adaptability to a wide range of climatic conditions. The rose also had to make a positive, attractive contribution to the chosen setting for it — as a colour maker (most of these roses bloom six to nine months), a cut flower, a border or hedge, as bedding, fence or walling plant, a pot plant, a pillar, trellis or ground cover. The size and growth habit of each rose should suit home gardens. Finally, the rose had to be widely available. The question of beauty took care of itself.

Roses are arranged in sections according to type — hybrid tea, floribunda, miniature and climbing — and within those divisions, according to colour. Standard or 'tree' roses are not shown separately as all roses may be grafted as standards. Below are explanatory notes on the headings and terminology used to discuss each rose.

NAME

Roses are listed under the commercial name by which they are best known. Sometimes more than one name is listed as a rose may be known by a different name in different countries. Raisers may sell the rights to name a rose in each country; or different names are given to avoid language difficulties. For example Duftwolke suits Germany but Fragrant Cloud is clearly more appropriate for Australia. To avoid the confusion of different names, in recent years the practice has begun of identifying a rose by the raiser's code name. See below, Hybridist's Code.

ORIGIN

This term refers to the 'parents' of the rose — the roses which were 'crossed' (hybridised) to produce a specific plant. Sometimes they are not listed as they have not been recorded with the International Registration Authority for Roses. Frequently, parentage is indicative of performance in the progeny and it is interesting (and comforting to some people) to realise that many 'old' roses, though no longer in catalogues, have played a part in breeding programmes.

HYBRIDISER

This is the name of the plant breeder who raised the rose. Currently there are fewer than fifty professional rose breeders in the world, understandable when one considers that it takes ten years to breed a rose. When the work is done there is nothing to guarantee popularity as roses, like clothes, are subject to fashion.

INTRODUCER

Some nurseries support their own rose hybridists and market their new roses. Independent hybridists can license nurseries to market their roses in return for a royalty on each rose sold.

YEAR

This is the year of introduction and it indicates how long a rose has remained popular. The year may vary slightly from country to country as introductions are rarely made simultaneously worldwide.

HYBRIDIST'S CODE

The first three letters of the code appear in capitals and

identify the hybridist. The other letters are his or her code for the rose. This code name for the rose identifies it throughout the world, even though the rose may also have a number of different names in different countries. This system is a comparatively recent introduction, and is not necessarily available for every rose.

SHADE TOLERANCE

Roses are sun lovers, however, many varieties will grow well in light to filtered shade. These are the varieties with a high degree of resistance to fungal diseases. In fact, in Mediterranean climates, shade during the hottest part of the summer day will prevent blooms 'burning'. This applies to all varieties subjected to very hot, dry climates, whether or not they are shade tolerant.

You can experiment with the placement of roses if you are uncertain about the degree of shade. If the position is unsuitable the bushes can be dug up and replanted easily during winter a year or two later, even many years later; though it is more difficult with old plants. Key phrases used throughout the book describe a rose's shade tolerance.

SANDY SOIL TOLERANCE

Sandy soils are those which are more sand than loam and have been built up with organic matter to suit roses. See maintenance section.

HEIGHT

Rose heights are variable and all, especially very tall varieties, can be reduced by pruning. If uniformity is needed, choose varieties from the one height range. (Heights given are the maximum for warm temperate areas. Where temperatures are below 20°C (68°F) for extended periods heights will be about one third less.)

Low	45–75 cm (17½–29 in) (includes all miniatures)
Small	1–1.067 m (yd)
Medium	1.29–1.372 m (yd)
Tall	over 1.387 m (yd)

FRAGRANCE

This term is answered with a straightforward 'Yes' or 'No'. Fragrance type cannot be defined. Like shop-bought perfume, each individual reacts differently to each rose scent.

DESCRIPTION

This section describes the rose's bud shape, flower form and colour, growth habit and foliage. 'Glossy' and 'leathery' indicate a good-looking, attractively textured foliage. These types are less susceptible to disease than thin, papery foliage. 'High centred' have the centre of the flower held well above the surrounding petals. In 'cupped' blooms all petals curve towards the centre and the outline of the rose is cup-shaped. 'Globular' flowers are even more rounded than 'cupped'. Unless otherwise stated the minimum flowering period is from spring to late autumn. Height and width will vary with conditions, care and climate. 'Repeat' blooming means a variety is quick to flower again after a flush of blooms is spent. 'Everblooming' means constantly in flower.

AWARDS

The following awards are the most sought after in the rose world and if a rose has won any of these it is a sure barometer of its value:

Bagatelle, Paris, Gold Medal
Geneva Gold Medal
National Rose Society (now Royal National Rose Society) of Great Britain Gold Medal
Portland, Oregon, Gold Medal
Rome Gold Medal
Madrid Gold Medal
Hague Gold Medal and Golden Rose
British Association of Rose Breeders' Award
From the American Rose Society:
John Cook Medal
Gertrude M. Hubbard Gold Medal
Dr W. Van Fleet Medal
David Fuerstenberg Prize
National Gold Medal Certificate
From the American Rose Foundation:
James Alexander Gamble Rose Fragrance Medal
All America Rose Selections Winner
American Rose Society Award of Excellence for Miniature Roses
In Australia:
Rose of the Year chosen by the Rose and Fruit Growers of New South Wales

VARIETIES

Under this heading come roses which usually are available in standard or 'tree' form and those which have developed a climbing form. Not every rose has a climbing form. Although only a few kinds are, any bush or floribunda rose may be grown as a standard.

CONDITIONS

This section states the optimum conditions for reasonable growth. Very few plants listed would fail to adapt to poorer or better conditions and are worth trying if an approximation of their requirements can be met.

Efficient drainage, sufficient sun for the variety, fertile soil that is kept well-watered and mulched are the main conditions for roses in sun or shade, in sandy or loamy soils. In light to filtered shade adequate disease-control measures will be necessary as shade favours fungal disease build-up. In sandy soil the incorporation of organic matter will provide food and help root anchorage.

LANDSCAPE USE
This section indicates the landscape purposes for which the rose is suited.

Use singly or in groups either with bush or floribunda roses and/or annuals for colour, cut blooms and scent. The roses described are at their best among other roses, not shrubs. This usage gives colour, fragrance and blooms for six to nine months of the year according to climate.

Another group more resistant to disease can be similarly used among small shrubs *or* roses. Including roses among shrubs is possible with many of the vigorous modern varieties.

Hedge Tidy, bushy, very free-flowering roses with the density and colour which makes an attractive hedge. Clipping is not necessary. A hedge may be mixed or of one variety. If mixed, plants of similar height should be chosen. Using one variety produces a greater concentration of colour.

Border Compact free-flowering bushes to edge garden beds and to grow under standards. Usually one variety only is used for mass colour but if heights and habits are compatible more than one can be used.

To Exhibit All rose types are exhibited at rose shows. Ability to hold form, the form itself, and stem quality are some of the attributes looked for when exhibiting roses. Almost all garden roses could be exhibited in at least one class at today's rose shows.

These should not be confused with those described as 'Exhibition' roses which usually are hybrid teas. They are produced singly, that is one rose to a stem, or they are disbudded to produce only one bloom of perfect form and quality on a stem. Examples of such roses are limited in this book because they are mainly suitable for the show bench rather than the home garden but the few included here will perform well under garden conditions.

Bedding Plant The aim of bedding is to achieve a concentration of colour by volume planting of the one variety of rose, usually a floribunda. Floribundas are chosen because most produce more flowers per stem than other rose types and so provide more colour.

They are well employed in large gardens and public plantings.

Screen Vigorous bushy varieties which could be a screen to 2 m (yd) high or less if pruned.

Mass Planting The term used for large-scale planting of the one variety of a high-growing bush rose. The objective is to mass colour.

For Commercial Cut Flower Production These are long-stemmed roses which open slowly and hold their form for days. Their growth habit is suitable for mass planting and rigorous picking.

Tub Plant This rose may be grown in tubs of 50 cm (19½ in) or more diameter. Group planting means placing two or more roses near one another. It emphasises the rose and makes maintenance easier. Several roses of the one variety together give more colour than assorted varieties.

To Climb on a Trellis, Pergola, Fence or Wall Climbing roses need support to climb. Wooden or wire fences, pergolas or trellises and masonry nails will hold the long canes. Alternatively, roses can be trained to follow the curving shape of chains between fence posts.

To Cover Columns or Pillars Pillar roses are distinctly different climbers which stay close to the support, accentuating without hiding it. Their close growth habit suits columns or pillars because it does not hide them by producing the long arms characteristic of climbing *bush* roses.

Standard Standard roses are like miniature trees. They are accent plants for formal situations such as beside a drive, along fences, near steps, in the middle or back row of a rose bed, or among shrubbery to allow room for shrubs or annuals below. They are convenient because the height of their stems places the bushes at working height and saves bending during pruning. Standards make maintenance easier as there are no thorns at ground level.

MAINTENANCE
The classic requirements of roses are ample, preferably day-long sun, efficient drainage, adequate water and a humus-rich, loamy soil. But roses are tenacious and adaptable plants capable of surviving in lesser conditions. This applies more to some than to others. Usually the general care instructions are sufficient for bushes growing in day-long sun. But if those same roses are shade tolerant and are given a position in shade, some extra feeding will be needed and disease control must be effective. Again some roses in sand

benefit from extra organic matter and mulching. Others need quick removal of spent flower heads if they are to produce another show of blooms quickly. This is called 'repeat' flowering or 'everblooming'. If the seed heads are allowed to set, repeat blooming may not occur. Yet other roses produce to capacity only if pruned by a third during summer after flowering.

Applicable additional maintenance practices are given under this heading. All roses need ample water, preferably in long weekly or biweekly soakings, a satisfactory pest and disease-control programme, suitable mulching, a loamy humus-rich soil and freedom from competition with grass roots.

H Y B R I D T E A
R O S E S

The hybrid tea is the most commonly grown garden rose today. It has well-shaped blooms on long stems and is most suitable for cut flowers. The first hybrid tea — a cross between a tea rose and a hybrid perpetual — was introduced in 1867. Some other outstanding hybrid teas not illustrated include:

• **WHITE** Elizabeth Harkness '69 & CLG '72. Crisp, creamy white buds, opening off-white with apricot shadings and fragrant.

John F. Kennedy '65. Large, high-centred white blooms; buds have a greenish tint.

• **YELLOW** Buccaneer. Buccaneer is noted for rampant growth and a sturdy constitution that allow it to grow happily under adverse conditions. Urn-shaped buds and thirty-petalled, 7.5–8.75 cm (3 in) cupped, fragrant, buttercup-yellow blooms almost cover the dark, leathery foliage, though they tend to droop.

Grandpa Dickson '66. Very large, high-centred, fragrant, yellow. RNRS Gold Medal '65; Hague Gold Medal and Golden Rose '66.

• **APRICOT/ORANGE** Dolly Parton '84. One of the most scented of all roses, this is huge — 12.5 cm (5 in) across — with up to thirty five petals so it appears full yet remains very shapely even when the blooms are fully opened. The colour is a soft light orange. It is a strong bush with semi-glossy mid-green foliage. American

Rose Centre Trial Ground Certificate (Bronze) 1982.

Just Joey '72. A wonderfully fragrant buff to apricot high-centred bloom which holds its shape for days. It is double with thirty petals. The foliage is glossy and leathery.

• **PINK** First Love '51. Pearly pink, tapered buds opening rose pink of unique form; prolific producer of cut flowers.

Royal Highness '62. Light blush-pink blooms of flawless form on long stems; large, high-centred and very fragrant. Portland Gold Medal '60; Madrid Gold Medal '62; AARS '63; ARS David Fuerstenberg Prize '64.

• **RED** Christian Dior '58 and CLG '66. High-centred to cupped, slightly fragrant, crimson-flushed-scarlet blooms. Geneva Gold Medal '58; AARS '62.

Sir Harry Pilkington '74. A very full bright-red rose 10–12.5 cm (4–5 in) across with thirty broad petals. Lightly fragrant blooms may be produced singly or several to a stem, and stand bad weather well.

Honor
(Jacolite; Michele Torr)

ORIGIN   Not available

HYBRIDISER   W. Warriner, USA

INTRODUCER   Jackson and Perkins, USA

YEAR   1980

SHADE TOLERANCE   None to light

SANDY SOIL TOLERANCE   No

HEIGHT   Medium

FRAGRANCE   Yes

DESCRIPTION   A crystal-white, large bloom up to 12 cm (5 in) wide with long strong stems. The buds are pointed and ovoid. The foliage is large and dark green on an upright bushy plant.

AWARDS   All America Rose Selection, 1980.

VARIETIES   This rose is also grown as a standard (tree rose).

CONDITIONS   Grow in sun or light to filtered shade in soil that is drained, fertile, well mulched and watered.

LANDSCAPE USE   Use singly or in groups either with bush or floribunda roses and/or annuals or among smaller shrubs for colour, cut blooms and scent; as an exhibition rose; as a standard; for mass planting.

MAINTENANCE   When grown in light to filtered shade some extra feeding and disease control, in addition to general care, may be needed.

PHOTOGRAPH: NICK BROOKE

Pascali

ORIGIN Queen Elizabeth x White Butterfly

HYBRIDISER Pepinières Louis Lens, France

INTRODUCER Alex Dickson & Sons Ltd, UK

YEAR 1963 (UK)

HYBRIDIST'S CODE LENip

SHADE TOLERANCE Light to filtered

SANDY SOIL TOLERANCE Yes

HEIGHT Medium to tall

FRAGRANCE No

DESCRIPTION A charming, medium-sized, high-centred, creamy white rose (almost ivory at its heart) which holds its shape well. Blooms have thirty pointed, reflexing petals and are carried on long, strong stems. Flowers are prolific and the bush repeat flowers quickly. Pascali is erect with mid-green foliage.

AWARDS Hague Gold Medal, 1963; Portland Gold Medal, 1967; All America Rose Selection, 1969.

VARIETIES Climbing and standard forms are grown.

CONDITIONS Grow in sun in soil that is drained, fertile, well mulched and watered, or in light to filtered shade with the same soil condition. In light to filtered shade effective drainage is even more important, especially in winter. Stands lesser soil conditions if drainage is satisfactory.

LANDSCAPE USE Use singly or in groups either with bush or floribunda roses and/or annuals for colour and cut blooms; as a hedge; a bushy and vigorous screen 2 m (yd) or less; for mass planting; as a commercial cut flower; as a climber on a trellis or pergola or against a fence or on a wall; as a standard.

MAINTENANCE When grown in light to filtered shade some extra feeding and disease control, in addition to general care, may be needed. Regular addition of organic matter to the soil and extra mulching will be beneficial.

PHOTOGRAPH: NICK BROOKE

Misty

ORIGIN   Mount Shasta x Matterhorn

HYBRIDISER   David L. Armstrong, USA

INTRODUCER   Armstrong Nurseries Inc, USA

YEAR   1965

SHADE TOLERANCE   None to light

SANDY SOIL TOLERANCE   Yes

HEIGHT   Tall

FRAGRANCE   Yes

DESCRIPTION   Cream centres blend into white outer petals on these tea-scented blooms which vary from cupped to formal and are charming in both shapes. The plump, pointed buds are carried on long, sturdy stems on a bush which is tall and robust with leathery, deep-green, disease-resistant foliage.

VARIETIES   It may be grown as a standard.

CONDITIONS   Drained, fertile, well-mulched and watered soil in sun. Stands lesser soil conditions if drainage is satisfactory.

LANDSCAPE USE   Use singly or in groups either with bush or floribunda roses and/or annuals or among smaller shrubs for colour, cut blooms and scent; a bushy screen 2 m (yd) or less; as a commercial cut flower; for mass planting.

MAINTENANCE   Follow general instructions. Additional organic matter in the soil and extra mulching will help.

PHOTOGRAPH: IVY HANSEN

Pristine

ORIGIN   White Masterpiece x First Prize

HYBRIDISER   W. A. Warriner, USA

INTRODUCER   Jackson & Perkins Co, USA

YEAR   1978

HYBRIDIST'S CODE   JACpico

SHADE TOLERANCE   Light to filtered

SANDY SOIL TOLERANCE   Yes

HEIGHT   Medium

FRAGRANCE   Yes

DESCRIPTION   Pristine is aptly named. The long buds form lightly fragrant, high-centred, nearly white blooms shaded light pink. These are large (12.5–15 cm (5–6 in) across) with twenty five to thirty overlapping petals. Pristine is classified as white though when first open there is so much pink that it could be labelled a gentle bicolour. The colours are unfading under all climatic conditions which is unusual in roses of such delicate shades. Dark, leathery foliage, a profuse blooming habit and a remarkably healthy compact bush complement the flowers.

VARIETIES   Climbing and standard forms are grown.

CONDITIONS   Grow in sun in soil that is drained, fertile, well mulched and watered, or in light to filtered shade with the same soil condition. In light to filtered shade effective drainage is even more important, especially in winter. Stands lesser soil conditions if drainage is satisfactory.

LANDSCAPE USE   Use singly or in groups either with bush or floribunda roses and/or annuals for colour, cut blooms and scent; as an exhibition rose; for mass planting; as a standard.

PHOTOGRAPH: NAN BARBOUR

MAINTENANCE   When grown in light to filtered shade some extra feeding and disease control, in addition to general care, may be needed. Regular addition of organic matter to the soil and extra mulching will be beneficial.

Sheer Bliss

ORIGIN White Masterpiece x Grand Masterpiece
HYBRIDISER W. Warriner, USA
INTRODUCER Jackson & Perkins, USA
YEAR 1987
HYBRIDIST'S CODE JACtro
SHADE TOLERANCE Light to filtered
SANDY SOIL TOLERANCE Yes
HEIGHT Tall
FRAGRANCE Yes
DESCRIPTION An elegant white rose with the palest of pink centres. The 10 cm (4 in) wide, spicily fragrant blooms are double, and of exhibition form and quality yet perfect for general garden use. They are produced singly on long strong stems. The foliage is mid green and matt, and growth is moderate on an upright bushy plant.
AWARDS Gold Medal Japan, 1984; All America Rose Selection, 1987.
VARIETIES May also be grown as a standard (tree).
CONDITIONS Grow in sun or light to filtered shade in soil that is drained, fertile, well mulched and watered.
LANDSCAPE USE Sheer Bliss is lovely either singly or in groups with other bush or floribunda roses and amongst annuals for colour and for cut blooms and scent. It is highly effective in a mass planting, as a hedge and is a superb exhibition rose. It may be grown as a standard or tree rose.
MAINTENANCE When grown in light to filtered shade some extra feeding and disease control, in addition to general care, may be needed.

PHOTOGRAPH: NICK BROOKE

Brigadoon

ORIGIN Pristine x unnamed seedling

HYBRIDISER W. Warriner, USA

INTRODUCER Bear Creek Nurseries, USA

YEAR 1992

HYBRIDIST'S CODE JACpal

SHADE TOLERANCE Light to filtered

SANDY SOIL TOLERANCE Yes

HEIGHT Medium

FRAGRANCE Yes

DESCRIPTION An outstanding rose which is basically cream blushing to strawberry coral at the edge of the petal. The pointed ovoid buds open slowly to very large, perfect high-centred blooms produced on long strong stems. It is a densely foliaged bushy plant with attractive glossy foliage.

AWARDS All America Rose Selection Award, 1992.

VARIETIES This rose may be grown as a standard.

CONDITIONS Grow in sun or light to filtered shade in soil that is drained, fertile, well mulched and watered.

LANDSCAPE USE Use singly or in groups either with bush or floribunda roses and/or annuals or among smaller shrubs for colour and cut blooms; to exhibit; for mass planting; as a standard.

MAINTENANCE When grown in light to filtered shade some extra feeding and disease control, in addition to general care, may be needed.

PHOTOGRAPH: DENSEY CLYNE

Diamond Jubilee

ORIGIN Marechal Niel x Feu Pernet-Ducher

HYBRIDISER E. S. Boerner, USA

INTRODUCER Jackson & Perkins Co, USA

YEAR 1947

SHADE TOLERANCE None to light

SANDY SOIL TOLERANCE Yes

HEIGHT Medium

FRAGRANCE Yes

DESCRIPTION A beautiful, scented, buff-yellow rose 12.5–15 cm (5–6 in) across with thirty five to fifty petals and a high, cupped centre which it retains even when the bloom is finished. Colour varies in density with the seasons but is always lovely and is unique. The blooms are at their best in autumn when the colour deepens and petal texture is strong with deep venation producing a luminous effect. The large buds are ovoid. The bush is upright and compact with dark, leathery foliage.

AWARDS All America Rose Selection, 1948.

VARIETIES This rose is frequently grown in a standard (tree) form.

CONDITIONS Grow in sun in soil that is drained, fertile, well mulched and watered, or in light to filtered shade with the same soil condition. In light to filtered shade effective drainage is even more important, especially in winter.

LANDSCAPE USE Use singly or in groups either with bush or floribunda roses and/or annuals or among smaller shrubs for colour, cut blooms and scent; to exhibit; for mass planting; as a standard.

MAINTENANCE Follow general instructions. Regular incorporation of additional organic matter to the soil and extra mulching will be beneficial.

PHOTOGRAPH: VALERIE SWANE

Amatsu-Otome

ORIGIN Chrysler Imperial x Doreen

HYBRIDISER T. Teranishi, Japan

INTRODUCER Itami Rose Nursery, Japan

YEAR 1960

SHADE TOLERANCE None to light

SANDY SOIL TOLERANCE Yes

HEIGHT Small to medium

FRAGRANCE Yes

DESCRIPTION A generous-flowering yellow. Nicely formed buds and blooms are produced freely on medium-length stems on a plant well covered in light-green foliage. Its repeat, free-flowering habit produces masses of blooms throughout the season. The blooms have good texture and last well when cut.

VARIETIES This rose is frequently grown in a standard (tree) form.

CONDITIONS Drained, fertile, well-watered and mulched soil in sun or very light shade. Stands lesser soil conditions if drainage is satisfactory.

LANDSCAPE USE Use singly or in groups either with bush or floribunda roses and/or annuals for colour, cut blooms and scent; as a hedge; to exhibit; for mass planting; as a standard.

MAINTENANCE Follow general instructions.

PHOTOGRAPH: JOHN CLUTTERBUCK

Kambala

ORIGIN   Gingersnap x Brandy
HYBRIDISER   Armstrong
Nurseries, USA
INTRODUCER   Swane's
Nurseries, Australia
YEAR   1988
HYBRIDIST'S CODE   AROheddo
SHADE TOLERANCE   None to
light
SANDY SOIL TOLERANCE   Yes
HEIGHT   Medium
FRAGRANCE   Yes
DESCRIPTION   A lovely, strongly
scented, many-petalled yellow rose
which produces several blooms to
a stem. These are at first high-
centred and become cupped with
age. Growth is dark green and
glossy on a robust bush.
VARIETIES   This rose is
sometimes grown as a standard
(tree rose).
CONDITIONS   Grow in sun or
light to filtered shade in soil that is
drained, fertile, well mulched and
watered.
LANDSCAPE USE   Use singly or
in groups either with bush or
floribunda roses and/or annuals
for colour, cut blooms and scent;
for mass planting; as a bushy and
vigorous hedge; as a standard.
MAINTENANCE   When grown in
light to filtered shade some extra
feeding and disease control, in
addition to general care, may be
needed.

PHOTOGRAPH: VALERIE SWANE

Lanvin

ORIGIN   Unnamed seedling x
Katherine Loker

HYBRIDISER   J. Christensen,
USA

INTRODUCER   Armstrong
Nurseries, USA

YEAR   1985

HYBRIDIST'S CODE   AROlemo

SHADE TOLERANCE   None to
light

SANDY SOIL TOLERANCE   Yes

HEIGHT   Medium

FRAGRANCE   Yes

DESCRIPTION   The buds are
conspicuously long and pointed.
Both buds and the yellow flowers
are shaded with chartreuse. The
high-centred, medium-sized double
blooms are fragrant and are
produced in sprays of three to five.
The dark-green foliage is semi-
glossy and tinted red on an upright
bushy plant.

VARIETIES   May also be grown as
a standard (tree).

CONDITIONS   Grow in sun or
light to filtered shade in soil that is
drained, fertile, well mulched and
watered.

LANDSCAPE USE   Use singly or
in groups either with bush or
floribunda roses and/or annuals
for colour and cut blooms; for
exhibition; for mass planting.

MAINTENANCE   When grown in
light to filtered shade some extra
feeding and disease control, in
addition to general care, may be
needed.

PHOTOGRAPH: VALERIE SWANE

Apollo

ORIGIN   High Time x Imperial Gold

HYBRIDISER   D. L. Armstrong, USA

INTRODUCER   Armstrong Nurseries Inc, USA

YEAR   1971

HYBRIDIST'S CODE   ARMolo

SHADE TOLERANCE   Light to filtered

SANDY SOIL TOLERANCE   Yes

HEIGHT   Tall

FRAGRANCE   Yes

DESCRIPTION   One of the best yellow roses from the viewpoint of constitution, bloom quality and quantity and repeat-flowering habit. It has slender, soft-yellow buds, barely tinged copper at their base. It is very free flowering with tall, straight stems topped with large, high-centred, mid-yellow, lightly fragrant blooms. These last well in the vase. The foliage is glossy, dark and leathery on a strong, bushy plant.

AWARDS   All America Rose Selection, 1972.

VARIETIES   It is frequently grown in a standard (tree) form.

CONDITIONS   Grow in sun in soil that is drained, fertile, well mulched and watered, or in light to filtered shade with the same soil condition. In light to filtered shade effective drainage is even more important, especially in winter.

LANDSCAPE USE   Use singly or in groups either with bush or floribunda roses and/or annuals or among smaller shrubs for colour,

PHOTOGRAPH: IVY HANSEN

cut blooms and scent; as a hedge; to exhibit; as a standard.

MAINTENANCE   When grown in light to filtered shade some extra feeding and disease control, in addition to general care, may be needed.

Broadway

ORIGIN (First Prize x Gold Glow) x Sutter's Gold

HYBRIDISER Anthony Perry, USA

INTRODUCER Co-operative Rose Growers

YEAR 1986

HYBRIDIST'S CODE BURway

SHADE TOLERANCE Light to filtered

SANDY SOIL TOLERANCE Yes

HEIGHT Medium

FRAGRANCE Yes

DESCRIPTION The colour is basically golden yellow blended with pink. The blooms open from pointed buds and are fragrant and very large (12-15 cm (5-6 in)) across. Foliage is dark green and semi-glossy on a strong bush. It is very free flowering and quick to repeat flower.

AWARDS All America Rose Selection, 1982.

VARIETIES May also be grown as a standard (tree).

CONDITIONS Grow in sun or light to filtered shade in soil that is drained, fertile, well mulched and watered.

LANDSCAPE USE Use singly or in groups either with bush or floribunda roses and/or annuals for colour, cut blooms and scent; to exhibit; for mass planting; as a hedge; as a standard.

MAINTENANCE When grown in light to filtered shade some extra feeding and disease control, in addition to general care, may be needed.

PHOTOGRAPH: IVY HANSEN

Orana Gold

ORIGIN   Freude x Landora
HYBRIDISER   Sam McGredy, NZ
YEAR   1990
HYBRIDIST'S CODE   Macerupt
SHADE TOLERANCE   Light to filtered
SANDY SOIL TOLERANCE   Yes
HEIGHT   Medium to tall
FRAGRANCE   No
DESCRIPTION   Shapely buds form high-centred, large blooms that are a blend of yellow, orange and red shades. These last well indoors and out, and the bush is very free flowering. The foliage is dark green on a sturdy, vigorous upright bush.
VARIETIES   May also be grown as a standard (tree).
CONDITIONS   Grow in sun or light to filtered shade in soil that is drained, fertile, well mulched and watered.
LANDSCAPE USE   Use singly or in groups either with bush or floribunda roses and/or annuals or among smaller shrubs for colour and cut blooms; as a hedge; for mass planting; as a standard rose.
MAINTENANCE   When grown in light to filtered shade some extra feeding and disease control, in addition to general care, may be needed.

PHOTOGRAPH: IVY HANSEN

Perfect Moment

ORIGIN New Day x a seedling
HYBRIDISER W. Kordes, Germany
INTRODUCER Kordes Sohne, Germany
YEAR 1991
HYBRIDIST'S CODE KOR wilma
SHADE TOLERANCE Light to filtered
SANDY SOIL TOLERANCE Yes
HEIGHT Medium
FRAGRANCE No
DESCRIPTION An attention-getting rose which is a combination of deep yellow with a broad, red edging. Nicely pointed buds unfurl slowly to a very large, flamboyantly coloured bloom with a perfect high centre. It is a compact bush with large, handsome, dark-green leaves that are strongly resistant to disease.
AWARDS All America Rose Selection Award, 1991.
VARIETIES This rose may be grown as a standard rose.
CONDITIONS Grow in sun or light to filtered shade in soil that is drained, fertile, well mulched and watered.

LANDSCAPE USE Use singly or in groups either with bush or floribunda roses and/or annuals or among smaller shrubs for colour and cut blooms; as a hedge; for exhibition; for mass planting and as a standard.
MAINTENANCE If grown in some shade, extra feeding and disease control measures, in addition to general care, will be necessary.

PHOTOGRAPH: DENSEY CLYNE

Peace
(Mme A. Meilland, Gioia, Gloria Dei)

ORIGIN (George Dickson x Souvenir de Claudius Pernet) x (Joanna Hill x Charles P. Kilham) x Margaret McGredy

HYBRIDISER Francis Meilland, France

INTRODUCER Conard-Pyle Co, USA

YEAR 1945

SHADE TOLERANCE None to light

SANDY SOIL TOLERANCE Yes

HEIGHT Medium

FRAGRANCE Yes

DESCRIPTION One of the world's best-loved roses; as nearly perfect as a rose can be. The greatest rose of all time, according to many rosarians. Peace has 15 cm (6 in) wide, high-centred, cupped, slightly fragrant blooms with forty to forty five petals. At first it is golden yellow, edged pink, changing each day until the pink dominates and the yellow pales. The flowers last well. After so many years there is still argument whether Peace is yellow or a bicolour. Once established (the first year is sometimes difficult) Peace is robust with large, glossy, dark, leathery foliage and strong stems.

AWARDS Portland Gold Medal, 1944; All America Rose Selection, 1946; American Rose Society

PHOTOGRAPH: NAN BARBOUR

National Gold Medal Certificate, 1947; National Rose Society Gold Medal, 1947; Golden Rose of the Hague, 1965.

VARIETIES Climbing and standard forms are grown.

CONDITIONS Drained, fertile, well mulched and watered soil in sun. Stands lesser soil conditions if drainage is satisfactory.

LANDSCAPE USE Use singly or in groups either with bush or floribunda roses and/or annuals or among smaller shrubs for colour, cut blooms and scent; as a hedge; to exhibit; as a climber on a trellis or pergola or against a fence or on a wall; as a standard; for mass planting.

MAINTENANCE Follow general instructions. Regular addition of organic matter to the soil and extra mulching will be beneficial.

Beauté

ORIGIN   Mme Joseph Perraud x
unnamed seedling
HYBRIDISER   Charles Mallerin,
France
INTRODUCER   Edition Française
de Roses, France
YEAR   1953
SHADE TOLERANCE   Light to
filtered
SANDY SOIL TOLERANCE   No
HEIGHT   Medium
FRAGRANCE   Yes
DESCRIPTION   Beauté is truly
named. It has long, spiralling buds
and large, precisely formed,
fragrant flowers. The distinct
colour is seen as light orange by
some, deep apricot with red
shadings by others and is classified
as a 'yellow blend'. In any case, it
is beautiful with an old-fashioned
appeal. It is sturdy with dark-green
foliage and a spreading habit.
VARIETIES   This rose is
frequently grown in a standard
(tree) form.
CONDITIONS   Grow in sun in
soil that is drained, fertile, well
mulched and watered, or in light
to filtered shade with the same soil
condition. In light to filtered shade
effective drainage is even more
important, especially in winter.
LANDSCAPE USE   Use singly or
in groups either with bush or
floribunda roses and/or annuals
for colour, cut blooms and scent;
to exhibit; for mass planting; as a
standard.

PHOTOGRAPH: NICK BROOKE

MAINTENANCE   When grown in
light to filtered shade some extra
feeding and disease control, in
addition to general care, may be
needed.

Lolita

ORIGIN   Colour Wonder x seedling

HYBRIDISER   Reimer Kordes, Germany

INTRODUCER   Alex Dickson & Sons Ltd, UK

YEAR   1973

HYBRIDIST'S CODE   KORlita, Litakor

SHADE TOLERANCE   Light to filtered

SANDY SOIL TOLERANCE   No

HEIGHT   Medium

FRAGRANCE   Yes

DESCRIPTION   The golden-bronze, cup-shaped blooms have twenty eight petals, are 12.5 cm (5 in) across and sweetly scented. Their colour is difficult to define and has also been described as golden apricot. As the blooms age the outer row of petals may carry salmon shadings. The buds are perfectly shaped and the flowers are long lasting in garden and vase. Lolita flowers continuously and very generously. It is a robust plant with healthy, leathery foliage.

AWARDS   RAFT Rose of the Year, 1981.

VARIETIES   This rose is frequently grown in a standard form.

CONDITIONS   Grow in sun in soil that is drained, fertile, well mulched and watered, or in light to filtered shade with the same soil condition. In light to filtered shade effective drainage is even more important, especially in winter.

PHOTOGRAPH: NICK BROOKE

Stands lesser soil conditions if drainage is satisfactory.

LANDSCAPE USE   Use singly or in groups either with bush or floribunda roses and/or annuals for colour, cut blooms and scent; to exhibit and as an exhibition rose; for mass planting; as a standard.

MAINTENANCE   When grown in light to filtered shade some extra feeding and disease control, in addition to general care, may be needed. Regular incorporation of additional organic matter to the soil and extra mulching will be beneficial.

Brandy

ORIGIN   First Prize x Golden Wave

HYBRIDISER   Jack L. Christensen, USA

INTRODUCER   Armstrong Nurseries Inc, USA

YEAR   1981

HYBRIDIST'S CODE   AROcad

SHADE TOLERANCE   Light to filtered

SANDY SOIL TOLERANCE   Yes

HEIGHT   Medium

FRAGRANCE   Yes

DESCRIPTION   Brandy is a rich, golden apricot as it unfolds, becoming lighter on the outside petals with age. The lovely buds slowly form classic, high-centred, fragrant blooms. Both bud and bloom stages last well in garden and vase. The unique colour and the quantity and quality of the flowers, combined with attractive mahogany foliage and healthy growth, account for its popularity.

AWARDS   All America Rose Selection, 1982.

VARIETIES   Frequently grown in a standard (tree) form.

CONDITIONS   Prefers day-long sun in soil that is drained, fertile, well mulched and watered but will grow in conditions of light to filtered shade.

LANDSCAPE USE   Use singly or in groups either with bush or floribunda roses for colour, cut blooms and scent; for exhibition; for bedding; as a standard.

MAINTENANCE   If grown in some shade, extra feeding and disease control measures will be needed, in addition to general care. Adding extra organic matter to the soil and extra mulching will be beneficial.

PHOTOGRAPH: IVY HANSEN

Marmalade

ORIGIN   Arlene Francis x Bewitched

HYBRIDISER   Herbert C. Swim and A. W. Ellis, USA

INTRODUCER   Armstrong Nurseries Inc, USA

YEAR   1977

SHADE TOLERANCE   None to light

SANDY SOIL TOLERANCE   Yes

HEIGHT   Tall

FRAGRANCE   Yes

DESCRIPTION   Truly named, this unusual rose has all the colours of slightly burnt marmalade — bright orange on the inner petal face and deep yellow on the reverse and shot with amber. The tea-scented blooms, 12.5 cm (5 in) across, and long, pointed buds are carried on tall, straight stems against light- to medium-green foliage on a robust bush.

VARIETIES   None.

CONDITIONS   Drained, fertile, well mulched and watered soil in sun. Stands lesser soil conditions if drainage is satisfactory.

LANDSCAPE USE   Use singly or in groups either with bush or floribunda roses and/or annuals for colour, cut blooms and scent; as a hedge; for mass planting.

MAINTENANCE   Follow general instructions. Prune throughout summer by keeping blooms picked and removing unwanted growth. Summer pruning encourages repeat flowering.

PHOTOGRAPH: NICK BROOKE

Royal Dane
(Troika)

ORIGIN Tropicana x (Baccara x Princesse Astrid)

HYBRIDISER Niels Poulsen, Denmark

INTRODUCER W. Kordes & Sohne, Germany

YEAR 1971

SHADE TOLERANCE Light to filtered

SANDY SOIL TOLERANCE Yes

HEIGHT Medium

FRAGRANCE Yes

DESCRIPTION A lovely, deliciously fragrant rose with exquisitely formed, high-centred blooms of coppery orange shaded here and there with apricot and salmon. Buds are long and pointed. The flowers are large (15 cm (6 in) across) and glow against the exceptionally dark, glossy, leathery foliage. Royal Dane is robust, upright and bushy and has been described as having 'just about everything — colour, fragrance, constitution and health'. It is highly resistant to black spot and mildew.

VARIETIES This rose is frequently grown in a standard form.

CONDITIONS Grow in sun in soil that is drained, fertile, well mulched and watered, or in light to filtered shade with the same soil condition. In light to filtered shade effective drainage is even more important, especially in winter.

LANDSCAPE USE Use singly or in groups either with bush or floribunda roses and/or annuals for colour, cut blooms and scent; as a hedge; to exhibit; for mass planting; as a commercial cut flower; as a standard.

PHOTOGRAPH: NICK BROOKE

MAINTENANCE Follow general instructions. Regular addition of organic matter to the soil and extra mulching will be beneficial.

Sutter's Gold

ORIGIN Charlotte Armstrong x Signora

HYBRIDISER Herbert C. Swim, USA

INTRODUCER Armstrong Nurseries Inc, USA

YEAR 1950

SHADE TOLERANCE Light to filtered

SANDY SOIL TOLERANCE Yes

HEIGHT Medium

FRAGRANCE Yes

DESCRIPTION Pointed buds are a colourful blend of orange and Indian red becoming glowing golden orange in the 10–12.5 cm (4–5 in), very fragrant, high-centred blooms. It is a tidy, upright bush with attractive, dark-green, leathery foliage and first-rate repeat-flowering habit which accounts for its long popularity among yellows.

AWARDS Portland Gold Medal, 1946; Bagatelle Gold Medal, 1948; Geneva Gold Medal, 1949; All America Rose Selection, 1950; James Alexander Gamble Rose Fragrance Medal, 1966.

VARIETIES Climbing and standard forms are grown.

CONDITIONS Grow in sun in soil that is drained, fertile, well mulched and watered.

LANDSCAPE USE Use singly or in groups either with bush or floribunda roses and/or annuals for colour, cut blooms and scent; as a hedge; to exhibit; for mass planting; as a climber on a trellis or pergola or against a fence or on a wall; as a standard.

MAINTENANCE When grown in light to filtered shade some extra feeding and disease control, in addition to general care, may be needed.

PHOTOGRAPH: VALERIE SWANE

Mojave

ORIGIN Charlotte Armstrong x Signora

HYBRIDISER Herbert C. Swim, USA

INTRODUCER Armstrong Nurseries Inc, USA

YEAR 1954

SHADE TOLERANCE None to light

SANDY SOIL TOLERANCE Yes

HEIGHT Medium

FRAGRANCE Yes

DESCRIPTION Mojave (pronounced Mo/ha/ve) is a brave mixture of bright Indian colours; fiery apricot orange, tinted nasturtium red and prominently veined. It has long, pointed buds and 10–11.5 cm (4–4½ in) wide, high-centred, twenty five-petalled flowers with a delectable scent. Glossy foliage, robust growth, very few thorns and its exceptional free-flowering habit account for its popularity over such a long period.

AWARDS Gold Medals Bagatelle and Geneva, 1953; All America Rose Selection, 1954.

VARIETIES Climbing and standard forms are grown.

CONDITIONS Drained, fertile, well mulched and watered soil in sun. Stands lesser soil conditions if drainage is satisfactory.

LANDSCAPE USE Use singly or in groups either with bush or floribunda roses and/or annuals or among smaller shrubs for colour, cut blooms and scent; to exhibit; for mass planting; as a climber on a trellis or pergola or against a fence or on a wall; as a standard.

MAINTENANCE Follow general instructions. Regular addition of organic matter to the soil and extra mulching will be beneficial.

PHOTOGRAPH: JOHN CLUTTERBUCK

Voodoo

ORIGIN   (Camelot x First Prize) x (Typhoo Tea x Lolita)

HYBRIDISER   J. Christensen, USA

INTRODUCER   Armstrong Nurseries Inc, USA

YEAR   1986

HYBRIDIST'S CODE   Aromiclea

SHADE TOLERANCE   Light to filtered

SANDY SOIL TOLERANCE   Yes

HEIGHT   Tall

FRAGRANCE   Yes

DESCRIPTION   A handsome rose with a rich fragrance, this has double (thirty five petals), exhibition-standard blooms which are a fusion of salmon yellow, orange and red. It has dark-green, glossy, medium-sized foliage and bushy upright growth.

AWARDS   All America Rose Selection, 1985.

VARIETIES   None.

CONDITIONS   Grow in sun or light to filtered shade in soil that is drained, fertile, well mulched and watered.

LANDSCAPE USE   Use singly or in groups, either with bush or floribunda roses and/or annuals for colour, cut blooms and scent. It can make a bushy vigorous screen; for mass planting and as an exhibition rose.

MAINTENANCE   When grown in light to filtered shade some extra feeding and disease control, in addition to general care, may be needed.

PHOTOGRAPH: DENSEY CLYNE

Carla

ORIGIN   Queen Elizabeth x The Optimist
HYBRIDISER   G. de Ruiter, Holland
INTRODUCER   Geo. J. Ball, USA
YEAR   1968
SHADE TOLERANCE   Light to filtered
SANDY SOIL TOLERANCE   No
HEIGHT   Medium
FRAGRANCE   Yes
DESCRIPTION   This rose is grown for the delicate colour — soft pink, shaded salmon — and perfect shape. Both are retained even when the bloom is old. Blooms have twenty six petals, are 8.75–12.5 cm (3–5 in) across and held on medium-length solid stems. Carla is better in autumn than in spring. The cool weather intensifies the colour and gives it a luminous quality. The bush is vigorous, repeat flowering and free blooming with attractive, dark-green foliage.
VARIETIES   Standard forms are grown.
CONDITIONS   Grow in sun in soil that is drained, fertile, well mulched and watered, or in light to filtered shade with the same soil condition. In light to filtered shade effective drainage is even more important, especially in winter.
LANDSCAPE USE   Use singly or in groups either with bush or floribunda roses and/or annuals for colour, cut blooms and scent; as a hedge; for mass planting; as a commercial cut flower; as a climber on a trellis or pergola; against a fence or on a wall; as a standard; to exhibit and as an exhibition rose.

MAINTENANCE   When grown in light to filtered shade some extra feeding and disease control, in addition to general care, may be needed.

PHOTOGRAPH: NICK BROOKE

Aotearoa

ORIGIN   Harmonie x Auckland
Metro

HYBRIDISER   Sam McGredy, NZ

INTRODUCER   Sam McGredy,
NZ

YEAR   1990

HYBRIDIST'S CODE   MACgenev.
Aotearoa is a Maori name which
translates as Land of the Long
White Cloud.

SHADE TOLERANCE   Light to
filtered

SANDY SOIL TOLERANCE   Yes

HEIGHT   Medium

FRAGRANCE   Yes

DESCRIPTION   Aotearoa is noted
for its fragrance. It is a high-
centred, long-stemmed, soft peach-
pink rose with large, double
blooms, attractive, glossy foliage
and strong bushy growth.

VARIETIES   May also be grown as
a standard (tree).

CONDITIONS   Grow in sun in
soil that is drained, fertile, well
mulched, and well watered. The
rose may also be grown in light to
filtered shade with the same soil
conditions although under these
conditions effective drainage is
even more important, especially in
winter.

LANDSCAPE USE   Use singly or
in groups either with bush or
floribunda roses and/or annuals
for colour, cut blooms and scent;
as a hedge; to exhibit and as an
exhibition rose.

MAINTENANCE   When grown in
light to filtered shade some extra
feeding and disease control, in
addition to general care, may be
needed.

PHOTOGRAPH: IVY HANSEN

Michelle Joy

ORIGIN Shreveport x unnamed seedling

HYBRIDISER Armstrong Nurseries, USA

INTRODUCER Swane's Nurseries, Australia

YEAR 1991

HYBRIDIST'S CODE Aroshrel

SHADE TOLERANCE Light to filtered shade

SANDY SOIL TOLERANCE Yes

HEIGHT Medium

FRAGRANCE Yes

DESCRIPTION This is a very large rose (12.5 cm (5 in) across) with many petals, light to deep peach pink in colour. Blooms are produced several to each stem. It has semi-glossy, mid-green foliage and bushy growth.

VARIETIES None.

CONDITIONS Grow in sun or light to filtered shade in soil that is drained, fertile, well mulched and watered.

LANDSCAPE USE Use singly or in groups with other bush or floribunda roses and/or annuals for colour and cut blooms; for mass planting; as a hedge.

MAINTENANCE When grown in light to filtered shade some extra feeding and disease control, in addition to general care, may be needed.

PHOTOGRAPH: IVY HANSEN

Tiffany

ORIGIN Charlotte Armstrong x Girona

HYBRIDISER Robert V. Lindquist, USA

INTRODUCER Howard Rose Co, USA

YEAR 1954

SHADE TOLERANCE Light to filtered

SANDY SOIL TOLERANCE Yes

HEIGHT Medium

FRAGRANCE Yes

DESCRIPTION The long, pointed buds develop into classic, high-centred, very fragrant, pale-rose to phlox-pink blooms. These are lasting cut flowers on erect, long stems. The habit is upright, repeat flowering and free blooming with dark foliage. Tiffany is lovely and, because it is easily cared for, remains one of the most popular pink garden roses.

AWARDS All America Rose Selection, 1955; American Rose Society David Furstenberg Prize, 1957; James Alexander Gamble Rose Fragrance Medal, 1962.

VARIETIES Climbing and standard forms are grown.

CONDITIONS Grow in sun in soil that is drained, fertile, well mulched and watered, or in light to filtered shade with the same soil condition. In light to filtered shade effective drainage is even more important, especially in winter.

LANDSCAPE USE Use singly or in groups either with bush or floribunda roses and/or annuals for colour, cut blooms and scent; as a hedge; to exhibit; for mass planting; as a commercial cut flower; as a climber on a trellis or pergola or against a fence or on a wall; as a standard.

PHOTOGRAPH: JOHN CLUTTERBUCK

MAINTENANCE When grown in light to filtered shade some extra feeding and disease control, in addition to general care, may be needed.

Chicago Peace

ORIGIN   A 'sport' of Peace
HYBRIDISER   Stanley C. Johnston, USA
INTRODUCER   Conard-Pyle Co, USA
YEAR   1962
SHADE TOLERANCE   None to light
SANDY SOIL TOLERANCE   Yes
HEIGHT   Medium
FRAGRANCE   Yes
DESCRIPTION   A large rose, 12.5–14 cm (4½–5½ in) across with fifty to sixty petals, high-centred or cupped, mostly phlox pink on a canary-yellow base. The buds are ovoid. The bush is robust and upright, flowers prolifically and is well covered in glossy, healthy, leathery foliage.
AWARDS   Portland Gold Medal, 1961.
VARIETIES   Climbing and standard (tree) forms are grown.
CONDITIONS   Drained, fertile, well watered and mulched soil in sun.
LANDSCAPE USE   Use singly or in groups either with bush or floribunda roses and/or annuals or among smaller shrubs for colour, cut blooms and scent; as a hedge; for exhibition; for mass planting; as a climber on a trellis or pergola or against a fence or wall; as a standard.
MAINTENANCE   Follow general instructions. Additional organic matter in the soil and extra mulching will help.

PHOTOGRAPH: NAN BARBOUR

59

Princess Margaret of England
(Princesse Margaret d'Angleterre)

ORIGIN   Queen Elizabeth x (Peace x Michele Meilland)
HYBRIDISER   Marie Louise Meilland, France
INTRODUCER   Universal Rose Selection, France
YEAR   1968
HYBRIDIST'S CODE   Meilista
SHADE TOLERANCE   None to light
SANDY SOIL TOLERANCE   No
HEIGHT   Tall
FRAGRANCE   Yes
DESCRIPTION   This has large, high-centred, lightly fragrant, phlox-pink flowers. It is an upright bush with leathery foliage, vigorous growth and a free-flowering habit. In spring flowers are borne both singly and several to a stem. In autumn they are carried singly and the colour is more intense.
VARIETIES   Also grown in a standard form.
CONDITIONS   Grow in sun in soil that is drained, fertile, well mulched and watered. Stands lesser soil conditions if drainage is satisfactory.
LANDSCAPE USE   Use singly or in groups either with bush or floribunda roses and/or annuals for colour, cut blooms and scent; as a hedge; to exhibit; for mass planting; as a climber on a trellis or pergola or against a fence or on a wall; as a standard.
MAINTENANCE   Follow general instructions.

PHOTOGRAPH: VALERIE SWANE

Portrait
(Stephanie de Monaco)

ORIGIN   Pink Parfait x Pink Peace

HYBRIDISER   C. Meyer, USA

INTRODUCER   Conard-Pyle Co, USA

YEAR   1972

HYBRIDIST'S CODE   Meypink

SHADE TOLERANCE   Light to filtered

SANDY SOIL TOLERANCE   Yes

HEIGHT   Tall

FRAGRANCE   Yes

DESCRIPTION   Ovoid buds open to fragrant blooms of mid and light pink with a satin blush on the edges. It blooms prolifically, repeat flowers consistently and has an excellent growth habit; upright and bushy with glossy, dark foliage, it is a mini-maintenance rose.

AWARDS   All America Rose Selection, 1972.

VARIETIES   This rose is frequently grown in a standard (tree) form.

CONDITIONS   Grow in sun in soil that is drained, fertile, well mulched and watered, or in light to filtered shade with the same soil condition. In light to filtered shade effective drainage is even more important, especially in winter.

LANDSCAPE USE   Use singly or in groups either with bush or floribunda roses and/or annuals for colour, cut blooms and scent; as a hedge; to exhibit; as a bushy and vigorous screen; for mass planting; as a commercial cut flower; as a standard.

MAINTENANCE   When grown in light to filtered shade some extra feeding and disease control, in addition to general care, may be needed.

PHOTOGRAPH: IVY HANSEN

Friendship

ORIGIN   Fragrant Cloud x Miss All American Beauty

HYBRIDISER   Robert V. Lindquist, USA

INTRODUCER   Conard-Pyle Co, USA

YEAR   1978

HYBRIDIST'S CODE   LINrick

SHADE TOLERANCE   Light to filtered

SANDY SOIL TOLERANCE   Yes

HEIGHT   Tall

FRAGRANCE   Yes

DESCRIPTION   Giant, very fragrant, deep-pink blooms develop from pointed buds. The flowers have twenty five to thirty petals and are 12.5–15 cm (5–6 in) across, cupped to flat in form and carried freely. The blooms, when full-blown, hold well both on the bush and in the vase making Friendship a rose of great decorative value. The abundant flowers, the large, dark-green foliage and a strong-growing, upright bush make this an ideal garden rose.

AWARDS   All America Rose Selection, 1979; RAFT Rose of the Year, 1979.

VARIETIES   This rose is frequently grown in a standard form.

CONDITIONS   Grow in sun in soil that is drained, fertile, well mulched and watered, or in light to filtered shade with the same soil condition. Stands lesser soil

PHOTOGRAPH: IVY HANSEN

conditions if drainage is satisfactory.

LANDSCAPE USE   Use singly or in groups either with bush or floribunda roses and/or annuals or among smaller shrubs for colour, cut blooms and scent; to exhibit; as a bushy and vigorous screen; for mass planting; as a standard.

MAINTENANCE   When grown in light to filtered shade some extra feeding and disease control, in addition to general care, may be needed. Adding additional organic matter to the soil and extra mulching will be beneficial. Summer pruning produces its best flowering habit.

Eiffel Tower

ORIGIN First Love x unnamed seedling

HYBRIDISER David L. Armstrong and Herbert C. Swim, USA

INTRODUCER Armstrong Nurseries Inc, USA

YEAR 1963

SHADE TOLERANCE Light to filtered

SANDY SOIL TOLERANCE Yes

HEIGHT Tall

FRAGRANCE Yes

DESCRIPTION Eiffel Tower is well named. The nearly thornless bush is upright and very tall and needs pruning to control its exuberant height. In the centre, at the back of a bed or as a screen it makes an impact with its non-stop flowering and long-lasting, exquisitely formed buds and flowers. The urn-shaped buds open gradually to large 8.25–12.5 cm (3–5 in), mid-pink fragrant flowers.

AWARDS Geneva Gold Medal, 1963; Rome Gold Medal, 1963.

VARIETIES This rose is also grown in a standard (tree) form.

CONDITIONS Grow in sun in soil that is drained, fertile, well mulched and watered, or in light to filtered shade with the same soil condition. In light to filtered shade effective drainage is even more important, especially in winter.

LANDSCAPE USE Use singly or in groups either with bush or floribunda roses and/or annuals for colour, cut blooms and scent; as a hedge; to exhibit; as a bushy and vigorous screen; for mass planting; as a standard.

MAINTENANCE When grown in light to filtered shade some extra feeding and disease control, in addition to general care, may be needed.

PHOTOGRAPH: IVY HANSEN

Electron
(Mullard Jubilee)

ORIGIN   Paddy McGredy x Prima Ballerina

HYBRIDISER   Sam McGredy IV, NZ

INTRODUCER   Samuel McGredy & Son Ltd, NZ

YEAR   1970

SHADE TOLERANCE   Light to filtered; at its best in day-long sun

SANDY SOIL TOLERANCE   Yes

HEIGHT   Medium

FRAGRANCE   Yes

DESCRIPTION   A very fragrant rose of classic form on long, strong stems. The long-lasting, high-centred, deep rose-pink blooms are 12.5 cm (5 in) across with thirty two petals. It grows and flowers freely, holding its shape even in prolonged periods of wet weather.

AWARDS   Gold Medal National Rose Society, 1969; The Hague, 1970; Belfast, 1972; All America Rose Selection, 1973.

VARIETIES   This rose is frequently grown in a standard form.

CONDITIONS   Grow in sun in soil that is drained, fertile, well mulched and watered, or in light to filtered shade with the same soil condition. In light to filtered shade effective drainage is even more important, especially in winter.

LANDSCAPE USE   Use singly or in groups either with bush or floribunda roses and/or annuals or among smaller shrubs for colour, cut blooms and scent; as a hedge; to exhibit; for mass planting; as a standard.

PHOTOGRAPH: IVY HANSEN

MAINTENANCE   When grown in light to filtered shade some extra feeding and disease control, in addition to general care, may be needed.

Showtime

ORIGIN   Kordes Perfecta x Granada

HYBRIDISER   Robert V. Lindquist, USA

INTRODUCER   Howard Rose Co, USA

YEAR   1969

SHADE TOLERANCE   Light to filtered

SANDY SOIL TOLERANCE   No

HEIGHT   Medium

FRAGRANCE   Yes

DESCRIPTION   Showtime is both a garden and exhibition rose. It has a fruity fragrance, is truly pink with an exquisite high-centred form. Buds and flowers open gradually and retain their shape for long periods. It repeat flowers readily. The foliage is very good-looking. It is glossy and leathery on a stocky, free-blooming bush.

VARIETIES   This rose is sometimes grown in a standard form.

CONDITIONS   Grow in sun in soil that is drained, fertile, well mulched and watered.

LANDSCAPE USE   Use singly or in groups either with bush or floribunda roses and/or annuals for colour, cut blooms and scent; as a hedge; to exhibit; for mass planting; as a standard.

MAINTENANCE   Follow general instructions. Keep Showtime free of spent flower heads to increase bloom production.

PHOTOGRAPH: NICK BROOKE

Century II

ORIGIN   Charlotte Armstrong x Duet

HYBRIDISER   David Armstrong, USA

INTRODUCER   Armstrong Nurseries Inc, USA

YEAR   1971

SHADE TOLERANCE   Light to filtered

SANDY SOIL TOLERANCE   Yes

HEIGHT   Medium

FRAGRANCE   Yes

DESCRIPTION   A splendid rose with graceful, long, pointed buds and fragrant, carmine-pink, cupped flowers which hold their form for days. They are produced on strong, tall stems. The bush repeat flowers soon after each flush of bloom. Century II is a first-rate cut flower. The attractive leathery, disease-resistant foliage complements a shapely bush which has a healthy constitution so that only minimal maintenance is necessary.

VARIETIES   This rose is frequently grown in a standard (tree) form.

CONDITIONS   Grow in sun in soil that is drained, fertile, well mulched and watered, or in light to filtered shade with the same soil condition. In light to filtered shade effective drainage is even more important, especially in winter.

LANDSCAPE USE   Use singly or in groups either with bush or floribunda roses and/or annuals or among smaller shrubs for colour, cut blooms and scent; as an exhibition rose; as a commercial cut flower; for mass planting; as a standard.

MAINTENANCE   When grown in light to filtered shade some extra feeding and disease control, in addition to general care, may be needed.

PHOTOGRAPH: IVY HANSEN

Maria Callas
(Miss All American Beauty)

ORIGIN Chrysler Imperial x Karl
Herbst
HYBRIDISER Marie Louise
Meilland, France
INTRODUCER Wheatcroft Bros,
UK; Conard-Pyle Co, USA
YEAR 1965 (UK)
HYBRIDIST'S CODE MeiDAUD
SHADE TOLERANCE Light to
filtered
SANDY SOIL TOLERANCE Yes
HEIGHT Medium
FRAGRANCE Yes
DESCRIPTION The giant,
cupped flowers, 12.5–15 cm (5–6 in)
across with fifty to sixty petals
hold their shape for days, very
gradually becoming full-blown, a
beautiful stage in the life of this
heavenly scented, dark-pink rose.
Just two blooms will make a
beautiful vase arrangement. Maria
Callas flowers abundantly and is a
tidy, plump bush.
AWARDS All America Rose
Selection, 1968.
VARIETIES Climbing and
standard forms are grown.
CONDITIONS Grow in sun in
soil that is drained, fertile, well
mulched and watered, or in light
to filtered shade with the same soil
condition. In light to filtered shade
effective drainage is even more
important, especially in winter.
Stands lesser soil conditions if
drainage is satisfactory.
LANDSCAPE USE Use singly or
in groups either with bush or
floribunda roses and/or annuals
for colour, cut blooms and scent;
as hedge; to exhibit; for mass
planting; as a climber on a trellis
or pergola; against a fence or on a
wall; as a standard.

PHOTOGRAPH: IVY HANSEN

MAINTENANCE When grown in
light to filtered shade some extra
feeding and disease control, in
addition to general care, may be
needed. Adding organic matter to
the soil and extra mulching will be
beneficial. Light summer pruning
keeps plants in continuous bloom.

Peter Frankenfeld

ORIGIN Parentage details not given to the International Registration Authority for Roses

HYBRIDISER Reimer Kordes, Germany

INTRODUCER Alex Dickson & Sons Ltd, UK

YEAR 1966

SHADE TOLERANCE None to light

SANDY SOIL TOLERANCE Yes

HEIGHT Medium

FRAGRANCE Yes

DESCRIPTION Beautiful, deep rose-pink-based petals reflex to form a base for the classic, perfect high-centred flowers. These hold their form for days, a quality which makes this rose popular on the show bench. The bush is strong growing with attractive foliage and is worthwhile under conditions of minimal care and outstanding when properly maintained.

VARIETIES Climbing and standard forms are grown.

CONDITIONS Grow in sun in soil that is drained, fertile, well mulched and watered. Stands lesser soil conditions if drainage is satisfactory.

LANDSCAPE USE Use singly or in groups either with bush or floribunda roses and/or annuals or among smaller shrubs for colour, cut blooms and scent; as a hedge; to exhibit; for mass planting; as a commercial cut flower; as a climber on a trellis or pergola or against a fence or on a wall; as a standard.

MAINTENANCE Follow general instructions. Regular addition of organic matter to the soil and extra mulching will be beneficial.

PHOTOGRAPH: VALERIE SWANE

Touch of Class
(Marechal de Clerc)

ORIGIN Micaela x (Queen Elizabeth x Romantica)
HYBRIDISER M. Kriloff, USA
INTRODUCER Armstrong Nurseries Inc, USA
YEAR 1984
HYBRIDIST'S CODE Kricarlo
SHADE TOLERANCE Light to filtered
SANDY SOIL TOLERANCE Yes
HEIGHT Medium to tall
FRAGRANCE Yes
DESCRIPTION This lightly fragrant rose has exhibition standard, many-petalled, long lasting pink flowers shaded with coral and cream. They are up to 12.5 cm (5 in) across with thirty three petals and high-centred form. The large foliage is dark green and semi-glossy. Growth is upright and bushy on a strong bush.
AWARDS All America Rose Selection, 1986; RAFT Rose of the Year in Australia, 1986.
VARIETIES May also be grown as a standard (tree).
CONDITIONS Grow in sun in soil that is drained, fertile, well mulched, and well watered, or in light to filtered shade with the same soil conditions. In light to filtered shade effective drainage is even more important especially in winter.
LANDSCAPE USE Use singly or in groups either with bush or floribunda roses and/or annuals for colour, cut blooms and scent; as a hedge; is an effective exhibition rose. It may be grown as a standard.
MAINTENANCE When grown in light to filtered shade some extra feeding and disease control, in addition to general care, may be needed.

PHOTOGRAPH: VALERIE SWANE

Paradise
(Burning Sky)

ORIGIN Swarthmore x unnamed seedling

HYBRIDISER O. L. Weeks, USA

INTRODUCER Conard-Pyle Co, USA

YEAR 1978

HYBRIDIST'S CODE WEzeip

SHADE TOLERANCE None to light

SANDY SOIL TOLERANCE No

HEIGHT Medium

FRAGRANCE Yes

DESCRIPTION A rose which is a unique colour combination: silvery lavender shaded ruby red on the petal edge. Paradise is richly scented and has long, pointed buds and large, twenty six- to thirty-petalled, full to cupped blooms, 8.75–11.75 cm (3–4½ in) across, which hold well. It blooms lavishly and has an erect habit with glossy, dark foliage. People have strong views about lavender or 'blue' roses, either for or against but never lukewarm. The graceful form, scent and the strawberry-red edge have won over many who were not fond of 'blue' roses.

AWARDS All America Rose Selection, 1979.

VARIETIES A standard (tree) form is grown.

CONDITIONS Drained, fertile, well mulched and watered soil in sun.

LANDSCAPE USE Use singly or in groups either with bush or floribunda roses and/or annuals for colour, cut blooms and scent; to exhibit; for mass planting; as a standard.

MAINTENANCE Follow general instructions. Regular addition of organic matter to the soil and extra mulching will be beneficial. The soft foliage may burn in hot climates if plants are allowed to dry out. They should be well mulched under these conditions.

PHOTOGRAPH: IVY HANSEN

Double Delight

ORIGIN Granada x Garden Party
HYBRIDISER Herbert C. Swim and A. W. Ellis, USA
INTRODUCER Armstrong Nurseries Inc, USA
YEAR 1977
HYBRIDIST'S CODE ANDeli
SHADE TOLERANCE Light to filtered
SANDY SOIL TOLERANCE Yes
HEIGHT Medium
FRAGRANCE Yes
DESCRIPTION The long buds are pointed to urn-shaped and open to very large, thirty five- to forty-petalled flowers 12.5 cm (5 in) across. The colouring is unique. There is a delectable, spicy fragrance to the high-centred, creamy white flowers edged with strawberry red and becoming red overall with age. It is sturdy and upright with a broad, bushy habit and masses of blooms. Double Delight has been the world's most popular rose for more than ten years.
AWARDS Gold Medal Baden Baden, 1976; All America Rose Selection, 1977; James Alexander Gamble Rose Fragrance Medal, 1986.
VARIETIES This rose is frequently grown in a standard (tree) form.
CONDITIONS Grow in sun in soil that is drained, fertile, well mulched and watered, or in light to filtered shade with the same soil condition. In light to filtered shade effective drainage is even more important, especially in winter.
LANDSCAPE USE Use singly or in groups either with bush or floribunda roses and/or annuals or among smaller shrubs for colour, cut blooms and scent; as a hedge; for exhibition; for mass planting; as a standard.
MAINTENANCE When grown in light to filtered shade some extra feeding and disease control, in addition to general care, may be needed. Regular incorporation of additional organic matter to the soil and extra mulching will be beneficial.

PHOTOGRAPH: IVY HANSEN

Mon Cheri

ORIGIN (Unnamed seedling of Bewitched x White Satin) x Double Delight

HYBRIDISER Jack L. Christensen, USA

INTRODUCER Armstrong Nurseries Inc, USA

YEAR 1981

SHADE TOLERANCE Light to filtered

SANDY SOIL TOLERANCE Yes

HEIGHT Medium

FRAGRANCE Yes

DESCRIPTION This magnificent rose is one of the first to bloom in spring. The huge, many-petalled, fragrant blooms are up to 15 cm (6 in) across. They begin as plump, pink buds and open to deep red on a lemon base. It is closely related to Double Delight and shares many of its qualities. It is a broad bush with semi-glossy foliage and a repeat, free-flowering habit.

AWARDS All America Rose Selection, 1982.

VARIETIES Frequently grown in a standard form.

CONDITIONS Prefers day-long sun in soil that is drained, fertile, well mulched and watered, but will grow in conditions of light to filtered shade.

LANDSCAPE USE Use singly or in groups either with bush or floribunda roses or among smaller shrubs for colour, cut blooms and scent; as a hedge; for exhibition; for mass planting; as a standard.

MAINTENANCE If grown in some shade extra feeding and disease control measures, in addition to general care, will be needed.

PHOTOGRAPH: VALERIE SWANE

Candy Stripe
(Lee Dee Bissett)

ORIGIN A 'sport' of Pink Radiance
HYBRIDISER R. Lindquist, USA
INTRODUCER Howard Rose Co, USA
YEAR 1963
SHADE TOLERANCE None to light
SANDY SOIL TOLERANCE No
HEIGHT Medium
FRAGRANCE Yes
DESCRIPTION An unusual rose likened by many to both carnations and tulips, though its classic shape does not resemble either. The plump, ovoid buds produce large flowers up to 15 cm (6 in) across with sixty petals. Candy Stripe is cupped, very fragrant and dusty pink streaked with lighter pink, almost white. It blooms very freely on a bushy plant with leathery, dark-green foliage.
VARIETIES None.
CONDITIONS Drained, fertile, well-watered and mulched soil in sun. Stands lesser conditions if drainage is effective.
LANDSCAPE USE Use singly or in groups either with bush or floribunda roses and/or annuals and among smaller shrubs for colour, cut blooms and scent; to exhibit; for mass planting.
MAINTENANCE Follow general instructions. Additional organic matter in the soil and extra mulching will help.

PHOTOGRAPH: NICK BROOKE

Anne Marie Trechslin
(Anne Marie)

ORIGIN   Sutter's Gold x (Demain x Peace)

HYBRIDISER   Francis Meilland, France

INTRODUCER   Universal Rose Selections, France

YEAR   1968

HYBRIDIST'S CODE   MEIfour

SHADE TOLERANCE   Light to filtered

SANDY SOIL TOLERANCE   Yes

HEIGHT   Medium to tall

FRAGRANCE   Yes

DESCRIPTION   A mix of glowing colours characterises this prolific, very fragrant rose. Technically it is described as 'madder red touched carmine' but the overall effect is rich coppery apricot. The buds are long and pointed; the flowers high centred and large, borne on very tall, reddish stems. The strong, healthy bush is low branching with handsome, dark, leathery foliage.

VARIETIES   This rose is frequently grown in a standard (tree) form.

CONDITIONS   Grow in sun in soil that is drained, fertile, well mulched and watered, or in light to filtered shade with the same soil condition. In light to filtered shade, effective drainage is even more important, especially in winter.

LANDSCAPE USE   Use singly or in groups either with bush or floribunda roses and/or annuals, or among smaller shrubs for colour, cut blooms and scent; as a bushy and vigorous hedge; for bedding; as a standard.

MAINTENANCE   When grown in light to filtered shade some extra feeding and disease control, in addition to general care, may be needed. Light summer pruning keeps this plant compact and gives a better repeat habit.

PHOTOGRAPH: IVY HANSEN

Red Devil
(Coeur d'Amour)

ORIGIN Silver Lining x Prima Ballerina

HYBRIDISER Alex Dickson & Sons Ltd, UK

INTRODUCER Jackson & Perkins Co, USA

YEAR 1970

HYBRIDIST'S CODE Dicam

SHADE TOLERANCE Light to filtered

SANDY SOIL TOLERANCE No

HEIGHT Tall

FRAGRANCE Yes

DESCRIPTION Red Devil is a must for those who exhibit roses and is frequently a successful contender at rose shows. The high-centred, fragrant, light-red blooms with lighter, silvery red on the reverse petals demand attention. At their centres they are reflexed with almost geometric precision. In addition to its show-business qualities, Red Devil performs well in the garden. It grows vigorously, has abundant bloom and attractive, glossy foliage.

AWARDS Gold Medal Japan, 1967; Gold Medal Belfast, 1969.

VARIETIES It may be grown as a standard.

CONDITIONS Grow in sun in soil that is drained, fertile, well mulched and watered, or in light to filtered shade with the same soil condition. In light to filtered shade effective drainage is even more important, especially in winter.

LANDSCAPE USE Use singly or in groups either with bush or floribunda roses and/or annuals for colour, cut blooms and scent; a bushy and vigorous screen; for mass planting; to exhibit.

MAINTENANCE When grown in light to filtered shade some extra feeding and disease control, in addition to general care, may be needed.

PHOTOGRAPH: VALERIE SWANE

Fragrant Cloud
(Nuage Parfume; Duftwolke)

ORIGIN Seedling x Prima Ballerina

HYBRIDISER Mathau Tantau, Germany, 1963

INTRODUCER Jackson & Perkins Co, USA

YEAR 1968

HYBRIDIST'S CODE TANellis

SHADE TOLERANCE Light to filtered

SANDY SOIL TOLERANCE Yes

HEIGHT Medium

FRAGRANCE Yes

DESCRIPTION A wonderfully scented, well-formed rose, coral red becoming geranium red, outstanding colours against its glossy, dark-green foliage. From ovoid buds the very large blooms (12.5 cm (5 in) across) with twenty five to thirty petals are freely borne in clusters of up to ten on each long, strong stem in a bush noted for robust, upright growth. Sam McGredy calls it 'the Bjorn Borg of Rosedom'.

AWARDS National Rose Society Gold Medal, 1963; Portland Gold Medal, 1967; James Alexander Gamble Rose Fragrance Medal, 1969.

VARIETIES This rose is frequently grown in a standard (tree) form.

CONDITIONS Grow in sun in soil that is drained, fertile, well mulched and watered or in light to filtered shade with the same soil condition.

LANDSCAPE USE Use singly or in groups either with bush or floribunda roses and/or annuals or among smaller shrubs for colour, cut blooms and scent; as a hedge; to exhibit; for mass planting; as a standard.

MAINTENANCE When grown in light to filtered shade some extra feeding and disease control, in addition to general care, may be needed. Regular incorporation of additional organic matter to the soil and extra mulching will be beneficial. This rose requires light summer pruning after each flowering to encourage repeat blooming.

PHOTOGRAPH: NAN BARBOUR

Samantha

ORIGIN Bridal Pink x seedling
HYBRIDISER W. A. Warriner, USA
INTRODUCER Jackson & Perkins Co, USA
YEAR 1974
HYBRIDIST'S CODE Jacmantha
SHADE TOLERANCE Light to filtered
SANDY SOIL TOLERANCE No
HEIGHT Tall
FRAGRANCE Yes
DESCRIPTION Samantha is an interesting rose. It was bred to grow as a cut flower under glass in the USA and Europe. Roses raised in glasshouses will be expensive so they must also be long lasting. Samantha was bred for the florist's trade. It is a prolific flowerer and can last over a week in the vase. Samantha has urn-shaped buds and is a medium-sized, many-petalled, high-centred, nicely fragrant red to medium-red rose. It grows satisfactorily outdoors, setting so many buds in spring that removal of some is advisable. In autumn it sets a single lovely bloom per stem. The foliage is dark green and the bush is vigorous and free blooming.
VARIETIES None
CONDITIONS Grow in sun in soil that is drained, fertile, well

PHOTOGRAPH: IVY HANSEN

mulched and watered, or in light to filtered shade with the same soil condition. In light to filtered shade effective drainage is even more important, especially in winter.
LANDSCAPE USE Use singly or in groups either with bush or floribunda roses and/or annuals for colour, cut blooms and scent; a bushy and vigorous screen; for mass planting; as a commercial cut flower.
MAINTENANCE When grown in light to filtered shade some extra feeding and disease control, in addition to general care, may be needed.

Olympiad

ORIGIN   Red Planet x Pharaoh
HYBRIDISER   Sam McGredy, NZ
INTRODUCER   Armstrong Nurseries Inc, USA
YEAR   1984
HYBRIDIST'S CODE   Macauck
SHADE TOLERANCE   Light to filtered
SANDY SOIL TOLERANCE   Yes
HEIGHT   Medium to tall
FRAGRANCE   Yes
DESCRIPTION   Medium-red, double (thirty five petals) blooms, have a light fragrance and elegant form. The mid-green, matt foliage is large and the growth is bushy and upright. It is one of the strongest and easiest-to-grow of all roses.
AWARDS   All America Rose Selection, 1984.
VARIETIES   May also be grown as a standard (tree).
CONDITIONS   Grow in sun or light to filtered shade in soil that is drained, fertile, well mulched and watered.
LANDSCAPE USE   Use singly or in groups either with bush or floribunda roses and/or annuals or among smaller shrubs for colour, and cut blooms; as a hedge or bushy vigorous screen; for mass planting; as a standard or tree (rose).
MAINTENANCE   When grown in light to filtered shade some extra feeding and disease control, in addition to general care, may be needed.

PHOTOGRAPH: VALERIE SWANE

Mister Lincoln

ORIGIN Chrysler Imperial x Charles Mallerin

HYBRIDISER Herbert C. Swim & O. L. Weeks, USA

INTRODUCER Conard-Pyle Co, USA

YEAR 1964

SHADE TOLERANCE Light to filtered

SANDY SOIL TOLERANCE Yes

HEIGHT Tall

FRAGRANCE Yes

DESCRIPTION A great red. The scent, velvety, rich-red colour, giant blooms, dark-green leathery foliage and very vigorous growth are outstanding. Urn-shaped buds form large, richly scented blooms on long, strong stems. Flowers are between 11.5–15 cm (4½–6 in) across with thirty to forty firm-textured petals and vary from high centred to cupped. The new growth is bright red and stretches out to set flower heads, the foliage gradually darkening as the buds commence forming and opening.

Mister Lincoln, Oklahoma and Papa Meilland — three great reds — all share the same parents.

AWARDS All America Rose Selection, 1965.

VARIETIES Climbing and standard forms are grown.

CONDITIONS Grow in sun in soil that is drained, fertile, well mulched and watered, or in light to filtered shade with the same soil condition. In light to filtered shade effective drainage is even more important, especially in winter. Stands lesser soil conditions if drainage is satisfactory.

LANDSCAPE USE Use singly or in groups either with bush or floribunda roses and/or annuals or among smaller shrubs for colour, cut blooms and scent; as a hedge; for mass planting; as a commercial cut flower; as a climber on a trellis or pergola or against a fence or on a wall; as a standard; as an exhibition rose.

MAINTENANCE When grown in light to filtered shade some extra feeding and disease control, in addition to general care, may be needed. The regular addition of organic matter to the soil and extra mulching will be beneficial.

PHOTOGRAPH: VALERIE SWANE

Papa Meilland

ORIGIN Chrysler Imperial x Charles Mallerin

HYBRIDISER Alain Meilland, France

INTRODUCER Universal Rose Selections, France; Wheatcroft Bros, UK; Wheatcroft & Sons, UK

YEAR 1963

HYBRIDIST'S CODE Meisar

SHADE TOLERANCE None to light

SANDY SOIL TOLERANCE Yes

HEIGHT Tall

FRAGRANCE Yes

DESCRIPTION One of a trio of elegant, red, scented roses all with the same parentage; see Mister Lincoln and Oklahoma. The gorgeous blooms are velvety dark crimson, very fragrant, high centred and large with thirty five petals. Buds are pointed. The petals are slightly pointed and nicely reflexed. In the fully blown bloom these frame a centre of golden stamens. The fragrance and colour of Papa Meilland are slightly stronger in late autumn and early winter. The strong-growing, upright bush blooms very freely and has glossy, olive-green, leathery foliage.

VARIETIES Climbing and standard forms are grown.

CONDITIONS Drained, fertile, well-mulched and watered soil in sun. Stands lesser soil conditions if drainage is satisfactory.

LANDSCAPE USE Use singly or in groups either with bush or floribunda roses and/or annuals for colour, cut blooms and scent; as a hedge; to exhibit and as an exhibition rose; a bushy and vigorous screen; for mass planting; as a commercial cut flower; as a climber on a trellis or pergola or against a fence or on a wall; as a standard.

MAINTENANCE Follow general instructions. Regular addition of organic matter to the soil and extra mulching will be beneficial.

PHOTOGRAPH: IVY HANSEN

Chrysler Imperial

ORIGIN   Charlotte Armstrong x Mirandy

HYBRIDISER   Dr W. E. Lammerts, USA

INTRODUCER   Germain's Inc, USA

YEAR   1952

SHADE TOLERANCE   None to light

SANDY SOIL TOLERANCE   No

HEIGHT   Medium

FRAGRANCE   Yes

DESCRIPTION   A magnificent red rose epitomising for many all that a rose should be. Long, pointed buds open to high-centred, large, forty- to fifty-petalled flowers 11.5–12.5 cm (4½–5 in) across. These are crimson red, shaded darker velvety red and have a strong, sweet scent. They last well on the bush or in the vase remaining beautiful when past their prime and their colour has changed to a rich purple-crimson hue. Dark semi-glossy foliage complements its vigorous compact habit.

AWARDS   Portland Gold Medal, 1951; All America Rose Selection, 1953; American Rose Society John Cook Medal, 1964; James Alexander Gamble Rose Fragrance Medal, 1965.

VARIETIES   Climbing and standard (tree) form grown.

CONDITIONS   Drained, fertile, well-watered and mulched soil in sun or light shade.

LANDSCAPE USE   Use singly or in groups either with bush or floribunda roses and/or annuals for colour, cut blooms and scent; as a hedge; to exhibit; for mass planting; as a commercial cut flower; as a climber on a trellis or pergola or against a fence or on a wall; as a standard.

MAINTENANCE   Follow general instructions.

PHOTOGRAPH: IVY HANSEN

Precious Platinum
(Red Star, Opa Potschke)

ORIGIN Red Planet x Franklin Engelmann

HYBRIDISER Dicksons of Hawlmark, UK

INTRODUCER Dicksons of Hawlmark, UK

YEAR 1974

SHADE TOLERANCE Light to filtered

SANDY SOIL TOLERANCE No

HEIGHT Medium

FRAGRANCE Yes

DESCRIPTION Cardinal-red blooms are 7.5 cm (2¾ in) across, high-centred, full and slightly fragrant with thick-textured petals. The quality blooms are produced in quantity, mostly one to each long stem and are excellent cut flowers. Precious Platinum's glossy foliage is highly resistant to fungus disease.

VARIETIES This rose is frequently grown in a standard form.

CONDITIONS Grow in sun in soil that is drained, fertile, well mulched and watered, or in light to filtered shade with the same soil condition. In light to filtered shade effective drainage is even more important, especially in winter.

LANDSCAPE USE Use singly or in groups either with bush or floribunda roses and/or annuals or among smaller shrubs for colour, cut blooms and scent; to exhibit; for mass planting; as a standard.

MAINTENANCE When grown in light to filtered shade some extra feeding and disease control, in addition to general care, may be needed. Regular addition of organic matter to the soil and extra mulching will be beneficial.

PHOTOGRAPH: IVY HANSEN

Bing Crosby

ORIGIN Unnamed seedling x First Prize

HYBRIDISER O. L. Weeks, USA

INTRODUCER O. L. Weeks, USA

YEAR 1981

SHADE TOLERANCE Light to filtered

SANDY SOIL TOLERANCE Yes

HEIGHT Medium

FRAGRANCE No

DESCRIPTION A colourful rose with magnificently large persimmon-red, consistently fine blooms formed from handsome, ovoid buds. Blooms are produced singly on long strong stems. It is vigorous with dark, glossy foliage. An excellent garden or exhibition rose.

AWARDS All America Rose Selection, 1981.

VARIETIES Frequently grown in a standard form.

CONDITIONS Prefers day-long sun in soil that is drained, fertile, well mulched and watered but will grow in conditions of light to filtered shade.

LANDSCAPE USE Use singly or in groups either with bush or floribunda roses and/or annuals or among smaller shrubs for colour, cut blooms; to exhibit; for mass planting; as a standard.

MAINTENANCE If grown in some shade, extra feeding and disease control measures will be needed and additional organic matter in the soil and extra mulching will be beneficial.

PHOTOGRAPH: IVY HANSEN

Grande Amore

ORIGIN Parentage details not available.

SHADE TOLERANCE Light to filtered.

SANDY SOIL TOLERANCE Yes

HEIGHT Medium

FRAGRANCE Yes

DESCRIPTION A gorgeous rose with rich lingering scent and large (12.5 cm (5 in)) many-petalled, crimson-red blooms which open slowly to their classic shape. It blooms very freely and is quick to repeat flower after each flush. The dark-green, leathery foliage and sturdy, compact shape are other good qualities.

VARIETIES It makes an attractive standard.

CONDITIONS Grow in sun in soil that is drained, fertile, well mulched and watered, or in light to filtered shade with the same soil condition where effective drainage is even more important, especially in winter. Stands lesser soil conditions if drainage is satisfactory.

LANDSCAPE USE Use singly or in groups either with bush or floribunda roses and/or annuals or among smaller shrubs for colour, cut blooms and scent; as a hedge; as an exhibition rose; for mass planting; for bedding.

MAINTENANCE When grown in light to filtered shade some extra feeding and disease control, in addition to general care, may be needed.

PHOTOGRAPH: IVY HANSEN

Ingrid Bergman

ORIGIN   Unnamed seedling x unnamed seedling

HYBRIDISER   D. T. Poulsen, Denmark

INTRODUCER   John Mattock Ltd, UK

YEAR   1983

HYBRIDIST'S CODE   Poulman

SHADE TOLERANCE   Light to filtered

SANDY SOIL TOLERANCE   Yes

HEIGHT   Medium

FRAGRANCE   Yes

DESCRIPTION   A lightly fragrant, medium-sized, warm dark-red, double rose which blooms freely and continuously and lasts well in the garden or as a cut flower. It has dark-green, semi-glossy foliage and vigorous upright growth.

AWARDS   Silver Medals in Rome and Geneva, 1984; Gold Medal Belfast, 1985.

VARIETIES   May also be grown as a standard (tree).

CONDITIONS   Grow in sun or light to filtered shade in soil that is drained, fertile, well mulched and watered.

LANDSCAPE USE   Use singly or in groups either with bush or floribunda roses and/or annuals for colour, and cut blooms; for mass planting; as a hedge.

MAINTENANCE   When grown in light to filtered shade some extra feeding and disease control, in addition to general care, may be needed.

PHOTOGRAPH: IVY HANSEN

Kentucky Derby

ORIGIN   John S. Armstrong x Grand Slam

HYBRIDISER   D. L. Armstrong, USA

INTRODUCER   Armstrong Nurseries Inc, USA

YEAR   1972

SHADE TOLERANCE   Light to filtered

SANDY SOIL TOLERANCE   Yes

HEIGHT   Tall

FRAGRANCE   Yes

DESCRIPTION   The huge (15 cm (6 in) wide), dark velvet-red, high-centred flowers are shaded an even deeper red. It is a healthy, almost rampant bush with glossy, leathery foliage and a repeat flowering habit.

VARIETIES   None

CONDITIONS   Grow in sun in soil that is drained, fertile, well mulched and watered, or in light to filtered shade with the same soil condition where effective drainage is important, especially in winter.

LANDSCAPE USE   Use singly or in groups either with bush or floribunda roses and/or annuals or among smaller shrubs for colour, cut blooms and scent; to exhibit; a bushy and vigorous screen capable of 2 m (yd) though it may be reduced to less; for mass planting.

MAINTENANCE   When grown in light to filtered shade some extra feeding and disease control, in addition to general care, may be needed.

PHOTOGRAPH: IVY HANSEN

Avon

ORIGIN   Nocturne x Chrysler Imperial
HYBRIDISER   Dennison Morey
INTRODUCER   Jackson & Perkins Co, USA
YEAR   1961
SHADE TOLERANCE   Light to filtered
SANDY SOIL TOLERANCE   Yes
HEIGHT   Medium
FRAGRANCE   Yes
DESCRIPTION   One of the truly great reds! A wealth of long, pointed buds open to large, very fragrant high-centred, beautifully formed blooms of unfading red from spring to autumn. They are 11.5–12.5 cm (4½–5 in) across, and are long-lasting cut flowers. It is a neat, vigorous, upright bush covered in leathery foliage. It has a good repeat flowering habit especially in hotter climates.
VARIETIES   Climbing and standard forms are grown.
CONDITIONS   Grow in sun in soil that is drained, fertile, well mulched and watered, or in light to filtered shade with the same soil condition. In light to filtered shade effective drainage is even more important, especially in winter.
LANDSCAPE USE   Use singly or in groups either with bush or floribunda roses and/or annuals or among smaller shrubs for colour, cut blooms and scent; as a hedge; to exhibit; for mass planting; as a commercial cut flower; as a climber on a trellis or pergola; or against a fence or on a wall; as a standard.
MAINTENANCE   When grown in light to filtered shade some extra feeding and disease control, in addition to general care, may be needed.

PHOTOGRAPH: IVY HANSEN

The Riverview Centenary Rose
(Riverview)

ORIGIN   Cara Mia x (Night and Day x Plain Talk)

HYBRIDISER   Jack L. Christensen, Armstrong Nurseries Inc, USA

INTRODUCER   St Ignatius College through Swane's Nurseries, Australia

YEAR   1980

SHADE TOLERANCE   Light to filtered

SANDY SOIL TOLERANCE   Yes

HEIGHT   Medium

FRAGRANCE   Yes

DESCRIPTION   The classic garden rose, repeat blooming, floriferous, robust and an excellent cut flower. It is a beautiful dark-red, high-centred, many-petalled and large (12.5–15 cm (5–6 in) across) rose. There is a barely noticeable scent. What it lacks in that direction is compensated by its long-lasting qualities on the bush and in the vase. The light-green foliage is closely placed on a broad, tidy, but compact bush. It is a robust grower making strong basal growth each year. A very carefree red which repeat flowers continuously. The blooms darken with age. It was introduced for St Ignatius College, Lane Cove, Sydney, Australia, better known as 'Riverview', to celebrate its centenary in 1980.

VARIETIES   This rose is frequently grown in a standard (tree) form.

CONDITIONS   Grow in sun in soil that is drained, fertile, well mulched and watered. Stands lesser soil conditions if drainage is satisfactory.

LANDSCAPE USE   Use singly or in groups either with bush or floribunda roses and/or annuals for colour and cut blooms; as a hedge; to exhibit; for mass planting; as a commercial cut flower; as a standard.

MAINTENANCE   When grown in light to filtered shade some extra feeding and disease control, in addition to general care, may be needed. Regular addition of organic matter to the soil and extra mulching will be beneficial.

PHOTOGRAPH: NICK BROOKE

Oklahoma

ORIGIN Chrysler Imperial x Charles Mallerin

HYBRIDISER Herbert C. Swim and O. L. Weeks, USA

INTRODUCER Weeks Wholesale Rose Grower, USA

YEAR 1963

SHADE TOLERANCE Light to filtered

SANDY SOIL TOLERANCE Yes

HEIGHT Medium to tall

FRAGRANCE Yes

DESCRIPTION One of the darkest reds. A magnificent rose, unforgettably perfumed, dark red and exquisitely high centred. Large blooms, 10–13.75 cm (4–5½ in) across, with forty to fifty five petals are long-lasting and hold their form even when past their prime. The bushy, robust plant flowers consistently and has attractive, dark, leathery foliage.

A point of interest is that this rose has the same parents as two other lovely reds, Mister Lincoln and Papa Meilland.

AWARDS Gold Medal Japan, 1963.

VARIETIES Climbing and standard forms are grown.

CONDITIONS Grow in sun in soil that is drained, fertile, well mulched and watered, or in light to filtered shade with the same soil condition. In light to filtered shade effective drainage is even more important, especially in winter. Stands lesser soil conditions if drainage is satisfactory.

PHOTOGRAPH: IVY HANSEN

LANDSCAPE USE Use singly or in groups either with bush or floribunda roses and/or annuals or among smaller shrubs for colour, cut blooms and scent; as a hedge; to exhibit; for mass planting; as a commercial cut flower; as a climber on a trellis or pergola or against a fence or on a wall; as a standard.

MAINTENANCE When grown in light filtered shade some extra feeding and disease control, in addition to general care, may be needed. Regular addition of organic matter to the soil and extra mulching will be beneficial.

Fragrant Plum

ORIGIN   Shocking Blue x Blue Nile x Ivory Tower

HYBRIDISER   Armstrong Nurseries Inc, USA

INTRODUCER   Armstrong Nurseries Inc, USA

YEAR   1988

HYBRIDIST'S CODE   Aroplumi

SHADE TOLERANCE   Light to filtered

SANDY SOIL TOLERANCE   Yes

HEIGHT   Medium

FRAGRANCE   Yes

DESCRIPTION   One of the most fragrant of all roses, this rose has deep-lilac blooms edged rose purple. They are high centred, and many petalled, holding their form for days. The foliage is mid green and semi-glossy and growth is bushy.

VARIETIES   May also be grown as a standard (tree).

CONDITIONS   Grow in sun or light to filtered shade in soil that is drained, fertile, well mulched and watered.

LANDSCAPE USE   Use singly or in groups either with bush or floribunda roses and/or annuals or among smaller shrubs for colour, cut blooms and above all for scent; as a hedge; for exhibition; and for mass planting.

MAINTENANCE   When grown in light to filtered shade some extra feeding and disease control, in addition to general care, may be needed.

PHOTOGRAPH: VALERIE SWANE

Blue Moon
(Mainzer Fastnach, Sissi, Tannacht, Blue Monday)

ORIGIN   Sterling Silver seedling x unknown seedling

HYBRIDISER   Mathau Tantau, Germany

INTRODUCER   Mathau Tantau, Germany

YEAR   1964

SHADE TOLERANCE   Light to filtered

SANDY SOIL TOLERANCE   Yes

HEIGHT   Medium to tall

FRAGRANCE   Yes

DESCRIPTION   Elegant, high-centred, long-lasting, fragrant, lilac blooms develop from long, pointed buds. These are exhibition quality, 11.5–12.5 cm (4½–5 in) across and produced on long stems bearing only a few thorns. In the vase both buds and blooms hold well. Blue Moon flowers freely and continuously and is seldom without a bloom. It is worth a place in the garden for the scent alone. The bluish-mauve colour evokes strong feeling — being liked or disliked with equal vigour but rarely regarded with indifference. The colour is lovely near deep reds or white. In dark rooms it appears almost grey. It has mid-green foliage and robust growth even in poor soil.

AWARDS   Gold Medal Rome, 1964.

VARIETIES   This rose is frequently grown in a standard (tree) form.

CONDITIONS   Grow in sun in soil that is drained, fertile, well mulched and watered, or in light to filtered shade with the same soil conditions. In light to filtered shade effective drainage is even more important, especially in winter.

PHOTOGRAPH: JOHN CLUTTERBUCK

LANDSCAPE USE   Use singly or in groups either with bush or floribunda roses and/or annuals or among smaller shrubs for colour, cut blooms and scent; for mass planting; a bushy and vigorous hedge or screen; as a commercial cut flower; as a standard; as an exhibition rose.

MAINTENANCE   When grown in light to filtered shade some extra feeding and disease control, in addition to general care, may be needed.

Big Purple

ORIGIN Purple Splendour x unknown seedling

HYBRIDISER Pat Stephens, NZ

INTRODUCER Sam McGredy, Roses International, NZ

YEAR 1990

HYBRIDIST'S CODE Stibigpu

SHADE TOLERANCE Light to filtered

SANDY SOIL TOLERANCE Yes

HEIGHT Tall

FRAGRANCE Yes

DESCRIPTION A magnificently large bloom with a heady scent. The large, purplish buds spiral open to high-centred purple blooms. It has greyish to dark-green foliage on an upright bushy plant.

VARIETIES May also be grown as a standard (tree).

CONDITIONS Grow in sun or light to filtered shade in soil that is drained, fertile, well mulched and watered.

LANDSCAPE USE Use singly or in groups either with bush or floribunda roses and/or annuals or among smaller shrubs for colour, cut blooms and scent; as a hedge; as an exhibition rose; for mass planting.

MAINTENANCE When grown in light to filtered shade some extra feeding and disease control, in addition to general care, may be needed.

PHOTOGRAPH: NICK BROOKE

FLORIBUNDA ROSES

Floribundas are shorter and bushier than the hybrid teas and bear several flowers in clusters. They flower for longer periods than the hybrid teas, but are not as suitable for use as cut flowers. Some other outstanding floribundas not illustrated include:

• **BUFF AND BONE** Iced Ginger '71. Buff blooms reflecting the deeper ginger-apricot shade on the reverse; very fragrant.

• **YELLOW** Katherine Loker '78. Pointed bud and outstanding classic flower form; fragrant butter-yellow blooms.

Whiskey '64. Large open, slightly fragrant, yellow shaded orange bronze; abundant blooms.

• **APRICOT/ORANGE** Ginger Meggs '71. Distinctive carrot-red, fragrant, freely produced blooms.

Orange Triumph '37. Small, semi-double, cupped, bright-orange, slightly fragrant blooms. NRS Gold Medal '37.

• **PINK** Anna Louisa '67. Soft-pink flowers in large clusters; free blooming.

Pink Chiffon '56. Classic shade of La France pink (petticoat pink); large-cupped to flat blooms and very fragrant.

• **RED/PURPLE** Evelyn Fison '62. This rose has scarlet clusters of slightly fragrant blooms. NRS Gold Medal '63.

Deep Purple '80. Well-formed, deep-purple buds and blooms; large and fragrant.

Iceberg
(Schneewittchen, Fee des Neiges)

ORIGIN Robin Hood x Virgo
HYBRIDISER Reimer Kordes, Germany
INTRODUCER R. Kordes, Germany
YEAR 1958
SHADE TOLERANCE Light to filtered
SANDY SOIL TOLERANCE Yes
HEIGHT Medium to tall
FRAGRANCE Yes
DESCRIPTION One of the most popular of all roses, Iceberg is also one of the most free-flowering, carrying ample clusters of fragrant, pure-white, open blooms. It is strong, bushy and upright with attractive light-green, glossy foliage. An excellent hedge if lightly trimmed frequently to maintain flowering.
AWARDS National Rose Society Gold Medal, 1958.
VARIETIES It is grown as a standard and there is a climbing form.
CONDITIONS Grow in sun in soil that is drained, fertile, well mulched and watered, or in light to filtered shade with the same soil condition. In light to filtered shade effective drainage is even more important, especially in winter.
LANDSCAPE USE Use singly or in groups either with bush or floribunda roses and/or annuals or among smaller shrubs for colour, cut blooms and scent; as a hedge; to exhibit; for bedding; for a tub plant; as a climber on a trellis or pergola; against a fence or on a wall.
MAINTENANCE When grown in light to filtered shade some extra feeding and disease control, in addition to general care, may be needed.

PHOTOGRAPH: IVY HANSEN

Crystalline

ORIGIN Bridal Pink x unnamed seedling

HYBRIDISER Armstrong Nurseries Inc, USA

INTRODUCER Armstrong Nurseries Inc, USA

YEAR 1988

HYBRIDIST'S CODE Arobipy

SHADE TOLERANCE Light to filtered

SANDY SOIL TOLERANCE Yes

HEIGHT Medium

FRAGRANCE Yes

DESCRIPTION A lovely long-stemmed rose carrying several blooms per stem. These are clear white and very fragrant with a high-centred form. It has light-green foliage and bushy growth. Among the best of the white roses.

VARIETIES May also be grown as a standard (tree).

CONDITIONS Grow in sun or light to filtered shade in soil that is drained, fertile, well mulched and watered.

LANDSCAPE USE Use singly or in groups, either with bush or floribunda roses and/or annuals for colour, cut blooms and scent; to exhibit; for mass planting; as a standard.

MAINTENANCE When grown in light to filtered shade some extra feeding and disease control, in addition to general care, may be needed.

PHOTOGRAPH: NICK BROOKE

Class Act

ORIGIN Sun Flare x unnamed seedling

HYBRIDISER W. Warriner, USA

INTRODUCER Bear Creek Nurseries, USA

YEAR 1989

HYBRIDIST'S CODE JACare

SHADE TOLERANCE Light to filtered

HEIGHT Medium

FRAGRANCE No

DESCRIPTION A charming, aptly named rose with pointed, cream-coloured buds which pop open into very large, semi-double, snowy white blooms showing bright-yellow stamens at their centres. There are several blooms to each strong stem. It is a dense, glossy green-foliaged bush with strong resistance to disease and a continuous blooming habit. It promises to be a rival for Iceberg.

AWARDS All America Rose Selection, 1989.

VARIETIES May also be grown as a standard (tree).

CONDITIONS Grow in sun or light to filtered shade in soil that is drained, fertile, well mulched and watered.

LANDSCAPE USE This rose lends itself to mass plantings since it flowers for almost ten months of the year in warm climates. It may be used singly or in groups either with bush or floribunda roses and/ or annuals or among smaller shrubs for colour and cut blooms. It makes an excellent hedge, and is suitable for bedding or as a large tub plant.

MAINTENANCE When grown in light to filtered shade some extra feeding and disease control, in addition to general care, may be needed.

PHOTOGRAPH: DENSEY CLYNE

Foster's Melbourne Cup
(Foster's Wellington Cup)

ORIGIN Sexy Rexy x Pot o' Gold
HYBRIDISER Sam McGredy, NZ
INTRODUCER Sam McGredy, NZ
YEAR 1988
SHADE TOLERANCE None to light
SANDY SOIL TOLERANCE Yes
HEIGHT Medium to tall
FRAGRANCE Yes
DESCRIPTION A petite and very pretty camellia-like white rose with a small high-pointed centre surrounded by slightly ruffled petals which open almost flat in the last stages when a centre of golden stamens is revealed. There are several flowers to each stem. It flowers as freely as Iceberg. The foliage is mid green and growth is compact.
VARIETIES May also be grown as a standard (tree).
CONDITIONS Grow in sun or light to filtered shade in soil that is drained, fertile, well mulched and watered.
LANDSCAPE USE Use as a hedge; as a border; for bedding; or as a container plant; or use singly or in groups either with bush or floribunda roses and/or annuals or among smaller shrubs for colour and cut blooms.
MAINTENANCE When grown in light to filtered shade some extra feeding and disease control, in addition to general care, may be needed.

PHOTOGRAPH: VALERIE SWANE

Valerie Swane

ORIGIN   Ivory Tower x Angel Face

HYBRIDISER   Armstrong Nurseries Inc, USA

INTRODUCER   Swane's Nurseries, Australia

YEAR   1988

HYBRIDIST'S CODE   AROkish

SHADE TOLERANCE   None to light

SANDY SOIL TOLERANCE   Yes

HEIGHT   Medium

FRAGRANCE   Yes

DESCRIPTION   A nicely fragrant, shapely, high-centred white rose which is ivory at its centre. Blooms are produced in clusters on strong stems. The buds are long and pointed and the bush is very free flowering. Foliage is glossy and mid green with upright growth.

VARIETIES   May also be grown as a standard (tree).

CONDITIONS   Grow in sun in soil that is drained, fertile, well mulched and watered.

LANDSCAPE USE   A rose to grow for its scent. Use singly or in groups either with bush or floribunda roses and/or annuals for colour, cut blooms and scent. It is suitable for mass planting, as an exhibition rose and as a standard rose.

MAINTENANCE   Follow general care instructions.

PHOTOGRAPH: VALERIE SWANE

Saratoga

ORIGIN   White Bouquet x Princess White

HYBRIDISER   E. S. Boerner, USA

INTRODUCER   Jackson & Perkins Co, USA

YEAR   1963

SHADE TOLERANCE   None to light

SANDY SOIL TOLERANCE   Yes

HEIGHT   Small

FRAGRANCE   Yes

DESCRIPTION   A very fragrant cluster rose carrying a profusion of lovely, white, cream-centred, gardenia-shaped blooms 10 cm (4 in) wide with thirty to thirty five petals softly contrasting with the plump, creamy buds. Aged blooms open to reveal golden stamens surrounded by clear-white petals. The plant has an excellent constitution and an upright, bushy shape.

AWARDS   All America Rose Selection, 1964.

VARIETIES   This rose is frequently grown in a standard (tree) form.

CONDITIONS   Grow in sun in soil that is drained, fertile, well mulched and watered. Stands lesser soil conditions if drainage is satisfactory.

LANDSCAPE USE   Use singly or in groups either with bush or floribunda roses and/or annuals for colour, cut blooms and scent; as a hedge; for bedding; for a tub plant; as a standard.

MAINTENANCE   Follow general instructions. Regular addition of organic matter to the soil and extra mulching will be beneficial.

PHOTOGRAPH: NICK BROOKE

Friesia
(Sunsprite)

ORIGIN Unnamed cultivar x Spanish Sun

HYBRIDISER Reimer Kordes, Germany

INTRODUCER Jackson & Perkins Co, USA

YEAR 1977

HYBRIDIST'S CODE KORresia

SHADE TOLERANCE None to light

SANDY SOIL TOLERANCE Yes

HEIGHT Small

FRAGRANCE Yes

DESCRIPTION To quote rose hybridist Sam McGredy: 'If you have room for only one yellow floribunda, it has to be Friesia.' Friesia is an unequalled yellow floribunda and carries profuse clusters of sweetly scented 8.5 cm (3 in) wide aureolin-yellow blooms each with thirty to forty petals. The colour is clear and vivid. Buds are ovoid to urn-shaped. Foliage is dark green on a dense, upright bush. Growth is as free as the flowering habit. Though bred for the glasshouse cut flower trade, Friesia performs beautifully in gardens.

AWARDS Gold Medal Baden Baden, 1972.

VARIETIES This rose is frequently grown in a standard (tree) form.

CONDITIONS Drained, fertile, well-watered and mulched soil in sun. Stands lesser soil conditions if drainage is satisfactory.

LANDSCAPE USE Brilliant as a bedding subject or hedge. Good alone or in groups with both bush and other floribunda roses for its colour, cut blooms and scent. It is an exceptional floribunda.

MAINTENANCE Follow general instructions. Regular incorporation of additional organic matter to the soil and extra mulching will be beneficial.

PHOTOGRAPH: JOHN CLUTTERBUCK

White Simplicity

ORIGIN   Sun Flare x Simplicity
HYBRIDISER   Armstrong Nurseries Inc, USA
YEAR   1990
HYBRIDIST'S CODE   Jacsnow
SHADE TOLERANCE   Light to filtered
SANDY SOIL TOLERANCE   Yes
HEIGHT   Small to medium
FRAGRANCE   Yes
DESCRIPTION   A continuous-blooming rose which needs only minimal care. This has long, pointed buds which form semi-double open blooms showing golden stamens. They have a slight fragrance and are produced in generous clusters. Foliage is mid green and shiny and growth is bushy. A companion rose is Simplicity which is pink.
VARIETIES   May also be grown as a standard (tree).
CONDITIONS   Grow in sun or light to filtered shade in soil that is drained, fertile, well mulched and watered.
LANDSCAPE USE   Use in a massed display or use singly or in groups with bush or floribunda roses and/or annuals for colour and cut blooms; as a hedge; and for bedding. It is particularly attractive in groupings or as a hedge/border.
MAINTENANCE   When grown in light to filtered shade some extra feeding and disease control, in addition to general care, may be needed.

PHOTOGRAPH: NICK BROOKE

Shining Hour

ORIGIN Sunbright x Sun Flare
HYBRIDISER W. Warriner, USA
INTRODUCER Bear Creek
Nurseries, USA
YEAR 1991
HYBRIDIST'S CODE JACyef
SHADE TOLERANCE Light to
filtered
SANDY SOIL TOLERANCE Yes
HEIGHT Tall
FRAGRANCE Yes
DESCRIPTION Pointed ovoid
buds open to large (10 cm (4 in)
wide), double, gleaming-yellow,
lightly fragrant blooms with thirty
petals. These are produced on long
strong stems. The glistening green
foliage has strong resistance to
disease. The bush is sturdy and
very free flowering from spring to
late autumn. It is one of the most
handsome yellow roses.
AWARDS All America Rose
Selection, 1991.
VARIETIES This rose may be
grown as a standard.
LANDSCAPE USE It's free-
flowering nature and highly
disease-resistant foliage make this
rose suitable for use as a hedge, or
in mass or group plantings. It may
also be used singly and under-
planted with annuals. It is an
excellent cut flower and is suitable
for exhibition. It makes a tall
standard.
MAINTENANCE If grown in
some shade extra feeding and
disease control measures, in
addition to general care, will be
necessary.

PHOTOGRAPH: NICK BROOKE

Gold Medal

ORIGIN Yellow Pages x unnamed seedling from Granada x Garden Party

HYBRIDISER Jack L. Christensen, USA

INTRODUCER Armstrong Nurseries Inc, USA

YEAR 1982, 1983 (USA)

HYBRIDIST'S CODE AROyqueli

SHADE TOLERANCE Light to filtered

SANDY SOIL TOLERANCE Yes

HEIGHT Tall

FRAGRANCE No

DESCRIPTION The very large, high-centred gold blooms are tinged with copper. It is a rewarding golden rose, which repeat flowers freely. Gold Medal grows very strongly and is a close, tidy bush with attractive light-green foliage. It is one of the most reliable roses in this colour.

VARIETIES Frequently grown in a standard form.

CONDITIONS Prefers day-long sun in soil that is drained, fertile, well mulched and watered but will grow in conditions of light to filtered shade.

LANDSCAPE USE Use singly or in groups either with bush or floribunda roses for colour and cut blooms.

MAINTENANCE If grown in some shade extra feeding and disease control measures, in addition to general care, will be needed.

PHOTOGRAPH: IVY HANSEN

Golden Gloves

ORIGIN (Sunsprite x Katherine Loker) x Gingersnap

HYBRIDISER Armstrong Nurseries Inc, USA

INTRODUCER Swane's Nurseries, Australia

YEAR 1991

SHADE TOLERANCE None to light

SANDY SOIL TOLERANCE Yes

HEIGHT Medium

FRAGRANCE No

DESCRIPTION A dainty, high-centred, continuous-blooming rose with deep old-gold blooms carried in generous clusters. The petals are pointed and the bloom opens in the last stages with an almost flat outer circle of petals. It has glossy mid-green foliage on a bushy plant with very few thorns.

VARIETIES May also be grown as a standard (tree).

CONDITIONS Grow in sun or light to filtered shade in soil that is drained, fertile, well mulched and watered.

LANDSCAPE USE Use singly or in groups either with bush or floribunda roses and/or annuals or among smaller shrubs for colour, cut blooms and scent; as a hedge; as a standard rose.

MAINTENANCE When grown in light to filtered shade some extra feeding and disease control, in addition to general care, may be needed.

PHOTOGRAPH: IVY HANSEN

Confetti

ORIGIN Jack O'Lantern x Zorina

HYBRIDISER Herbert Swim and Jack L. Christensen, USA

INTRODUCER Armstrong Nurseries Inc, USA

YEAR 1983

HYBRIDIST'S CODE AROjechs

SHADE TOLERANCE Light to filtered

SANDY SOIL TOLERANCE Yes

HEIGHT Small

FRAGRANCE No

DESCRIPTION A brilliant-gold rose with rolled edges brushed scarlet. Each strong stem carries a mass of cupped flowers against dark-green, glossy foliage. Growth is vigorous and flowering is continuous.

VARIETIES None

CONDITIONS Prefers day-long sun in soil that is drained, fertile, well mulched and watered but will grow in conditions of light to filtered shade.

LANDSCAPE USE Use for colour and cut blooms; makes an excellent border; for bedding; and as tub plant. Use singly or in groups either with bush or floribunda roses.

MAINTENANCE If grown in some shade extra feeding and disease control measures, in addition to general care, will be needed.

PHOTOGRAPH: VALERIE SWANE

Red Gold
(Rouge et Or)

ORIGIN   (Karl Herbst x Masquerade) x Faust x Piccadilly
HYBRIDISER   Alex Dickson, UK
INTRODUCER   Jackson & Perkins Co, USA
YEAR   1971
HYBRIDIST'S CODE   Dicor
SHADE TOLERANCE   None to light
SANDY SOIL TOLERANCE   No
HEIGHT   Medium
FRAGRANCE   Yes
DESCRIPTION   A prolific, wonderfully colourful rose with ovoid buds, sturdy bushy habit and glossy, leathery foliage. The slightly fragrant flowers are gold edged with red. The red edging intensifies as the flowers age. The petals drop cleanly and the flowering recommences freely. The colours and the quantity of bloom carried in large clusters are spectacular.
AWARDS   All America Rose Selection, 1971.
VARIETIES   Climbing and standard (tree) forms are grown.
CONDITIONS   Grow in sun in soil that is drained, fertile, well mulched and watered.
LANDSCAPE USE   Use singly or in groups either with bush or floribunda roses and/or annuals for colour, cut blooms and scent; as a hedge; to exhibit; for bedding; for a tub plant; as a climber on a trellis or pergola; or against a fence or on a wall.
MAINTENANCE   Follow general instructions.

PHOTOGRAPH: VALERIE SWANE

Arizona
(Werina, Tocade)

ORIGIN (Fred Howard x Golden Scepter) x Golden Rapture x (Fred Howard x Golden Scepter) x Golden Rapture

HYBRIDISER O. L. Weeks, USA

INTRODUCER Conard-Pyle Co, USA

YEAR 1975

SHADE TOLERANCE Light to filtered

SANDY SOIL TOLERANCE Yes

HEIGHT Medium to tall

FRAGRANCE Yes

DESCRIPTION An impressive multi-coloured rose. A golden bronze that is a suffusion of shades of apricot, yellow, pink and orange red. Ovoid buds become medium-sized, perfectly formed, high-centred flowers on long stems. Arizona is 'everblooming' and blooms very generously. It is robust with dark glossy, leathery foliage on a bushy plant.

AWARDS All America Rose Selection, 1975.

VARIETIES This rose is frequently grown in a standard (tree) form.

CONDITIONS Grow in sun in soil that is drained, fertile, well mulched and watered, or in light to filtered shade with the same soil condition.

LANDSCAPE USE Use singly or in groups either with bush or floribunda roses and/or annuals or among smaller shrubs for colour, cut blooms and scent; as a hedge; to exhibit; for mass planting; as a commercial cut flower; as a standard.

MAINTENANCE When grown in light to filtered shade some extra feeding and disease control, in addition to general care, may be needed. In humid climates this rose may be subject to mildew.

PHOTOGRAPH: NICK BROOKE

Young-At-Heart
(Origami)

ORIGIN Coquette x Zorina
HYBRIDISER W. Warriner, Armstrong Nurseries Inc, USA
INTRODUCER Swane's Nurseries, Australia
YEAR 1989
HYBRIDIST'S CODE Arocharm
SHADE TOLERANCE Light to filtered
SANDY SOIL TOLERANCE Yes
HEIGHT Small to medium
FRAGRANCE Yes
DESCRIPTION A long-lasting, very free-flowering, many-petalled rose which is peach, almost apricot in colour. The form is high-centred and the blooms are produced singly or in clusters on strong stems. It was introduced in Australia as the National Heart Foundation's rose in 1989.
AWARDS Rose of the Year in Australia, 1989.
VARIETIES May also be grown as a standard or tree rose.
CONDITIONS Grow in sun or very light to filtered shade in soil that is drained, fertile, well mulched and watered.
LANDSCAPE USE Use singly or in groups either with bush or floribunda roses and/or annuals or among smaller shrubs for colour, cut blooms and scent; as a hedge; to exhibit; for mass planting; as a standard.

PHOTOGRAPH: VALERIE SWANE

MAINTENANCE When grown in light to filtered shade some extra feeding and disease control, in addition to general care, may be needed.

Catherine McCauley

ORIGIN   Gingersnap x Brandy x Sunsprite (Friesia)
HYBRIDISER   W. Warriner, Bear Creek Nurseries, USA
INTRODUCER   Swane's Nurseries, Australia on behalf of The Sisters of Mercy
YEAR   1992
HYBRIDIST'S CODE   JACIBRAS
SHADE TOLERANCE   Light to filtered
SANDY SOIL TOLERANCE   Yes
HEIGHT   Small

FRAGRANCE   Yes
DESCRIPTION   Long pointed buds open to small, high-centred blooms produced in exceptionally long trusses which last for more than a week in the vase. Because it is continuous-blooming this rose is rarely without a flower. The foliage is mid green and the bush is neat and rounded with a robust habit.
VARIETIES   May also be grown as a standard or tree rose.

CONDITIONS   Grow in sun or light shade in soil that is well drained, fertile, mulched and adequately watered.
LANDSCAPE USE   Grow as a cut flower (lasts a week in the vase); as a border or low hedge; in mass; in group plantings or in large pots.
MAINTENANCE   When grown in light to filtered shade some extra feeding and disease control, in addition to general care, will be needed.

PHOTOGRAPH: DENSEY CLYNE

Marina

ORIGIN Colour Wonder x unnamed seedling

HYBRIDISER Reimer Kordes, Germany

INTRODUCER W. Kordes Sohne, Germany

YEAR 1974

HYBRIDIST'S CODE Rinakor

SHADE TOLERANCE Light to filtered

SANDY SOIL TOLERANCE Yes

HEIGHT Medium to tall

FRAGRANCE Yes

DESCRIPTION A wonderfully colourful rose of brilliant, non-fading orange hues on a gold base. The massive clusters of blooms are made up of prettily formed individual flowers, each with thirty to forty four petals. It is striking, especially in group plantings. Marina has healthy foliage, is repeat flowering and robust.

AWARDS All America Rose Selection, 1981.

VARIETIES None.

CONDITIONS Prefers day-long sun in soil that is drained, fertile, well mulched and watered but will grow in conditions of light to filtered shade.

LANDSCAPE USE Use singly or in groups either with bush or floribunda roses or among smaller shrubs for colour, cut blooms and scent; as a hedge; for bedding.

PHOTOGRAPH: VALERIE SWANE

MAINTENANCE If grown in some shade extra feeding and disease control measures, in addition to general care, will be needed. Regular addition of organic matter to the soil and extra mulching will be beneficial.

Sundowner

ORIGIN Bond Street x Peer Gynt
HYBRIDISER Sam McGredy IV, NZ
INTRODUCER Fred Edmunds Roses, USA
YEAR 1978
HYBRIDIST'S CODE MACcheup
SHADE TOLERANCE Light to filtered
SANDY SOIL TOLERANCE Yes
HEIGHT Tall
FRAGRANCE Yes
DESCRIPTION A magnificent sunset-coloured rose glowing with deep orange and shades of yellow and gold lightened with salmon pink. The colours change as the bloom ages, salmon dominating the outer edge of the petals. Sundowner is heavily fragrant with pointed buds and large, 12.5 cm (5 in), classic blooms. Foliage is leathery on a tall, free-flowering and vigorous bush.
AWARDS All America Rose Selection, 1979.
VARIETIES None.
CONDITIONS Grow in sun in soil that is drained, fertile, well mulched and watered, or in light to filtered shade with the same soil condition. In light to filtered shade effective drainage is even more important, especially in winter.
LANDSCAPE USE Use singly or in groups either with bush or floribunda roses and/or annuals for colour, cut blooms and scent; for mass planting; a bushy and vigorous screen 2 m (yd) or less; to exhibit; as a standard.
MAINTENANCE When grown in light to filtered shade some extra feeding and disease control, in addition to general care, may be needed.

PHOTOGRAPH: NAN BARBOUR

Charisma

ORIGIN   Gemini x Zorina
HYBRIDISER   E. G. Hill, Cal, USA
INTRODUCER   Conard-Pyle Co, USA
YEAR   1977
SHADE TOLERANCE   Light to filtered
SANDY SOIL TOLERANCE   No
HEIGHT   Small
FRAGRANCE   Yes
DESCRIPTION   An exuberant rose with colourful scarlet and yellow blooms which attract attention. These are 5–6.5 cm (2–2½ in) across, high-centred, with thirty five to forty five petals and are produced in long trusses. The glossy, leathery foliage, generous blooming habit and robust growth make it an excellent border and the ideal subject for dull corners.
AWARDS   All America Rose Selection, 1978.
VARIETIES   None.
CONDITIONS   Grow in sun in soil that is drained, fertile, well mulched and watered, or in light to filtered shade with the same soil condition. In light to filtered shade effective drainage is even more important, especially in winter.
LANDSCAPE USE   Use as a border; for bedding; as a hedge; or singly or in groups either with bush or floribunda roses and/or annuals or among smaller shrubs for colour, cut blooms and scent.
MAINTENANCE   Follow general instructions and add additional organic matter to the soil and mulch heavily.

PHOTOGRAPH: NAN BARBOUR

Apricot Nectar

ORIGIN Unnamed seedling x Spartan

HYBRIDISER E. S. Boerner, USA

INTRODUCER Jackson and Perkins Co, USA

YEAR 1965

SHADE TOLERANCE Light to filtered

SANDY SOIL TOLERANCE Yes

HEIGHT Medium

FRAGRANCE Yes

DESCRIPTION A charming rose with ovoid buds which form large (10–11.5 cm (4–4½ in) wide) apricot-pink flowers with a golden base to their petals and a strong fruity fragrance. It has glossy dark-green foliage and bushy growth.

AWARDS All America Rose Selection, 1966.

VARIETIES This rose is frequently grown in a standard (tree) form.

CONDITIONS Grow in sun or light to filtered shade in soil that is drained, fertile, well mulched and watered.

LANDSCAPE USE Use singly or in groups either with bush or floribunda roses and/or annuals or among smaller shrubs for colour, cut blooms and scent; as a hedge; as a border; for bedding.

MAINTENANCE When grown in light to filtered shade some extra feeding and disease control, in addition to general care, may be needed.

PHOTOGRAPH: IVY HANSEN

Kirsten

ORIGIN   Unnamed seedling x Berolina

HYBRIDISER   Pernille and Morgens N. Olesen; Poulsen, Denmark

INTRODUCER   Poulsen, Denmark

YEAR   1988

SHADE TOLERANCE   Light to filtered

SANDY SOIL TOLERANCE   Yes

HEIGHT   Medium

FRAGRANCE   No

DESCRIPTION   A pretty, soft-pink to champagne-coloured rose which retains its form and lasts well in the vase. From pointed buds emerge double blooms about 5 cm (2 in) wide with a high centre surrounded by rather flat layers of petals. The buds show colour at an early stage. It has matt, mid-green foliage and a bushy habit. A popular rose with European brides.

VARIETIES   May also be grown as a standard (tree).

CONDITIONS   Grow in sun or light to filtered shade in soil that is drained, fertile, well mulched and watered.

LANDSCAPE USE   Use singly or in groups either with bush or floribunda roses and/or annuals for colour, cut blooms and mass planting. It is outstanding as a cut flower both for the home and on a commercial scale; as a standard (or tree) rose; in tubs.

MAINTENANCE   When grown in light to filtered shade some extra feeding and disease control, in addition to general care, may be needed.

PHOTOGRAPH: IVY HANSEN

Aquarius

ORIGIN (Charlotte Armstrong x Contrast) x (Fandango x World's Fair x Floradora)

HYBRIDISER D. L. Armstrong, USA

INTRODUCER Armstrong Nurseries Inc, USA

YEAR 1971

HYBRIDIST'S CODE ARMaq

SHADE TOLERANCE Light to filtered

SANDY SOIL TOLERANCE Yes

HEIGHT Tall

FRAGRANCE Yes

DESCRIPTION Aquarius is for those who like their roses to 'hold' for long periods. From bud to full bloom it does just that, carrying the high-centred, fragrant blooms on tall, strong stems. The plump buds become perfect forty two-petalled blooms (8.75–10.25 cm (3½–4 in)) of soft pink, blushed with pale pink and edged with rose. In autumn, the colouring is almost luminous and even more lovely than in spring. The bush blooms generously, is quick to repeat flower and is very erect, a vigorous grower with dark-green, leathery foliage.

AWARDS All America Rose Selection, 1971.

VARIETIES None.

CONDITIONS Grow in sun in soil that is drained, fertile, well mulched and watered, or in light to filtered shade with the same soil condition. In light to filtered shade effective drainage is even more important, especially in winter.

LANDSCAPE USE Use singly or in groups either with bush or floribunda roses and/or annuals, among smaller shrubs, for colour, cut blooms and scent; to exhibit; as a bushy and vigorous hedge; for mass planting; as a commercial cut flower.

MAINTENANCE When grown in light to filtered shade some extra feeding and disease control, in addition to general care, may be needed.

PHOTOGRAPH: NICK BROOKE

Simplicity

ORIGIN   Iceberg x unnamed seedling

HYBRIDISER   W. Warriner, USA

INTRODUCER   Jackson & Perkins Co, USA

YEAR   1979

HYBRIDIST'S CODE   JACink

SHADE TOLERANCE   Light to filtered

SANDY SOIL TOLERANCE   Yes

HEIGHT   Medium to tall

FRAGRANCE   No

DESCRIPTION   A continuous-blooming rose with soft-pink blooms. This is one of the world's most popular and versatile roses due to its ever-blooming nature, highly disease-resistant foliage and exceptional hardiness.

VARIETIES   None.

CONDITIONS   Grow in sun or light to filtered shade in soil that is drained, fertile, well mulched and watered.

LANDSCAPE USE   This is an outstanding rose for landscaping. It can be allowed to grow to hide fences or can be clipped down to border height. It is lovely alone or planted in mass, and makes an excellent companion plant to White Simplicity.

MAINTENANCE   If grown in some shade extra feeding and disease control measures, in addition to general care, will be necessary.

PHOTOGRAPH: IVY HANSEN

Sonia
(Sweet Promise)

ORIGIN Zambra x (Baccara x White Knight)

HYBRIDISER A. Meilland, France

INTRODUCER Conard-Pyle Co, USA

YEAR 1974

HYBRIDIST'S CODE Meihelvet

SHADE TOLERANCE Light to filtered

SANDY SOIL TOLERANCE No

HEIGHT Medium

FRAGRANCE Yes

DESCRIPTION Elongated buds form large, 10–11.5 cm (4–4½ in), thirty-petalled, high-centred blooms with a very fruity fragrance. Blooms are an unusual soft pink suffused with coral. They hold their form for days and are exceptional cut flowers. The bushes repeat flower quickly outdoors and under glasshouse conditions. Sonia is valued for its unique colour. The dark foliage is glossy and leathery on a neat bush.

VARIETIES Climbing and standard (tree) forms are grown.

CONDITIONS Grow in sun in soil that is drained, fertile, well mulched and watered, or in light to filtered shade with the same soil condition. In light to filtered shade effective drainage is even more important, especially in winter.

LANDSCAPE USE Use singly or in groups either with bush or floribunda roses and/or annuals for colour, cut blooms and scent; as a hedge; to exhibit; for mass planting; as a commercial cut flower; as a climber on a trellis or pergola; against a fence or on a wall; as a standard.

MAINTENANCE When grown in light to filtered shade some extra feeding and disease control, in addition to general care, may be needed.

PHOTOGRAPH: NICK BROOKE

Mary MacKillop

ORIGIN Not available

HYBRIDISER Armstrong Nurseries Inc, USA

INTRODUCER Swane's Nurseries, Australia

YEAR 1989

SHADE TOLERANCE Light to filtered

SANDY SOIL TOLERANCE Yes

HEIGHT Medium

FRAGRANCE Yes

DESCRIPTION The long-lasting, shell-pink blooms are edged with rose pink on their outer petals and are produced singly or in clusters of two to three each stem. The buds are pointed and form high-centred fragrant blooms which are particularly long-lasting in the vase. It has mid-green foliage and compact bushy growth. The rose was named for Mary MacKillop co-founder of The Sisters of St Joseph of the Sacred Heart, whose cause for canonization as Australia's first saint is before Rome.

VARIETIES May also be grown as a standard (tree).

CONDITIONS Grow in sun or light to filtered shade in soil that is drained, fertile, well mulched and watered.

LANDSCAPE USE Use singly or in groups with other roses of similar height either in a bed of their own or amongst other plants; as a hedge; for mass planting; as a standard or tree rose.

MAINTENANCE When grown in light to filtered shade some extra feeding and disease control, in addition to general care, may be needed.

PHOTOGRAPH: NICK BROOKE

Sonoma

ORIGIN   Sumatra x Circus
HYBRIDISER   David L. Armstrong, USA
INTRODUCER   Armstrong Nurseries Inc, USA
YEAR   1973
SHADE TOLERANCE   None to light
SANDY SOIL TOLERANCE   No
HEIGHT   Low
FRAGRANCE   Yes
DESCRIPTION   A dainty bush bearing clusters of medium-sized, fragrant, high-centred blooms shading from pink to salmon pink. Though small the bush is vigorous, bears generously and is quick to repeat flower, qualities which suit borders and bedding schemes.
VARIETIES   None.
CONDITIONS   Grow in sun in soil that is drained, fertile, well mulched and watered.
LANDSCAPE USE   Use singly or in groups with other roses of similar height or as underplanting to standards; as a border; for bedding; for a tub plant.
MAINTENANCE   Follow general instructions.

PHOTOGRAPH: NAN BARBOUR

119

Gay Princess

ORIGIN   Spartan x The Farmer's Wife

HYBRIDISER   E. S. Boerner, USA

INTRODUCER   Jackson & Perkins Co, USA

YEAR   1967

SHADE TOLERANCE   Light to filtered

SANDY SOIL TOLERANCE   Yes

HEIGHT   Small

FRAGRANCE   Yes

DESCRIPTION   A strong-growing, leathery foliaged rose with a pleasing bushy habit, almost covered with generous clusters of fragrant shell-pink blooms. Urn-shaped buds open to cupped, perfectly formed, large flowers which retain their shape for many days. The autumn flowers have more intense colour than spring flowers.

AWARDS   All America Rose Selection, 1967.

VARIETIES   May be grown as a standard rose.

CONDITIONS   Grow in sun in soil that is drained, fertile, well mulched and watered, or in light to filtered shade with the same soil condition. In light to filtered shade effective drainage is even more important, especially in winter.

LANDSCAPE USE   Use singly or in groups either with bush or floribunda roses and/or annuals or among smaller shrubs for colour, cut blooms and scent; as a hedge; to exhibit; for bedding; for a tub plant.

MAINTENANCE   When grown in light to filtered shade some extra feeding and disease control, in addition to general care, may be needed. Plants require light pruning after each flowering in order to stop seed heads forming.

PHOTOGRAPH: IVY HANSEN

Tournament of Roses

ORIGIN   Impatient x unnamed seedling

HYBRIDISER   W. Warriner, USA

INTRODUCER   Bear Creek Nurseries, USA

YEAR   1989

HYBRIDIST'S CODE   JACient

SHADE TOLERANCE   Light to filtered

SANDY SOIL TOLERANCE   Yes

HEIGHT   Medium to tall

FRAGRANCE   Yes

DESCRIPTION   Pointed ovoid coral buds open to lightly fragrant, two-toned, soft coral-pink blooms with thirty five to forty petals and up to 10 cm (4 in) across in size. These are produced on long strong stems. The foliage is glossy green and highly resistant to disease. It becomes a vigorous bushy plant.

AWARDS   All America Rose Selection, 1989.

VARIETIES   May also be grown as a standard (tree).

CONDITIONS   Grow in sun in soil that is drained, fertile, well mulched, and well watered, or in light to filtered shade with the same soil conditions though then effective drainage is even more important.

LANDSCAPE USE   Use singly or in groups either with bush or floribunda roses and/or annuals for colour and cut blooms; as a hedge; as an exhibition rose.

MAINTENANCE   When grown in light to filtered shade some extra feeding and disease control, in addition to general care, may be needed.

PHOTOGRAPH: VALERIE SWANE

Pink Parfait

ORIGIN   First Love x Pinocchio
HYBRIDISER   Herbert C. Swim, USA
INTRODUCER   Armstrong Nurseries Inc, USA
YEAR   1960
SHADE TOLERANCE   None to light
SANDY SOIL TOLERANCE   No
HEIGHT   Medium
FRAGRANCE   Yes
DESCRIPTION   Pink Parfait is a study in pinks varying from medium to light. Blooms are numerous and the bush repeat flowers quickly. Each flower has twenty to twenty five petals, is 8.75–10 cm (3½–4 in) across and is high-centred or cupped and near perfect in form. Blooms are slightly fragrant and last well indoors and in the garden. Leathery foliage is light green and semi-glossy on a tidy, plump bush.
AWARDS   Portland Gold Medal, 1959; All America Rose Selection, 1961; National Rose Society Gold Medal, 1962.
VARIETIES   This rose is frequently grown in a standard form.
CONDITIONS   Grow in sun in soil that is drained, fertile, well mulched and watered.
LANDSCAPE USE   Use singly or in groups either with bush or floribunda roses and/or annuals for colour, cut blooms and scent; as a hedge; to exhibit; for mass planting; as a standard.
MAINTENANCE   Follow general instructions.

PHOTOGRAPH: VALERIE SWANE

Pleasure

ORIGIN Seedling x Intrigue
HYBRIDISER W. Warriner, USA
INTRODUCER Bear Creek
Nurseries, USA
YEAR 1990
HYBRIDIST'S CODE JACpif
SHADE TOLERANCE Light to
filtered
SANDY SOIL TOLERANCE Yes
HEIGHT Medium
FRAGRANCE Yes
DESCRIPTION A warm-pink rose
with beautiful form and abundant
blooms carried continuously. The
blooms are medium to large,
double with thirty to thirty five
petals and have a slight fragrance.
Growth is compact and the foliage
is dark green and highly resistant
to disease.
AWARDS All America Rose
Selection, 1990.
VARIETIES May also be grown as
a standard (tree).
CONDITIONS Grow in sun or
light to filtered shade in soil that is
drained, fertile, well mulched and
watered.
LANDSCAPE USE Delightful as a
border, this rose may also be used
singly or in groups with bush or
floribunda roses; for colour and
cut blooms; for bedding; as a
standard.
MAINTENANCE When grown in
light to filtered shade some extra
feeding and disease control, in
addition to general care, may be
needed.

PHOTOGRAPH: DENSEY CLYNE

Queen Elizabeth

ORIGIN   Charlotte Armstrong x Floradora

HYBRIDISER   Dr W. E. Lammerts, USA

INTRODUCER   Germain's Inc, USA

YEAR   1954

SHADE TOLERANCE   Light to filtered

SANDY SOIL TOLERANCE   Yes

HEIGHT   Tall

FRAGRANCE   Yes

DESCRIPTION   The best rose in the world — at the age of twenty six Queen Elizabeth was voted that by the World Federation of Rose Societies meeting in South Africa in 1980. Whether cared for or ignored, Queen Elizabeth flowers magnanimously and is so robust and prolific that both the hybrid tea and floribunda classes failed to fit it and a new class — grandiflora — was created especially to classify this rose. Height is 2–3 m (yd) if hard pruned, or up to 5 m (yd) with light pruning. Pointed buds open to large carmine-pink and dawn-pink, fragrant blooms 8.75–10 cm (3½–4 in) wide with thirty seven to forty petals varying from high-centred to cupped. These are carried either singly or in clusters. They are luminous indoors and are a long-lasting cut flower.

AWARDS   All America Rose Selection, 1955; National Rose Society Gold Medal, 1955; American Rose Society Gertrude M. Hubbard Gold Medal, 1957; American Rose Society National Gold Medal Certificate, 1960; Golden Rose of the Hague, 1968.

VARIETIES   Climbing and standard forms are grown though as a standard it should be used where its height is an advantage.

CONDITIONS   Grow in sun in

PHOTOGRAPH: VALERIE SWANE

soil that is drained, fertile, well mulched and watered, or in light to filtered shade with the same soil condition. In light to filtered shade effective drainage is even more important, especially in winter. Stands lesser soil conditions if drainage is satisfactory.

LANDSCAPE USE   Use singly or in groups either with bush or floribunda roses and/or annuals for colour, cut blooms and scent; as a hedge; to exhibit; as a bushy and vigorous screen 2 m (yd) or

less; for mass planting; as a commercial cut flower; as a climber on a trellis or pergola or against a fence or on a wall; as a standard.

MAINTENANCE   Minimal. Care as outlined under general instructions will usually be sufficient in all situations but extra disease control and feeding in shade will pay dividends, as will the addition of organic matter to sandy soil.

Regensberg

ORIGIN   Geoff Boycott x Old Master

HYBRIDISER   Sam McGredy IV, NZ

INTRODUCER   McGredy Roses International, NZ

YEAR   1979

HYBRIDIST'S CODE   MACyoumis

SHADE TOLERANCE   None to light

SANDY SOIL TOLERANCE   No

HEIGHT   Low

FRAGRANCE   Yes

DESCRIPTION   Regensberg is named after the pretty Swiss village where the rose painter Lotte Gunthart lives. A rose with a nostalgic quality. It looks old-fashioned but is ultra-modern and trend-setting, a member of a group of colourful, low-growing floribundas. Regensberg is exceptionally free flowering and remains very low. It is an excellent border rose and packs much colour in the small space it needs. The classic, fragrant, rose-pink blooms are 11.5 cm (4½ in) across with twenty one petals showing white at their base. Old blooms reveal a centre of golden stamens. Buds are long and pointed.

AWARDS   Gold Medal Baden Baden, 1980.

VARIETIES   A standard form is grown.

CONDITIONS   Grow in sun in soil that is drained, fertile, well mulched and watered.

LANDSCAPE USE   Use singly or in groups either with bush or floribunda roses and/or annuals for colour, cut blooms and scent; as a border; for bedding; for a tub plant; as a standard.

MAINTENANCE   Follow general instructions.

PHOTOGRAPH: VALERIE SWANE

Olé

ORIGIN   Roundelay x El Capitan
HYBRIDISER   David L. Armstrong, USA
INTRODUCER   Armstrong Nurseries Inc, USA
YEAR   1964
SHADE TOLERANCE   Light to filtered
SANDY SOIL TOLERANCE   Yes
HEIGHT   Medium
FRAGRANCE   Yes
DESCRIPTION   Shapely buds form bright, red, fragrant, forty five- to fifty five-petalled blooms varying in shape from high-centred to cupped and carried on tall stems. It has glossy foliage. The hybrid-tea-type flowers are massed on each stem. The bush is decked with blooms from spring to autumn.
VARIETIES   Standard and climbing forms are available.
CONDITIONS   Grow in sun in soil that is drained, fertile, well mulched and watered, or in light to filtered shade where drainage is important in winter.
LANDSCAPE USE   Use singly or in groups either with bush or floribunda roses and/or annuals for colour, cut blooms and scent; as a hedge; to exhibit; for mass planting; as a climber on a trellis or pergola or against a fence or on a wall.
MAINTENANCE   When grown in light to filtered shade some extra feeding and disease control, in addition to general care, may be needed.

PHOTOGRAPH: NICK BROOKE

Bloomin' Easy

ORIGIN Trumpeter x Simplicity
HYBRIDISER Armstrong Nurseries Inc, USA
INTRODUCER Armstrong Nurseries Inc, USA
YEAR 1990
HYBRIDIST'S CODE Arotrusim
SHADE TOLERANCE Light to filtered
SANDY SOIL TOLERANCE Yes
HEIGHT Tall
FRAGRANCE Yes
DESCRIPTION A rose for those who cannot grow roses! Bloomin' Easy carries four or five lightly scented red blooms to each stem. They are high-centred and hold form well. The plant blooms continuously and becomes an upright bush which makes an excellent screen.
VARIETIES None.
CONDITIONS Grow in sun or light to filtered shade in soil that is drained, fertile, well mulched and watered.
LANDSCAPE USE An excellent screen or hedge rose which may be grown with or without pruning.
MAINTENANCE When grown in light to filtered shade some extra feeding and disease control, in addition to general care, may be needed.

PHOTOGRAPH: IVY HANSEN

Scarlet Queen Elizabeth

ORIGIN   Korona x seedling x Queen Elizabeth

HYBRIDISER   Patrick Dickson, UK

INTRODUCER   Alex Dickson & Sons Ltd, UK

YEAR   1963

SHADE TOLERANCE   Light to filtered

SANDY SOIL TOLERANCE   Yes

HEIGHT   Tall

FRAGRANCE   Yes

DESCRIPTION   The striking, globular, flame-scarlet blooms are slightly fragrant and produced in generous clusters on very long, strong stems. They stand hot weather well and are long-lasting as a cut flower. The bush repeat flowers and is especially effective as a screen plant. It is a particularly vigorous, easy-to-care-for bush with good-looking, dark-green, shining foliage.

AWARDS   The Hague Gold Medal and Golden Rose of the Hague, 1973.

VARIETIES   None.

CONDITIONS   Grow in sun in soil that is drained, fertile, well mulched and watered, or in light to filtered shade with the same soil condition. In light to filtered shade effective drainage is even more important, especially in winter.

LANDSCAPE USE   Use singly or in groups either with bush or floribunda roses and/or annuals or among smaller shrubs for colour, cut blooms and scent; as a hedge or bushy and vigorous screen 2 m (yd) or less; for mass planting.

PHOTOGRAPH: NAN BARBOUR

MAINTENANCE   When grown in light to filtered shade some extra feeding and disease control, in addition to general care, may be needed.

Satchmo

ORIGIN   Evelyn Fison x Diament
HYBRIDISER   Sam McGredy IV, NZ
INTRODUCER   Samuel McGredy & Son Ltd, NZ
YEAR   1970
SHADE TOLERANCE   None to light
SANDY SOIL TOLERANCE   Yes
HEIGHT   Small
FRAGRANCE   Yes
DESCRIPTION   Satchmo has strong growth, a lavish flowering habit and bright-scarlet flowers and glossy, dark-green foliage. The buds produce dazzling twenty five-petalled blooms 7.5 cm (2¾ in) across. They are carried in masses on long, erect stems, the flowers sitting just above the bush.
AWARDS   The Hague Gold Medal, 1970.
VARIETIES   It may be grown as a standard.
CONDITIONS   Grow in sun in soil that is drained, fertile, well mulched and watered.
LANDSCAPE USE   Use singly or in groups either with bush or floribunda roses and/or annuals for colour, cut blooms and scent; for bedding; for a tub plant. It is the ideal hedge rose because of its habit, height and consistent flowering.
MAINTENANCE   Follow general instructions. Additional organic matter in the soil and extra mulching will help.

PHOTOGRAPH: NICK BROOKE

Roundelay

ORIGIN   Charlotte Armstrong x Floradora

HYBRIDISER   Herbert C. Swim, USA

INTRODUCER   Armstrong Nurseries Inc, USA

YEAR   1954

SHADE TOLERANCE   Light to filtered

SANDY SOIL TOLERANCE   Yes

HEIGHT   Tall

FRAGRANCE   Yes

DESCRIPTION   A grand rose especially for non-gardeners because it is particularly vigorous, prolific and repeat flowering. The large, long-lasting, high-centred to flat, fragrant, thirty five- to forty-petalled blooms are currant red to rich cardinal red. Buds are plump. The foliage is dark and handsome and the blooms are so well arranged on the stems and so numerous that one stem becomes a graceful arrangement.

AWARDS   Geneva Gold Medal, 1954.

VARIETIES   It may be grown as a standard.

CONDITIONS   Grow in sun in soil that is drained, fertile, well mulched and watered, or in light to filtered shade with the same soil condition. In light to filtered shade effective drainage is even more important, especially in winter.

LANDSCAPE USE   Use singly or in groups either with bush or floribunda roses and/or annuals for colour, cut bloom and scent; as a hedge or bushy and vigorous screen 2 m (yd) or less; for mass planting; as a commercial cut flower.

PHOTOGRAPH: NICK BROOKE

MAINTENANCE   When grown in light to filtered shade some extra feeding and disease control, in addition to general care, may be needed.

Marlena

ORIGIN   Gertrud Westphal x Lilli Marlene

HYBRIDISER   Reimer Kordes, Germany

INTRODUCER   Alex Dickson & Sons Ltd, UK

YEAR   1964, UK

SHADE TOLERANCE   Light to filtered

SANDY SOIL TOLERANCE   Yes

HEIGHT   Small

FRAGRANCE   No

DESCRIPTION   A border and/or bedding rose to grow for its non-stop, free-flowering qualities. A compact, rounded bush covered in clusters of flat, eighteen-petalled, crimson-scarlet blooms.

VARIETIES   None

CONDITIONS   Grow in sun in soil that is drained, fertile, well mulched and watered, or in light to filtered shade with the same soil condition where drainage is important in winter.

LANDSCAPE USE   Use singly or in groups with other roses of similar height; or as underplanting to standards; as a border; for bedding; for a tub plant.

MAINTENANCE   When grown in light to filtered shade some extra feeding and disease control may be needed.

PHOTOGRAPH: IVY HANSEN

Lilli Marlene
(Lilli Marleen)

ORIGIN (Our Princess x Rudolph Timm) x Ama

HYBRIDISER Reimer Kordes, Germany

INTRODUCER Samuel McGredy & Son Ltd, NZ

YEAR 1959

HYBRIDIST'S CODE KORlima

SHADE TOLERANCE Light to filtered

SANDY SOIL TOLERANCE Yes

HEIGHT Medium

FRAGRANCE Yes

DESCRIPTION A bountiful rose producing great clusters of cupped, fragrant, velvety crimson blooms overlaid with spectrum red. They glow with colour and are 8 cm (3 in) across, have twenty five petals and develop from ovoid buds. As they age the golden stamens are seen. It is a many-branched, free-blooming bush with handsome, leathery foliage. To quote rose hybridist Sam McGredy: 'It has a faultless even habit, is quick to repeat, holds its head high above the foliage and flowers in torrents.'

AWARDS Golden Rose of the Hague, 1966.

VARIETIES It may be grown as a standard.

CONDITIONS Grow in sun in soil that is drained, fertile, well mulched and watered, or in light to filtered shade with the same soil condition. In light to filtered shade effective drainage is even more important, especially in winter. Stands lesser soil conditions if drainage is satisfactory.

PHOTOGRAPH: NICK BROOKE

LANDSCAPE USE Use singly or in groups either with bush or floribunda roses and/or annuals or among smaller shrubs for colour, cut blooms and scent; as a hedge; to exhibit; for bedding; for a tub plant.

MAINTENANCE When grown in light to filtered shade some extra feeding and disease control, in addition to general care, may be needed.

Lagerfeld

ORIGIN Blue Nile x (Ivory Tower x Angel Face)

HYBRIDISER J. Christensen, USA

INTRODUCER Armstrong Roses Inc, USA

YEAR 1985

HYBRIDIST'S CODE Arolaqueli

SHADE TOLERANCE Light to filtered

SANDY SOIL TOLERANCE Yes

HEIGHT Medium

FRAGRANCE Yes

DESCRIPTION The blooms are elegant; silvery lavender with a high centre and are as much as 12.5 cm (5 in) across. They have an outstanding fragrance and are produced in sprays of five to fifteen. Medium-sized foliage is green and matt on an upright bushy plant with relatively few thorns.

VARIETIES This rose is sometimes grown as a standard (tree rose).

CONDITIONS Grow in sun or light to filtered shade in soil that is drained, fertile, well mulched and watered.

LANDSCAPE USE Use singly or in groups either with bush or floribunda roses and/or annuals for colour, cut blooms and delicious scent. It is suitable for mass planting and as a standard.

MAINTENANCE When grown in light to filtered shade some extra feeding and disease control, in addition to general care, may be needed.

PHOTOGRAPH: VALERIE SWANE

Hans Christian Andersen

ORIGIN   Royal Occasion x unnamed seedling

HYBRIDISER   Pernille and Morgens N. Olesen, Poulsen, Denmark

INTRODUCER   Poulsen, Denmark

YEAR   1987

SHADE TOLERANCE   Light to filtered

SANDY SOIL TOLERANCE   Yes

HEIGHT   Medium to tall

FRAGRANCE   Yes

DESCRIPTION   A particularly strong and very free-flowering rose with dark-red, semi-double 5 cm (2 in) wide blooms in clusters of three to ten on strong stems. Foliage is dark and glossy with a red shine. The plant is vigorous and bushy and stands city conditions well.

VARIETIES   None.

CONDITIONS   Grow in sun or light to filtered shade in soil that is drained, fertile, well mulched and watered.

LANDSCAPE USE   Use singly or in groups either with bush or floribunda roses and/or annuals or among smaller shrubs for colour, cut blooms, and scent; as a hedge; for bedding; as a tub plant.

MAINTENANCE   When grown in light to filtered shade some extra feeding and disease control, in addition to general care, may be needed.

PHOTOGRAPH: IVY HANSEN

MINIATURE ROSES

Miniature roses are miniature-flowered plants which, in bush form, are under 75 cm (29 in) in height. The origin of the miniature rose is uncertain, however, the strongest theory is that the hybrid was developed from a Chinese species.

Some other outstanding miniatures not illustrated include:

• **WHITE** Green Ice. Pretty pointed buds open to small, double, very full flowers, white to soft green at their centres. It flowers continuously.

Snow Carpet. A very profuse rose with a distinct, low, ground-covering habit. The pure white, small flowers have fifty five petals and are slightly fragrant.

• **YELLOW** Hopscotch. In a collection of miniatures, the clarity of the canary-yellow and lemon buds and blooms of Hopscotch is a foil for other colours.

Sunspray. Yellow, in blazing intensity, is a feature of the buds and blooms of Sunspray.

• **APRICOT/ORANGE** Baby Bettina '81. Semi-double, coral-orange blooms.

• **PINK** Ocarina. A rounded little bush, continuously covered with a superabundance of small, fragrant, coral-pink flowers.

Perla de Montserrat '45. Semi-double, rose-pink-edged pearl blooms of exquisite form.

• **RED** Beauty Secret '65. Pointed buds open to small, high-centred, bright-red, very fragrant blooms.

Royal Salute. The full rose-red, thirty-petalled flowers are 3.75 cm (1¼ in) across and are carried in colourful clusters on strong stems.

Amorette
(Amoru, Amoretta, Snowdrop)

ORIGIN   Rosy Jewel x Zorina
HYBRIDISER   G. de Ruiter, Holland
INTRODUCER   G. de Ruiter, Holland
YEAR   1977
SHADE TOLERANCE   Light to filtered
SANDY SOIL TOLERANCE   Yes
HEIGHT   Low
FRAGRANCE   Yes
DESCRIPTION   A delight even among the many delights of miniatures. The fragrant, creamy white double blooms are numerous on a stocky stemmed, vigorous bush. Healthy, dark-green foliage and free, continuous blooming habit are other attributes.
VARIETIES   Frequently grown in a standard (tree) form.
CONDITIONS   Prefers day-long sun in soil that is drained, fertile, well mulched and watered but will grow in conditions of light to filtered shade.
LANDSCAPE USE   Use singly or in groups with other roses of similar height or as underplanting to standards; as a border; to exhibit; for bedding; as a commercial cut flower; for a tub plant; as a standard.
MAINTENANCE   When grown in some shade extra feeding and disease control measures, in addition to general care, will be needed.

PHOTOGRAPH: VALERIE SWANE

Ko's Yellow

ORIGIN (New Penny x Banbridge) x (Border Flame x Manx Queen)

HYBRIDISER Sam McGredy IV, NZ

INTRODUCER Sam McGredy Roses International, NZ

YEAR 1978

HYBRIDIST'S CODE MACkosyel

SHADE TOLERANCE Yes

SANDY SOIL TOLERANCE Light to filtered

HEIGHT Low

FRAGRANCE No

DESCRIPTION A miniature with pure hybrid-tea form and clear yellow, thirty nine-petalled flowers produced in large clusters. Free-flowering habit, glossy, dark foliage and strong stems make it a fine cut flower. The compact bush is quick to repeat flower after each wave of flowering.

VARIETIES This rose is frequently grown in a standard (tree) form.

CONDITIONS Grow in sun in soil that is drained, fertile, well mulched and watered, or in light to filtered shade with the same soil condition. In light to filtered shade effective drainage is even more important, especially in winter. Stands lesser soil conditions if drainage is satisfactory.

PHOTOGRAPH: NICK BROOKE

LANDSCAPE USE Use singly or in groups with other roses of similar height or as underplanting to standards; as a border; to exhibit; for bedding; as a commercial cut flower; for a tub plant; as a standard.

MAINTENANCE When grown in light to filtered shade some extra feeding and disease control, in addition to general care, may be needed.

Guletta
(Rugul)

ORIGIN   Rosy Jewel x Allgold
HYBRIDISER   G. de Ruiter, Holland
INTRODUCER   G. de Ruiter, Holland
YEAR   1974
SHADE TOLERANCE   None to filtered
SANDY SOIL TOLERANCE   Yes
HEIGHT   Low
FRAGRANCE   Yes
DESCRIPTION   A petite and very pretty, semi-double yellow with an old rose fragrance. Bright-green foliage, abundant flowers and repeat-flowering habit place this among the best of the yellow miniatures.
VARIETIES   This rose is frequently grown in a standard (tree) form.
CONDITIONS   Prefers day-long sun in soil that is drained, fertile, well mulched and watered but will grow in conditions of light to filtered shade.
LANDSCAPE USE   Use singly or in groups with other roses of similar height or as underplanting to standards; as a border; to exhibit; for bedding; as a commercial cut flower; for a tub plant; as a standard.
MAINTENANCE   If grown in some shade extra feeding and disease control measures, in addition to general care, will be needed.

PHOTOGRAPH: NICK BROOKE

Cricket

ORIGIN Anytime x (Zorina x Golden Wave)
HYBRIDISER Jack L. Christensen, USA
INTRODUCER Armstrong Nurseries Inc, USA
YEAR 1978
HYBRIDIST'S CODE AROket
SHADE TOLERANCE Light to filtered
SANDY SOIL TOLERANCE Yes
HEIGHT Low
FRAGRANCE No
DESCRIPTION Cricket is a delight. Its tangerine buds and ripe, lightly fragrant orange blooms must have inspired the name because they are so bright

that they seem to leap out at you. It is prolific and blooms continuously. Each strong stem carries multi-heads of twenty five-petalled blooms, 3.75 cm (1¼ in) across, each a mini replica of a classically formed hybrid tea.
VARIETIES This rose is frequently grown in a standard (tree) form and there is a climbing form.
CONDITIONS Grow in sun in soil that is drained, fertile, well mulched and watered, or in light to filtered shade with the same soil condition. In light to filtered shade effective drainage is even more important, especially in winter.

LANDSCAPE USE Use singly or in groups with other roses of similar height or as underplanting to standards; as a border; to exhibit; for bedding; as a commercial cut flower; for a tub plant; as a standard.
MAINTENANCE When grown in light to filtered shade some extra feeding and disease control, in addition to general care, may be needed.

PHOTOGRAPH: VALERIE SWANE

Petite Folie
(Meiherode)

ORIGIN (Dany Robin x Fire King) x (Cricri x Perla de Montserrat)

HYBRIDISER A. Meilland, France

INTRODUCER Universal Rose Selections, France

YEAR 1968

SHADE TOLERANCE Light to filtered

SANDY SOIL TOLERANCE Yes

HEIGHT Low

FRAGRANCE Yes

DESCRIPTION The combination of light, fruity fragrance and bright flowers, vermilion on their faces, backed by carmine on the reverse, partly accounts for the popularity of this beautiful rose. The non-stop flowering habit, sturdy growth and handsome, leathery foliage also help Petite Folie to remain a best-seller as a cut flower and a border rose.

VARIETIES This rose is frequently grown in a standard form.

CONDITIONS Grow in sun in soil that is drained, fertile, well mulched and watered, or in light to filtered shade with the same soil condition. In light to filtered shade effective drainage is even more important, especially in winter.

LANDSCAPE USE Use singly or in groups with other roses of similar height or as underplanting to standards; as a border; to exhibit; for bedding; as a commercial cut flower; for a tub plant; as a standard.

MAINTENANCE When grown in light to filtered shade some extra feeding and disease control, in addition to general care, may be needed.

PHOTOGRAPH: VALERIE SWANE

Holy Toledo

ORIGIN Gingersnap x Magic Carousel

HYBRIDISER Jack L. Christensen, USA

INTRODUCER Armstrong Nurseries Inc, USA

YEAR 1978

HYBRIDIST'S CODE ARObri

SHADE TOLERANCE Light to filtered

SANDY SOIL TOLERANCE Yes

HEIGHT Low

FRAGRANCE No

DESCRIPTION Each miniature bud and bloom has the refined shape of an exhibition hybrid tea rose. The ovoid, pointed buds open to flowers 3.75–5 cm (1¼–2 in) across with twenty five to thirty imbricated (overlapping) petals of brilliant apricot orange, shaded yellow orange on the reverse. These are borne profusely and continuously in multi-heads on strong stems and last well in the vase. Glossy, dark foliage and a vigorous, tidy, bushy habit make it suitable for borders.

AWARDS All America Rose Selection Award of Excellence, 1980.

VARIETIES This rose is frequently grown in a standard form.

CONDITIONS Grow in sun in soil that is drained, fertile, well mulched and watered, or in light to filtered shade with the same soil condition. In light to filtered shade effective drainage is even more important, especially in winter. Stands lesser soil conditions if drainage is satisfactory.

LANDSCAPE USE Use singly or in groups with other roses of similar height or as underplanting to standards; as a border; to exhibit; for bedding; as a commercial cut flower; for a tub plant; as a standard.

MAINTENANCE Regular incorporation of additional organic matter to the soil and extra mulching will be beneficial.

PHOTOGRAPH: VALERIE SWANE

Starina

ORIGIN (Dany Robin x Fire King) x Perla de Montserrat

HYBRIDISER Marie Louise Meilland, France

INTRODUCER Conard-Pyle Co, USA

YEAR 1965

HYBRIDIST'S CODE Meigabi

SHADE TOLERANCE Light to filtered

SANDY SOIL TOLERANCE Yes

HEIGHT Low

FRAGRANCE No

DESCRIPTION Tried and proven true, this lovely little rose flowers continuously and lavishly and lasts in garden or vase. The hybrid tea form of the orange-scarlet flowers is shown to advantage against glossy, dark-green foliage. Growth is robust.

VARIETIES This rose is frequently grown in a standard rose form.

CONDITIONS Grow in sun in soil that is drained, fertile, well mulched and watered, or in light to filtered shade with the same soil condition. In light to filtered shade effective drainage is even more important, especially in winter.

LANDSCAPE USE Use singly or in groups with other roses of similar height or as underplanting to standards; as a border; to exhibit; for beding; as a commercial cut flower; for a tub plant; as a standard.

MAINTENANCE When grown in light to filtered shade some extra feeding and disease control, in addition to general care, may be needed.

PHOTOGRAPH: NICK BROOKE

Kaikoura

ORIGIN   Anytime x Matangi
HYBRIDISER   Sam McGredy IV, NZ
INTRODUCER   Sam McGredy Roses International, NZ
YEAR   1978
HYBRIDIST'S CODE   MACwalla
SHADE TOLERANCE   Light to filtered
SANDY SOIL TOLERANCE   Yes
HEIGHT   Low
FRAGRANCE   Yes
DESCRIPTION   A pleasing, free-flowering orange vermilion, slightly fragrant with double blooms with twenty seven petals. A robust bush. The foliage is glossy and dark green. A first-rate cut flower.
VARIETIES   This rose is frequently grown in a standard (tree) form.
CONDITIONS   Prefers day-long sun in soil that is drained, fertile, well mulched and watered but will grow in conditions of light to filtered shade if the soil is drained effectively, especially in winter.

LANDSCAPE USE   Use singly or in groups with other roses of similar height or as underplanting to standards; as a border; to exhibit; for bedding; as a commercial cut flower; for a tub plant; as a standard.
MAINTENANCE   If grown in some shade extra feeding and disease control measures, in addition to general care, will be needed.

PHOTOGRAPH: VALERIE SWANE

Otago

ORIGIN   Anytime x Minuette
HYBRIDISER   Sam McGredy IV, NZ
INTRODUCER   Sam McGredy Róses International, NZ
YEAR   1978
HYBRIDIST'S CODE   MACnecta
SHADE TOLERANCE   Light to filtered
SANDY SOIL TOLERANCE   Yes
HEIGHT   Low
FRAGRANCE   Yes
DESCRIPTION   This appealing miniature has the classic form of a high-centred hybrid tea rose plus fragrance. The salmon-orange flowers have thirty five petals, are very full and hold well. It is a bushy, free-blooming, healthy plant.
VARIETIES   This rose is frequently grown in a standard form.
CONDITIONS   Prefers day-long sun in soil that is drained, fertile, well mulched and watered but will grow in conditions of light to filtered shade if the soil is drained effectively, especially in winter.
LANDSCAPE USE   Use singly or in groups with other roses of similar height or as underplanting to standards; as a border; to exhibit; for bedding; as a commercial cut flower; for a tub plant; as a standard.
MAINTENANCE   If grown in some shade extra feeding and disease control measures, in addition to general care, will be needed.

PHOTOGRAPH: NICK BROOKE

Mary Marshall

ORIGIN Little Darling x Fairy Princess

HYBRIDISER Ralph S. Moore, USA

INTRODUCER Sequoia Nursery, USA

YEAR 1970

SHADE TOLERANCE Light to filtered

SANDY SOIL TOLERANCE Yes

HEIGHT Low

FRAGRANCE Yes

DESCRIPTION The buds are long and pointed and the cupped, fragrant flowers are pink with a yellow base to each of the forty pointed petals. The difficult to define colour is sometimes described as coral pink. Mary Marshall is a pretty and rewarding rose with hybrid tea form and is very free flowering and continuously in flower. It has been endowed with small, leathery, green foliage and a robust, bushy habit.

AWARDS American Rose Society Award of Excellence for Miniature Roses, 1975.

VARIETIES This rose is frequently grown in a standard form.

CONDITIONS Grow in sun in soil that is drained, fertile, well mulched and watered, or in light

PHOTOGRAPH: IVY HANSEN

to filtered shade with the same soil condition. In light to filtered shade effective drainage is even more important, especially in winter.

LANDSCAPE USE Use singly or in groups with other roses of similar height or as underplanting to standards; as a border; to exhibit; for bedding; as a commercial cut flower; for a tub plant; as a standard.

MAINTENANCE When grown in light to filtered shade some extra feeding and disease control, in addition to general care, may be needed.

Foxy Lady

ORIGIN   Gingersnap x Magic Carousel

HYBRIDISER   Jack L. Christensen, USA

INTRODUCER   Armstrong Nurseries Inc, USA

YEAR   1980

HYBRIDIST'S CODE   AROshrim

SHADE TOLERANCE   None to light

SANDY SOIL TOLERANCE   Yes

HEIGHT   Low

FRAGRANCE   No

DESCRIPTION   A classic miniature, shrimp-pink rose 3.75 cm (1¼ in) across with twenty to twenty-eight imbricated (overlapping) petals. Flowers are carried in such profusion that they hide the foliage. The high-centred form is charming. Small foliage, robust growth, the free, recurrent-flowering habit and pretty, pointed, ovoid buds make this a desirable rose.

VARIETIES   This rose is frequently grown in a standard (tree) form.

CONDITIONS   Grow in sun in soil that is drained, fertile, well mulched and watered, or in light to filtered shade with the same soil condition. In light to filtered shade effective drainage is even more important, especially in winter.

LANDSCAPE USE   Use singly or in groups with other roses of similar height; or as underplanting to standards; as a border; to exhibit; for bedding; as a commercial cut flower; for a tub plant; as a standard.

MAINTENANCE   When grown in light to filtered shade some extra feeding and disease control, in addition to general care, may be needed.

PHOTOGRAPH: NICK BROOKE

Magic Carousel

ORIGIN   Little Darling x Westmont

HYBRIDISER   Ralph S. Moore, USA

INTRODUCER   Sequoia Nursery & Mini Roses, USA

YEAR   1972

HYBRIDIST'S CODE   MORrusel

SHADE TOLERANCE   None to light

SANDY SOIL TOLERANCE   Yes

HEIGHT   Low

FRAGRANCE   Yes

DESCRIPTION   The ideal form of a high-centred hybrid tea rose is repeated in this delightful white bloom edged with red. Small, glossy, leathery foliage clothes a vigorous dwarf bush which blooms generously and repeat flowers quickly.

AWARDS   American Rose Society Award of Excellence for Miniature Roses, 1975.

VARIETIES   This rose is frequently grown in a standard form.

CONDITIONS   Grow in sun in soil that is drained, fertile, well mulched and watered, or in light to filtered shade with the same soil condition. In light to filtered shade effective drainage is even more important, especially in winter.

LANDSCAPE USE   Use singly or in groups with other roses of similar height or as underplanting to standards; as a border; to exhibit; for bedding; as a commercial cut flower; for a tub plant; as a standard.

MAINTENANCE   When grown in light to filtered shade some extra feeding and disease control, in addition to general care, may be needed.

PHOTOGRAPH: VALERIE SWANE

Little Red Devil

ORIGIN Gingersnap x Magic Carousel

HYBRIDISER Jack L. Christensen, USA

INTRODUCER Armstrong Nurseries Inc, USA

YEAR 1980

HYBRIDIST'S CODE AROvidil

SHADE TOLERANCE Light to filtered

SANDY SOIL TOLERANCE Yes

HEIGHT Low

FRAGRANCE Yes

DESCRIPTION This is one of the pleasing roses from the cross between Gingersnap and Magic Carousel; another was Holy Toledo. Little Red Devil deserves top billing. From pointed, ovoid buds open slightly fragrant, medium-red flowers 3.75 cm (1¼ in) across, each with thirty five to fifty beautifully imbricated petals. The closely packed flower clusters have strong stems and cut well. The foliage is small on a bushy, vigorous plant which is free flowering and quick to repeat flower after each flush.

VARIETIES This rose is frequently grown in a standard form.

CONDITIONS Grow in sun in soil that is drained, fertile, well mulched and watered, or in light to filtered shade with the same soil condition. In light to filtered shade effective drainage is even more important, especially in winter.

LANDSCAPE USE Use singly or in groups, with other roses of similar height or as underplanting to standards; as a border; to exhibit; for bedding; as a commercial cut flower; for a tub plant; as a standard.

PHOTOGRAPH: NAN BARBOUR

MAINTENANCE When grown in light to filtered shade some extra feeding and disease control, in addition to general care, may be needed.

Lavender Lace

ORIGIN   Ellen Poulsen x Debbie
HYBRIDISER   Ralph S. Moore, USA
INTRODUCER   Sequoia Nursery, USA
YEAR   1968
SHADE TOLERANCE   Light to filtered
SANDY SOIL TOLERANCE   Yes
HEIGHT   Low
FRAGRANCE   Yes
DESCRIPTION   This was the first mauve miniature rose and is still superior in this colour. The dainty lavender flowers are fragrant, with the high-centred form of the hybrid teas. Flowers are abundant and the flowering habit is recurrent. The foliage of Lavender Lace is small and glossy on a plant which is vigorous and bushy.
VARIETIES   This rose is frequently grown in a standard form.
CONDITIONS   Grow in sun in soil that is drained, fertile, well mulched and watered, or in light or filtered shade with the same soil condition. In light to filtered shade effective drainage is even more important, especially in winter.
LANDSCAPE USE   Use singly or in groups with other roses of similar height or as underplanting to standards; as a border; to exhibit; for bedding; as a commercial cut flower; for a tub plant; as a standard.
MAINTENANCE   When grown in light to filtered shade some extra feeding and disease control, in addition to general care, may be needed.

PHOTOGRAPH: VALERIE SWANE

CLIMBING AND PILLAR ROSES

Most climbing roses developed spontaneously as a variation or 'sport' on the parent bush. Pillar roses are natural climbers with a less vigorous habit suitable for twining around columns and pergolas. Some other outstanding climbing and pillar roses not illustrated include:

• **YELLOW** Casino '63. Buttercup-yellow, large well-formed fragrant blooms; recurrent flowering. NRS Gold Medal, '63.

• **PINK** Clair Matin. Dainty pointed buds open to 5 to 7.5 cm (2 to 3 in) pink blooms with twelve to eighteen petals from cupped to flat in form and with a sweet-briar fragrance.

Renae. A very fragrant pink cluster rose, each bloom 6.25 cm (2½ in) across, open with thirty eight to forty five petals. Repeat flowering.

• **RED** Don Juan '58. Large cupped, rich velvety red with a delightful fragrance.

Nancy Hayward '37. Rich, bright-cerise, single, open blooms; very vigorous.

• **MULTI-COLOUR** Joseph's Coat '64. Yellow and red, semi-double, fragrant blooms in clusters.

Rosa Banksiae 'Lutea'
(Yellow Banks' Rosa; Banksia Rose)

PHOTOGRAPH: WALTER KNIGHT

ORIGIN Not known

HYBRIDISER A form of the species rose *Rosa banksiae*

INTRODUCER It was introduced to cultivation in 1824

SHADE TOLERANCE Light to filtered

SANDY SOIL TOLERANCE Yes

HEIGHT Climber

FRAGRANCE No

DESCRIPTION This charming nineteenth-century rose is more than a little responsible for keeping public interest in 'old' roses alive. In late spring it wears a cloak of small, yellow, cupped flowers and these are in nodding groups on short pedicels along arching branches. Though vase life is limited their inclusion among mixed flowers is light and graceful. Few other cut flowers have so many flowers and such long, easily arranged stems. The bush is robust, almost rampant but easily controlled with hard pruning, or it can be left unpruned. It will grow through trees with speed or it may be kept pruned to a bush 2–4 m (yd) high. It is very healthy, almost evergreen, and does not require spraying for fungal diseases. Though robust it is not troublesome.

VARIETIES This may be pruned and grown as a shrub. Very similar to this rose and an effective companion for it is the parent White Banks' Rose, *Rosa banksiae* with double white blooms.

CONDITIONS Grow in sun in soil that is drained, fertile, well mulched and watered.

LANDSCAPE USE A bushy and vigorous screen 2 m (yd) or less; to climb on a trellis or pergola or against a fence or on a wall.

MAINTENANCE Follow general instructions.

151

Golden Showers

ORIGIN   Charlotte Armstrong x Captain Thomas

HYBRIDISER   Walter Lammerts, USA

INTRODUCER   Germain's Inc, USA

YEAR   1956

SHADE TOLERANCE   None to light

SANDY SOIL TOLERANCE   Yes

HEIGHT   Climber

FRAGRANCE   Yes

DESCRIPTION   A pretty rose carrying masses of fragrant, daffodil-yellow flowers, high-centred at first then becoming flat revealing a crown of golden stamens. The flowers are produced singly or in clusters on strong stems. Golden Showers blooms recurrently from early spring to late autumn. The bush is vigorous with dark, glossy foliage.

AWARDS   All America Rose Selection, 1957; Portland Gold Medal, 1957.

VARIETIES   None.

CONDITIONS   Drained, fertile, well-watered and mulched soil in sun.

LANDSCAPE USE   Climber on a trellis or pergola; against a fence or on a wall; to cover columns or pillars.

MAINTENANCE   Follow general instructions. Additional organic matter in the soil and extra mulching will help.

PHOTOGRAPH: VALERIE SWANE

Handel

ORIGIN   Columbine x Heidelberg
HYBRIDISER   Sam McGredy IV,
NZ
INTRODUCER   McGredy Roses
International, NZ
YEAR   1965
SHADE TOLERANCE   Light to
filtered
SANDY SOIL TOLERANCE   Yes
HEIGHT   2–3 m (yd)
FRAGRANCE   No
DESCRIPTION   A frilly, cream
and pink flower edged deeper rose.
The large (8.25 cm (3 in)) blooms
have twenty two petals and appear
semi-double. It has a free, recurrent
flowering habit and robust growth.
The glossy foliage is olive green.
VARIETIES   None.
CONDITIONS   Prefers day-long
sun in soil that is drained, fertile,
well mulched and watered, but
will grow in conditions of light to
filtered shade if the soil is drained
effectively, especially in winter.
Stands lesser soil conditions if
drainage is satisfactory.
LANDSCAPE USE   To climb on a
trellis or pergola; against a fence or
on a wall; to cover columns or
pillars.
MAINTENANCE   If grown in
some shade extra feeding and
disease control measures, in
addition to general care, will be
needed.

PHOTOGRAPH: NICK BROOKE

Blossomtime

ORIGIN   New Dawn x unnamed hybrid tea

HYBRIDISER   Conrad O'Neal, USA

INTRODUCER   Boxley Nursery Inc, USA

YEAR   1951

SHADE TOLERANCE   Light to filtered

SANDY SOIL TOLERANCE   Yes

HEIGHT   Climber (or tall shrub 2–3 m (yd))

FRAGRANCE   Yes

DESCRIPTION   A very fragrant, high-centred, two-toned pink rose 10 cm (4 in) across with thirty five to forty petals. The buds are pointed and the blooms are produced in clusters of three to eight. It is a pretty and very colourful rose which repeat flowers freely and is hardy and easy to grow.

VARIETIES   Though a climber this rose can be pruned to shrub proportions.

CONDITIONS   Prefers day-long sun in soil that is drained, fertile, well watered and mulched but will grow in conditions of light to filtered shade if the soil is drained effectively, especially in winter. Stands lesser soil conditions if drainage is satisfactory.

LANDSCAPE USE   A bushy and vigorous hedge or screen; to climb on a trellis or pergola or against a fence or on a wall.

MAINTENANCE   Follow general instructions.

PHOTOGRAPH: IVY HANSEN

Cecile Brunner Climbing
(Mignon, Mlle Cecile Brunner, Mme Cecile Brunner, Sweetheart Rose, Buttonhole Rose)

ORIGIN   Probably a polyantha x Mme de Tartas

HYBRIDISER   Vve (Widow) Ducher, France

INTRODUCER   Pernet Ducher, France

YEAR   1881

SHADE TOLERANCE   Light to filtered

SANDY SOIL TOLERANCE   No

HEIGHT   Climbing

FRAGRANCE   Yes

DESCRIPTION   A well-loved, time-honoured rose once much used in bridal bouquets and still popular in flower arrangements. The buds are long and pointed. The fragrant flowers are small, double, open and pink on a creamy yellow ground. The foliage is soft and reddish. It is a sturdy, free-blooming climber with few thorns.

VARIETIES   None.

CONDITIONS   Prefers day-long sun in soil that is drained, fertile, well watered and mulched but will grow in conditions of light to filtered shade if the soil is drained effectively, especially in winter. Stands lesser soil conditions if drainage is satisfactory.

LANDSCAPE USE   A bushy and vigorous screen or hedge; to climb on a trellis or pergola; against a fence or on a wall; as a shrub.

MAINTENANCE   Follow general instructions.

PHOTOGRAPH: NICK BROOKE

Titian

ORIGIN   A 'sport' of the Australian-raised floribunda of the same name

HYBRIDISER   F. L. Reithmuller (of the parent floribunda), Australia

INTRODUCER   R. Kordes, Germany

YEAR   1964

SHADE TOLERANCE   Light to filtered

SANDY SOIL TOLERANCE   Yes

HEIGHT   Climber

FRAGRANCE   Yes

DESCRIPTION   A climbing cluster or pillar rose with recurrent-flowering habit, bearing lavish quantities of large, light-red to crimson-pink blooms. It makes a colourful display and is easy to grow.

VARIETIES   The parent of this rose was a floribunda which is not grown today.

CONDITIONS   Grow in sun in soil that is drained, fertile, well mulched and watered, or in light to filtered shade with the same soil condition where effective drainage is important, especially in winter.

LANDSCAPE USE   Climber on a trellis or pergola; against a fence or on a wall; to cover columns or pillars.

MAINTENANCE   When grown in light to filtered shade some extra feeding and disease control, in addition to general care, may be needed.

PHOTOGRAPH: IVY HANSEN

Paul's Scarlet Climber

ORIGIN Paul's Carmine Pillar x Rêve d'Or

HYBRIDISER W. Paul, UK

INTRODUCER William Paul & Son Ltd, UK

YEAR 1916

SHADE TOLERANCE Light to filtered

SANDY SOIL TOLERANCE Yes

HEIGHT Climber

FRAGRANCE Yes

DESCRIPTION At its best in spring when almost covered in bloom. The large clusters of vivid-scarlet blooms, shaded crimson, do not fade or burn.

AWARDS National Rose Society Gold Medal, 1915; Bagatelle Gold Medal, 1918.

VARIETIES None.

CONDITIONS Grow in sun in soil that is drained, fertile, well mulched and watered. Or in light to filtered shade with the same soil condition where good drainage is important, especially in winter.

LANDSCAPE USE Climber on a trellis or pergola; against a fence or on a wall; to cover columns or pillars.

MAINTENANCE Extra feeding and disease control is needed when grown in light to filtered shade.

PHOTOGRAPH: NICK BROOKE

Altissimo

ORIGIN   Tenor x (unlisted)
HYBRIDISER   Georges Delbard, France
INTRODUCER   R. & G. Cuthbert Ltd, UK
YEAR   1966
SHADE TOLERANCE   Light to filtered
SANDY SOIL TOLERANCE   Yes
HEIGHT   Climber
FRAGRANCE   Yes
DESCRIPTION   A rampant grower with large (10–12.5 cm (4–5 in)) seven-petalled, single blood-red blooms with crimson overtones in shapes varying from cupped to flat and showing golden stamens. It flowers abundantly and repeat flowers. It has few equals as a cover on columns and pillars. The dark-green foliage is disease resistant.
VARIETIES   None.
CONDITIONS   Grow in sun in soil that is drained, fertile, well mulched and watered, or in light to filtered shade with the same soil condition. In light to filtered shade effective drainage is even more important, especially in winter.
LANDSCAPE USE   A bushy and vigorous screen 2 m (yd) or less; as a climber on a trellis or pergola or against a fence or on a wall; to cover columns or pillars.
MAINTENANCE   When grown in light to filtered shade some extra feeding and disease control, in addition to general care, may be needed.

PHOTOGRAPH: NICK BROOKE

Black Boy

ORIGIN Etoile de France x Bardou Job
HYBRIDISER Alister Clark, Australia
INTRODUCER National Rose Society of South Australia
YEAR 1919
SHADE TOLERANCE Light to filtered
SANDY SOIL TOLERANCE Yes
HEIGHT Climber
FRAGRANCE Yes
DESCRIPTION A vigorous climber with large, plump buds and big, dark-red blooms becoming darker in summer. The foliage is light green, wrinkled and sparse. It is a very popular climber with few thorns and an early, continuous flowering habit. Contrary to popular opinion there is no bush form of Black Boy.
VARIETIES None.
CONDITIONS Grow in sun in soil that is drained, fertile, well mulched and watered, or in light to filtered shade with the same soil condition. In light to filtered shade effective drainage is even more important, especially in winter.
LANDSCAPE USE Climber on a trellis or pergola; against a fence or on a wall; to cover columns or pillars.
MAINTENANCE When grown in light to filtered shade some extra feeding and disease control, in addition to general care, may be needed.

PHOTOGRAPH: WALTER KNIGHT

PESTS AND DISEASES

Even with minimal care roses are capable of surviving to a great age, but basic care should include protection against diseases and pests. Like every other garden plant roses attract their share of pests and are hosts to disease organisms. Keeping the rose garden free of spent foliage or flowers, prunings and dead wood, is an important protective measure.

In humid climates, particularly those with dewy mornings or overnight rain, controlling the fungus disease black spot is an essential part of growing healthy roses. Black spot and mildew can also be discouraged by using drip irrigation. It is less of a problem in hot dry climates which partly accounts for the large size and good health of roses in such climates.

In all climates roses can be affected by diseases induced through the deficiency of one or more chemical nutrients, eg, phosphate, magnesium, iron, manganese, potassium etc. In saline soils nutrient deficiencies are more of a problem than they are in neutral to acid soils. Taking pH readings will indicate whether a garden bed is becoming too acid or too alkaline. Usually foliage colour and condition will show which nutrient is lacking or excessive.

Some symptoms are similar for a variety of rose problems. 'Dieback', the gradual browning of shoots, is a symptom of the disease known by that name, but not all browning of the shoots is 'dieback'. Disease identification needs more than a cursory investigation in order to ensure the right conclusion is reached. Then the correct treatment can be applied. Pesticides are ineffective against disease, and fungicides will not control pests. To overcome the identification problem more 'complete' sprays containing both an insecticide and a fungicide are being marketed. But when a problem is severe specific treatments are preferable and less wasteful.

The loss of young, newly planted roses is usually caused by handling, not disease. It is vital to water and then store newly purchased roses in a cool draught-free room (eg, a laundry) until they are planted. If they are in a bundle water can be trickled down the centre to dampen the tops, wet the roots and then drain away. Leaving roses in the boot (trunk) of the car for a few days, or on the verandah or against a warm wall where sun and wind can reach them, causes drying out and death two or three months later. Before it reaches you the rose has been disturbed by the nurseryman who has dug, pruned and parcelled it. Roses move readily and tolerate this handling. Nevertheless shock is inevitable. Drying the bushes, either through wind or sun or failure to keep the roots wet and covered, aggravates the shock.

After planting (into damp soil) two or three weekly soakings are essential. Drainage must be effective so that excess water is not being trapped in the hole. Insufficient water in the first three months will slowly kill new roses, so will poor drainage at any time. Digging deep holes into the subsoil and filling these with fresh soil or compost often creates a well which holds water and is a breeding ground for root-rot diseases.

Fertilising new roses can cause losses. It is better to prepare the ground before planting as detailed in General Planting Instructions, but failing that, avoid adding fertiliser or manures at planting time. When applied in excess the roots will be 'burnt' and the plant, unable to take in nutrients, will die. Fertilising after the first flowers have appeared is soon enough. It is essential that it be applied to damp ground as dry soil intensifies the 'burning' action of fertiliser. Mulching with old, composted manures, grass clippings or hay is very important. Lucerne hay is highly recommended as it provides nutrients to the soil and encourages earthworm activity. Mulching keeps weeds down and retains moisture and a cool root zone. A beneficial fungus grows under mulch which can digest up to 98% of the nematode population. Lucerne hay is nitrogen-rich, but in the case of other mulches, blood and bone can be sprinkled on top to replace any nitrogen lost through mulching.

Rose health deteriorates and flowering is reduced when disease is not checked. It may be difficult initially to tell the difference between the effects of disease and damage from pests. Pests and their damage can be seen (perhaps with the aid of a magnifying glass) whereas only the effects of disease are visible.

A regular feeding programme for established roses keeps the bushes healthy and this reduces the incidence of some pests which prefer to attack weak or debilitated plants as part of nature's plan to support the survival of the fittest. Maintaining good health and keeping the garden free of diseased debris are worthwhile disease-control measures.

Foliage Diseases

SYMPTOMS

Evident in summer: ragged-edged, black or dark-brown spots often with yellow surround which can be up to 1 cm (½ in) across. May also appear on the bark of susceptible old and neglected bushes. Foliage yellows and falls littering soil below the bush. The defoliated plants make weak growth which is prone to winter frost damage. Flowering is reduced: blooms are smaller.

CAUSE

Black spot fungus disease.

Dew on foliage for four hours or more at low night temperatures encourages black spot. The spores on affected foliage are capable of over-wintering on spent foliage left on the ground. When summer comes they begin their life cycle again.

PROTECTION

Good health and garden cleanliness are best protection. Keep roses well fed, watered and mulched; remove and dispose of fallen foliage and prunings.
Some varieties are more susceptible than others. Select less disease-prone cultivars for humid climates. Plant in sunny positions with ample space around each rose to ensure satisfactory air circulation. Avoid watering in the evening with overhead sprinklers in warm humid weather.
After winter pruning spray with a homemade bordeaux spray. Lime sulphur spray may be used only before new growth appears after winter pruning. Triforine may be used at three-weekly intervals from late spring to autumn. Alternatively, spray during this period with Mancozeb, or a similar fungicide or alternate these if the disease becomes very difficult to control. An organic alternative during the flowering season is to use a seaweed spray such as Maxicrop, or a homemade fungicide consisting of fresh chamomile, chives, lavender flowers, casuarina needles and plenty of horseradish leaves covered with water and left until the liquid is light brown. Use as a spray every two weeks.
Spray at 14-day intervals depending on need with 'complete' rose sprays containing both fungicide and insecticide.

SYMPTOMS	CAUSE	PROTECTION
Leaf fall	See black spot, anthracnose, powdery mildew rust and downy mildew. Leaf fall is a sign of each of these diseases and could indicate that the spray programme needs improvement. It may also mean that organic phosphate insecticides are being used too frequently or in too high a concentration. Over application of fertiliser may also cause sudden leaf drop.	If applicable, improve spray programme, first checking equipment. Often the distribution of the spray is faulty and though spray is being applied, insufficient is reaching the plant. Replace organic phosphate sprays with inorganic treatments (at more frequent intervals) until the bushes recover. Try to leach excess fertiliser away by watering but avoid 'drowning' the bushes.
Leaf burn — browning foliage. Looks and feels burnt.	Strong concentrations of fungicides or rose sprays. Using sulphur and karathane preparations at normal strength will also cause burning if the next day is hot and sunny.	Apply fungicides late in the day or in the early evening.
The underside of rose foliage is dusted with bright orange powdery spots or pustules. The leaves become speckled with yellow then become completely yellow and fall prematurely and the shoots become deformed and snap off easily. The rusty spots contain the fungal spores of the disease. They spread over the foliage through spring and summer. In late summer in a further stage of the disease dark brown or black spore-bearing bodies appear together with the orange spots. Rust spores are capable of over-wintering on the fallen foliage.	Rust (*Phragmidium mucronatum*) Source of infection is other infected plants and over-wintering spores. The disease is distributed by wind and is more prevalent in hot humid weather.	Collect and dispose of all fallen foliage, prunings and affected leaves and plant parts in autumn. Avoid adding excess nitrogen and potash to the soil. Spray with Mancozeb or Triforine. Dust with sulphur every seven days in humid weather. Regular use of lucerne hay as mulch can help eliminate the problem. Comfrey can also be used.
Irregular purplish-red to dark brown angular spots appear on the foliage. On the undersides of the foliage below the spots a downy fungal growth commences during humid weather. The young foliage may fall readily. On the stems and flower stalks purple spotting, streaking and blotching occurs and the young shoots die back.	Downy mildew (*Peronospora spasa*) The source of infection is other infected plants and plant parts. The disease is spread by wind and is more prevalent in humid weather. Some varieties are more susceptible than others.	Early detection and destruction of all infected foliage, flowers and prunings in autumn is the best organic means of control. Otherwise spray thoroughly, making sure to cover stems and undersurfaces of leaves with Zineb or copper oxychloride as soon as noticed. Repeat spraying after one week if weather is wet. Mixing the two sprays is also

SYMPTOMS

Continued
Spotting can extend to the calyces and dead brown areas will form on the petals.
Flowers become deformed when the flower buds are infected.

Small ash grey spots with well-defined black margins appear on the foliage and occasionally on the young green stems and the flowers. As they age their centres fall away leaving only the black margins. Yellowing of the foliage follows though it does not fall as much as it does with black spot.

A powdery dusting of white or greyish spots covers the leaves, calyxes, shoots and sometimes the flower buds. Flowers and foliage can be malformed and fallen leaves may be wrinkled and reddish coloured.
Young growth is the most susceptible.
Some rose varieties are more mildew-prone than others.
Source of infection is other infected plants.

CAUSE

Anthracnose (*Sphaceloma rosarum*)

Spread by wind and more prevalent in cool humid weather.

Powdery mildew (*Oidium* sp.)

Encouraged by humid conditions, moderate temperatures 21°–27°C (70°–81°F) and over-application of nitrogen in the feeding programme producing lush growth which helps the disease to spread. The fungus over-winters in the leaf buds and when spring and summer temperatures are suitable it begins a new cycle of infection.

PROTECTION

Continued
effective, using equal quantities of both in soluble powder form.

Spray with copper oxychloride if necessary. If a black spot control programme is being followed it will also control this disease and separate sprays will not be needed.

Best protection is to choose from the mildew-resistant varieties. Hybridists have produced so many resistant varieties that powdery mildew is not the problem it once was.
Cleanliness helps. Removal and burning of old prunings and fallen foliage in winter and other seasons reduces the carry-over source of the disease.
Avoid over-application of fertiliser with a high nitrogen content. Organic sprays which can be used include chamomile tea, or a brew of horsetail or casuarina needles. In severe cases use bordeaux or 'complete' rose sprays alternating them with organic products if necessary.

Flower Disease

SYMPTOMS

The buds brown and decay and the petals of partially opened flowers brown and shrivel. Then a furry-grey fungal growth covers these damaged areas.
On fully opened flowers the petals develop small reddish rings in light coloured varieties or creamy-white rings in dark roses.

CAUSE

Grey mould and petal spot (*Botrytis cinerea*)

The source of infection is dead and decaying plant debris and infected flowers.
The disease is spread by wind and is more prevalent in cool, humid conditions. It attacks many plants besides roses and colonises on decaying plant debris.

PROTECTION

Keep plants free of dead and decaying foliage, flowers and prunings.

Stem Disease

SYMPTOMS	CAUSE	PROTECTION
Pale yellow or reddish spots appear on the bark, enlarging and browning with age. Eventually the bark cracks and becomes sunken with tiny black pin-point structures on the infected areas. Some varieties are more susceptible than others. In those with high resistance the fungus will stop where the branch joins the main stem but in others it will continue down the stem, eventually killing the plant.	Canker and dieback fungus (*Coniothyrium fuckelii*) This fungus disease is confined to roses. It is spread by wind or water splash. The source of infection is often the dead tissue on the plant.	Cut off diseased branches with a slanting cut several centimetres (1 in) below the infected area and just above a bud. The cut must be clean without frayed edges. Using sharp secateurs is the best way to achieve this.
Infected plants produce very few flowers and are stunted, with large wart-like growths at the base of the stem, on the roots and sometimes on the branches.	Crown gall bacterium (*Agrobacterium radiobacter* var. *tumefaciens*) The source of infection is infested soil. The disease is spread by taking infected plants into uninfested soil.	Remove and dispose of diseased plants. Do not replant into affected area unless new plants have been treated with Nogall. Examine roses for galls, on delivery before planting.
The foliage wilts and branches die back often on one side of the plant while the rest of the plant remains healthy. The disease discolours the affected woody tissue.	Verticillium wilt fungus (*Verticillium dahliae*) The source of infection is infested soil and the fungus is spread by the introduction of infested plants into clean soil. Its host range is wide and includes a very large number of garden plants and weeds.	Remove and dispose of infected plants. Treat the soil with a fumigant, before replanting with susceptible species. Fumigation is unnecessary if resistant species are replanted.
The cuttings have areas of olive green, dark brown or black. They fail to make roots (or make very few), and die. Disease may be evident before the cuttings are planted.	Black rot fungus (*Chalaropsis thielavioides*) This is a disease of rose cuttings and is aggravated by keeping cuttings under wet conditions for prolonged periods.	Store only clean cuttings. Do not store under wet conditions. This is a propagation problem confined to rootstocks.

Root Disease

SYMPTOMS	**CAUSE**	**PROTECTION**
The bushes are stunted and yellow. The roots are covered with a mass of bead-like swellings.	Nematodes (*Meliodogyne hapla* or *M. javanica*) The source of infection is infested soil and infested seedlings of others species. It is spread by footwear, drainage water and garden tools. Nematodes prefer light soils and warm weather and can be harboured by a wide range of plants including weeds, ornamentals and vegetables.	Avoid infested soils and be careful to check newly purchased plants for infection. Use the non-fumigant nematicide fenamiphose (Nemacur (R)) before planting and/or on growing plants. Marigolds are said to be a deterrent if grown beside rose bushes, and in winter all parts of the marigold can be chopped up and used as mulch around the bush. Soaking the soil beneath the plant with a thick syrup of dissolved sugar is said to dehydrate the nematodes. A companion planting of mustard or french lavender is also recommended.

Non-Parasitic Disorders

SYMPTOMS	**CAUSE**	**PROTECTION**
Leaves have dark brownish-yellow markings between the veins which can also be yellowish: leaf edges are sometimes shrivelled.	Usually indicates chloride toxicity. Often occurs in seaside areas or where water is heavily chlorinated. Chlorinated swimming pool water splashed over roses frequently will cause chloride toxicity.	Avoid fertilisers containing muriate of potash (potassium chloride) particularly in seaside areas.
Small yellow-green leaves, sometimes spotted red; foliage which falls prematurely.	Nitrogen deficiency	Wet the root area then water in a complete water-soluble plant food.
New roses planted in old soil may fail to grow satisfactorily, and, in the worst cases, will gradually turn brown and die.	Replant. The disease is due to planting in rose-sick soil which has used all or most of the nutrients needed by the rose.	Dig out old roses and remove their surrounding soil to a spade or a spade and a half depth and a width of 1 m (yd). Replace with suitable soil containing ample organic matter.

Nutrient Disorders

SYMPTOMS	**CAUSE**	**PROTECTION**
Small dark-green leaves with purplish tints mostly on the undersurface, and poor stunted growth. Foliage drops after yellowing along leaf margins.	Phosphate deficiency	Water in a handful of superphosphate per square metre (yard) or use phosphorous-rich compounds such as blood and bone or ground eggshells, ground bones or poultry manure.

SYMPTOMS	CAUSE	PROTECTION
Flowers are small and lacking quality; leaf margins are dead, occasional purpling of foliage; poor colour, weak stems.	Potassium deficiency	Apply rose food or water in a level tablespoon of potassium sulphate per square metre (yard). A short term solution is to use a seaweed-based foliar spray. Adding wood ash or urine may have some benefit.
Yellowing between veins and towards the centre of the leaf, mostly on older foliage. Stunted growth with few flower breaks.	Magnesium deficiency	Dissolve one teaspoon of Epsom salts in a watering can of water and apply to ground underneath the foliage. Small additions of dolomite or lime will be beneficial.
Yellowing occurs around leaf edges and extends inwards between the veins usually on the old foliage. Reduced growth.	Manganese deficiency	Soil probably contains too much lime. Using lucerne hay as a mulch will probably correct this deficiency. If not, water generously and if the rose does not improve apply manganese sulphate at the rate of one tablespoon per watering can to the area below the foliage.
Overall distinctive yellowing is noticeable on the new growth. Green veins with chlorotic areas between them on some leaves.	Iron deficiency	Avoid adding too much lime to the soil; correct deficiency with iron chelates at recommended rate. Good mulching practices should make iron more available to the plant. Harvest the leaves of cultivated dandelions and use chopped up as mulch.
Yellowing of leaf veins and later along the midrib.	Roots are suffering from oxygen deficiency due to soil being too wet or over-compacted.	Improve the soil drainage. Roses will not grow in badly drained areas. Dig and loosen soil and improve its texture and aeration by digging in organic material. Apply an organic mulch. Do not use water which contains detergents.
Misshapen, abnormally dark-green leaves.	Soil may be too acid. Or it may be over-fed with nitrogen which can cause deficiencies of boron and molybdenum.	A pH meter will determine soil acidity. If acid correct by applying lime, otherwise water in a trace element mixture plus one heaped teaspoon each of superphosphate and potassium sulphate per square metre (yard) and use complete fertilisers in future.

Virus Diseases

SYMPTOMS

These are variable and include vein banding, a yellow band along the veinal network of the leaflet, or an isolated area or the margins. Yellow (chlorotic) mottling of minor veins which gradually becomes a general chlorosis. Line pattern: closely placed lines of creamy-white or pale-green tissue.

Young spring leaflets curl downwards 'balling' the leaf and giving the plant a wilted look. The brittle leaves fall easily and the defoliated shoots die back. Young new plants produce yellowish-green new growth which dies during the current season. Old established plants after a setback grow at a reduced rate and have hard yellowish foliage but continue to flower. Warm temperatures mask the symptoms and during summer growth may be normal. Symptoms are most evident during cool spring and autumn periods.

CAUSE

Rose mosaic virus

Spread by propagation from infected plants.

Rose wilt virus

The disease is spread by propagation material from infected plants and by the aphid *Macrosiphum rosae* which is known to transmit the disease to healthy plants. The rose rootstock *Rosa multiflora* is suspected of being a symptomless carrier of the disease.

PROTECTION

Do not use infected plants as a source of propagating material.

Dig up and dispose of infected plants. Do not take budwood from infected plants. Destroy all rootstocks on which buds did not grow. Keep mother blocks for budwood and rootstocks free of diseases and insects and spray regularly to control aphids.

Rose Pests

SYMPTOMS

Small insects which develop large dense colonies on shoots and flower buds. By sucking the sap from both they cause deformation of flowers and foliage.

CAUSE

Aphids (*Macrosiphum rosae* and other aphid spp.)

PROTECTION

They are easily dislodged with pyrethrum or garlic sprays or soapy water or can be rubbed off by hand. Predatory ladybirds feed on rose aphids. So do some small birds. Try growing chives, onions, parsley, garlic, marigolds, cotton lavender (santolina), strawberries, lemon balm, lavender, nasturtiums, thyme or hyssop as companion plants to repel aphids. 'Complete' rose sprays also contain insecticides to kill aphids or Malathion or any general purpose insecticide can be used.

SYMPTOMS	CAUSE	PROTECTION
Black or brown weevils about 10 mm (½ in) long infest the flowers making holes in the petals.	Rose weevils (*Asynonychus cervinus*)	Difficult to control because they work from inside the bud. Destroy nearly finished flowers as these may harbour the weevils. Spray with any recommended insecticide.
Small dark-brown insects about 1 mm long and with fringed wing tips. They suck sap from flowers and foliage preferring flowers just about to open. The damaged petals have a crumpled look, or they may be shrivelled or transparent or fused in bud form.	Thrips (*Thrips* spp.)	Spray with recommended insecticides such as Rogor or Malathion. Misting the foliage in hot weather helps to control thrips. Try organic sprays of soap, onion or derris, or spray with a powerful jet of water to dislodge them. Companion plants are marigolds, tobacco, nasturtiums and pyrethrum daisies.
The centre of the bud is partly eaten and there is a small entry hole on a side of the bud.	Leaf roller or tortrix moth caterpillar. A small, very fast-moving insect which hides itself in the end of a rolled webbed leaf.	Spray with a recommended insecticide such as Carbaryl very late in the afternoon so as not to affect bees, or remove and dispose of affected foliage.
Stems covered with flaky scales.	Rose scale	Spray after pruning with lime sulphur or if foliage is present paint it on making sure to avoid the leaves, otherwise they will burn. The lime sulphur spray with white oil (one part to a hundred) also helps control summer fungal diseases and black spot, etc. Do not use oil sprays if temperature is in excess of 24°C (75°F) as they can burn foliage. Try rubbing off the scale by hand, or use a toothbrush dipped in soapy water to scrub scale loose. Nicotine and quassia sprays may also be used.
Succulent new growth is eaten.	Some large birds and small animals including possums seem to regard roses as a delicacy.	Spray foliage with deterrent sprays. Results can be less than satisfactory as the spray is not long lasting. A spray made from quassia chips may be effective.

SYMPTOMS	CAUSE	PROTECTION
Neat circle shapes cut from the foliage. Depredations are usually more curious than harmful.	Leaf cutting 'bees' (really wasps). Grasshoppers have a similar effect.	Find and remove bee nests or use a butterfly net! Identify the type of grasshopper and select an appropriate spray. Horehound may be effective in repelling grasshoppers.
Leaves look dull as though suffering from lack of moisture, the undersides are covered with minute webs, tiny mites and their even smaller eggs.	Two-spotted (red spider) mites.	Use ovacides (which are effective against the eggs) or adulticides (which are effective at all active stages). Use predatory mites (mites will not reproduce in temperatures below 20°C (68°F) or above 35°C (95°F) or spray or dust with sulphur or use the residual spray Kelthane or Maverick (these are also hazardous to the predatory mites). Most (not all) fungicides are safe for use with predators. An organic spray of derris or milk used regularly on the underside of leaves can help control this mite. Ladybirds and lacewing larvae are other natural predators.
Chewed foliage or petals producing a tattered effect.	Caterpillars, earwigs or grasshoppers.	Pick off caterpillars but try to leave some as later they become butterflies. Usually caterpillars are not too destructive. If necessary use Dipel.

Rose spraying can be simplified by using 'complete' sprays which contain ingredients to control all the foregoing pests and diseases (except birds and possums). Or the specific sprays given can be added to most insecticides (check for compatibility first) to combine pest and disease control in the one spray.

    Regulations regarding chemicals may vary between states and countries and alter from time to time. This advice is given in good faith. All chemicals must be applied strictly in accordance with the manufacturer's recommendations.

APPENDIX 2

MORE ROSES
NEW AND OLD

In this section I have listed some other outstanding roses, grouped according to type. The name of the rose is followed by the classification where relevant, the date of origination or introduction, a brief description and any awards it may have won.

CLASS ABBREVIATIONS

CLG . . . . Climbing
R . . . . Rambler
W . . . . Weeping Standard

AWARDS

Bagatelle, Paris, Gold Medal
Geneva Gold Medal
National Rose Society (now Royal National Rose Society) of Great Britain Gold Medal
Portland, Oregon, Gold Medal
Rome Gold Medal
Madrid Gold Medal
Hague Gold Medal and Golden Rose
From the American Rose Society:
John Cook Medal
Gertrude M. Hubbard Gold Medal
Dr W. Van Fleet Medal
David Fuerstenberg Prize
National Gold Medal Certificate
From the American Rose Foundation:
James Alexander Gamble Rose Fragrance Medal
All America Rose Selections Winner
American Rose Society Award of Excellence for Miniature Roses

AARS . . . . All America Rose Selections
ARS . . . . American Rose Society
NRS (RNRS) . . . . . National Rose Society of Great Britain, now Royal National Rose Society

RAFT . . . . Rose and Fruit Tree Growers of New South Wales Rose of the Year Selection

Hybrid Teas

RED

Baronne Edmond de Rothschild '68 & CLG '74. Large, ruby red with silvery reverse blooms; very fragrant.

Bing Crosby '75. Large blooms in deep persimmon red. AARS '81.

Cara Mia '69. Deep blood-red buds and rich-red blooms; sweet briar fragrance.

Champs-Elysees '57 & CLG '69. Large cupped, rich crimson red; slightly fragrant. Madrid Gold Medal '57.

Daily Mail Scented Rose '27 & CLG '30. Very fragrant, crimson blooms shaded maroon and vermilion; reverse dark crimson. Awarded Daily Mail Cup '27.

Ena Harkness '46 & CLG '54. Large, high-centred, crimson scarlet. NRS Gold Medal '54; Portland Gold Medal '55.

Espéranza HT '66. Deep Chinese-lacquer-red blooms in large clusters. Hague Gold Medal '68.

Etoile de Hollande '19. Large cupped, bright red, very fragrant.

John S. Armstrong '61. Large, high-centred to cupped, dark-red fragrant blooms.

John Waterer '70. Velvety, scarlet-crimson, spiralled blooms in classic form.

Josephine Bruce '40. Rich, deep-crimson, fragrant blooms; profuse bloomer.

Pharaoh '67. Intense blood red with scarlet reverse; fragrant and high-centred. Geneva Gold Medal '67; Madrid Gold Medal '67; Hague Gold Medal '67.

Rubaiyat '46. Large, high-centred, very fragrant, rose red with a lighter reverse. Portland Gold Medal '45; AARS '47.

Samourai '66. Large-cupped, crimson-scarlet, slightly fragrant blooms. Madrid Gold Medal '66; AARS '68.

Shot Silk '24. High-centred, fragrant, cherry cerise with golden yellow at base. NRS Gold Medal '23.

Super Star '60 & CLG '65. Well-formed vermilion blooms unshaded and non-fading, almost iridescent; fruity fragrance. Prone to mildew in humid climates. Bagatelle Gold Medal '60; NRS Gold Medal '60; Geneva Gold Medal '60; Portland Gold Medal '60; Golden Rose of the Hague '63; AARS '63; ARS '67.

Tassin '42. Very fragrant, very large, darker scarlet edge and with cardinal-red centre.

Texas Centennial '35 & CLG '36. Vermilion red with some gold, centre lighter; fruity fragrance; very long stems.

Uncle Walter '63. Large high-centred crimson scarlet; free bloomer.

Wendy Cussons '63 & CLG '67. Rose-red, very fragrant, high-centred blooms. NRS Gold Medal '59; Golden Rose of the Hague '64; Portland Gold Medal '64.

PINK

Admiral Rodney '73. Large, conical, very fragrant, pale rose-pink blooms with deeper pink reverse.

Arianna '68. Carmine rose, suffused Chinese coral; high-centred blooms; large and slightly fragrant. Bagatelle Gold Medal '65; Rome Gold Medal '65; Hague Gold Medal '65.

Bewitched '67. Large, fragrant pure-pink flowers; urn-shaped buds, high-centred blooms. AARS '67; Portland Gold Medal '67.

Blessings '67. Large, fragrant, translucent coral-pink blooms; very free blooming.

Bobby Charlton '74. A very large bloom (15 cm (6 in)) with thirty five to forty petals and a spicy fragrance. It is a deep pink with a silvery pink reverse to the petals.

Camelot '64. Luminous, coral-pink, cupped bloom clusters; spicy fragrance. AARS '65.

Charlotte Armstrong '40 & CLG '42. Long, pointed blood-red buds open to cerise-pink fragrant blooms. AARS '41; ARS John Cook Medal '41; ARS David Fuerstenberg Prize '41; Portland Gold Medal '41; ARS Gertrude M. Hubbard Medal '45; NRS Gold Medal '50.

China Doll '46 & CLG '77. Large clusters of rose-pink yellow-based blooms; cupped and slightly fragrant.

Colour Magic '78. Aromatic pink rose with old-world charm. The long spiral buds form large open blooms 12.5 cm (5 in) across with twenty–thirty broad petals.

Columbus Queen '62. Large, high-centred to cupped light pink with darker reverse. Geneva Gold Medal '61.

Comtesse Vandal '32 & CLG '36. Large, high-centred, fragrant, salmon pink with coppery pink reverse. Bagatelle Gold Medal '31.

Coronado '61. Long buds on long stems, opening to cerise pink with yellow reverse; high-centred blooms and fragrant.

Dainty Bess '25 & CLG '35. Fragrant, soft rose pink, very distinct darker stamens. NRS Gold Medal '25.

Dame Edith Helen '26 & CLG '30. Very large cupped, fragrant, glowing pink. NRS Gold Medal '26.

Duet '60. Large, light pink with dark pink reverse. AARS '61.

Fortuna '27. SD. Fruity fragrance, rose pink becoming lighter; gold anthers; dwarf bush. NRS Gold Medal '27.

Ginger Rogers '69. Loosely formed, fragrant, salmon-pink blooms.

Grace de Monaco '56. Fragrant, light-rose pink, very large, well-formed blooms.

Harmonie '54. Light-red buds opening pink; bicolour; fragrant blooms on long, almost thornless, stems.

Helen Traubel '51. Large, high-centred becoming flat, broad-petalled blooms in soft pink to apricot; fragrant. Rome Gold Medal '51; AARS '52.

Herzog von Windsor (syn Duke of Windsor) '69. Very fragrant, bright salmon pink; large double well-formed blooms.

Isabel de Ortiz '62. Long-stemmed, strawberry-pink blooms with a silvery vanilla reverse. Madrid Gold Medal '61; NRS Gold Medal '62.

Memoriam '61. High-centred, fragrant pastel pink to nearly white. Portland Gold Medal '60.

Michele Meilland '45. Delicate soft pink and lilac with deeper centre tones.

Mme Butterfly '18 & CLG '26. Fragrant, light pink tinted gold, lighter centre; very well formed.

Perfume Delight '73. Classic, high-centred bud and cupped bloom of brilliant deep pink; very fragrant. AARS '74.

Portrait '71. Long, pointed buds; blooms full, fragrant, creamy pink, outer petals flushed deep pink. AARS '72.

Shannon '65. Very large, deep glowing-pink blooms; holds well.

Silver Jubilee '78. A gentle rose, the delicate shades of pink apricot, peach and cream deepen during warmer weather. This scented rose is elegant with a classic high-centred form 12.5 cm (5 in) across and carrying thirty three petals.

Swarthmore '63. Large blooms 10 cm (4 in) across, have forty five to fifty petals, and are high centred, slightly fragrant and rose red or deep pink to cherry red. There is a distinctive, smoky edge to the unfurling petals.

Sylvia '78. A beautiful luminous pink rose with a hint of yellow at the petal base. Forty petals are arranged around a classic high centre. The sweetly fragrant blooms are long lasting and the stems tall and straight.

The Doctor '36 & CLG '50. Very fragrant, satin-pink, well-formed, very large blooms; dwarf bushy shrub. NRS Gold Medal '38.

Yankee Doodle '65. Bud urn shaped; large blooms in tints of peachy pink and apricot. AARS '76.

BLUE

Blue Nile Large, high-centred, intensely fragrant, rich lavender-mauve blooms. Has won European Gold Medals.

Charles de Gaulle '74. Large, full, globular then cupped, deep lilac-blue blooms; very fragrant.

Lady X '66 & CLG '76. Long, pointed buds; soft lilac-mauve, high-pointed blooms with long, almost thornless stems; exhibition rose.

Lavender Mist '62. Lavender with deeper edge to petals; large, scented blooms.

Lilac Time '56. High-centred, fragrant, lilac; free blooming.

Vol de Nuit (Night Flight) '78. High-centred blooms of clear deep mauve with reflexed petals; very fragrant. Rome Gold Medal '79.

WHITE

Honor '80. Loose, slightly fragrant, crystal-white blooms with occasional pale-pink blush; long-stemmed elegant buds. AARS '80.

Matterhorn '65. Large, high-centred white; bears abundant blooms. AARS '66.

Mount Shasta '63. Long, pointed buds; fragrant, cupped, white blooms.

Sweet Afton '64. Off-white with pale blush pink on reverse; high-centred and fragrant; abundant blooms.

Virgo '47 & CLG '57. Bud often blush pink; large, high-centred, slightly fragrant, exquisitely formed pure-white blooms, sometimes blush pink. NRS Gold Medal '49.

White Lightnin' '80. Sparkling white, very fragrant, shapely buds and blooms.

Youki San '65. Large, very fragrant white blooms.

YELLOW

Adolf Horstmann '71. The large, handsome blooms are 12.5 cm (5 in) across, high-centred, lightly fragrant and a rich yellow orange, tinted deeply orange on opening.

Canary '29. High, spiralled centre, light canary and deepening yellow, lightly flushed pink; fragrant blooms.

Dr A. J. Verhage '63 & CLG '62. Buttercup-yellow, waved petals; large, very fragrant blooms.

Eclipse '35. Long, pointed buds; fragrant high-centred, open blooms of golden yellow. Portland Gold Medal '35; Rome Gold Medal '35; Bagatelle Gold Medal '36; ARS David Fuerstenberg Prize '38.

Golden Masterpiece '54 & CLG '57. Long, pointed buds; large high-centred blooms, deep yellow and fragrant.

Grand'mère Jenny '50 & CLG '58. High-centred, fragrant, apricot-yellow edged and suffused pink. NRS Gold Medal '50; Rome Gold Medal '55.

Helmut Schmidt '82. Pure clear-yellow, beautifully formed blooms. Very free-flowering. RAFT Rose of the Year '83.

King's Ransom '61. Long tapering buds; clear golden-yellow blooms; fragrant, profuse. AARS '62.

Kordes' Golden Times '70. Non-fading luminous golden yellow, perfumed blooms.

Kordes' Perfecta '57. Very fragrant, high-centred, cream tipped, and flushed crimson and suffused yellow on long stems. NRS Gold Medal '57; Portland Gold Medal '58.

Northern Lights '69. Primrose yellow, sometimes flushed pink; pointed centres; very fragrant.

Oldtimer '69. Lovely old-gold colour and sweet fragrance.

Peer Gynt '68. Large, full, crisp blooms of light gold; edges pick up reddish tints.

Souv de Mme Boullet '21 & CLG '30. Deep-yellow, long, pointed, large, full and beautifully formed blooms.

Summer Sunshine '62. Large, high-centred to cupped, pure golden-yellow blooms; floriferous and slightly fragrant.

Sunblest '70. Deep golden-chrome-yellow blooms on good stems; fragrant large blooms.

Whisky Mac '67. Large well formed, very fragrant, bronze yellow.

ORANGE/APRICOT

Ambassador '79. Apricot buds opening to large, full to cupped, light orange shading golden yellow.

Apricot Delight '73. Long buds; apricot petals flushed rich deep apricot; fragrant blooms.

Aztec '57. Scarlet-orange, large, high-centred flowers; fragrant with abundant blooms.

Bettina '53 & CLG '58. Deep orange-apricot, well-formed fragrant blooms.

Brandenburg '65. Large, high-centred, deep orange salmon, darker reverse.

Dickson's Wonder '80. Rich bright salmon orange; very fragrant.

Doris Tysterman '75. Large full tangerine colour; edged orange with a slight fragrance.

Folklore '77. Large, high-centred, very fragrant orange and orange blends. RAFT Rose of the Year '78.

Fred Edmunds '43. Large, cupped, spicily fragrant, brilliant ochre-orange blooms. Portland Gold Medal '42; AARS '44.

Hot Pewter '78. Bright clear orange, very large blooms.

Lady Rose '79. Large, high-centred, fragrant, shining salmon orange with a yellow base.

Mission Bells '49. Large, high-centred, rich salmon orange; slight fragrance.

Mrs Sam McGredy '29 & CLG '37. High-centred, fragrant scarlet-copper-orange blooms, reverse flushed red; long stems. NRS Gold Medal '29.

President Herbert Hoover '30. Large, open spicily fragrant, orange rose and gold with lighter gold reverse. ARS Gertrude M. Hubbard Gold Medal '34; ARS John Cook Medal '35.

Soaring Wings '78. Large, high-centred, fragrant amber orange, flushed flame with a yellow base.

Wiener Charme (Vienna Charm) '63 & CLG '72. Large, high-centred, coppery-orange fragrant blooms.

Yankee Doodle '65. Peach pink and sherbert orange tinted fire-cracker red; large, slightly fragrant blooms. AARS '76.

MULTI-COLOUR

Alpine Sunset '73. Very full blooms in autumn shades of apricot, peach, yellow and cream and very fragrant.

American Heritage '65. Large, high-centred blooms in blendings of ivory, yellow. AARS '66.

Ambossfunken (syn Anvil Sparks) '61. Fragrant blooms of tangerine-striped yellow; large, well formed, fragrant.

Champion '76. Creamy yellow flushed red and pink blooms are very large, very full and fragrant.

Cherry Vanilla '73. Cupped blooms are fragrant and pink with creamy yellow centres.

El Dorado '72. Large, open, high-centred, very fragrant blooms in mingling shades of gold and pink, edged reddish.

Fred Gibson '66. Light honey apricot with pastel-pink flush; full, slightly fragrant; exhibition blooms.

Granada '63. An unusual and very gay, many-flowered, multi-coloured rose with richly fragrant blooms. The urn-shaped buds form large high-centred flowers 10 to 12.5 cm (4–5 in) across with eighteen to twenty five petals. These open to a blend of rose, nasturtium red and lemon yellow.

Headline '78. This vibrant rose glows with colour. The background is yellow, highlighted with a suffusion of carmine producing a multi-coloured effect. The shapely, large blooms are high-centred with reflexed petals.

Love '80. Elegantly quilled, crimson and white blooms atop long straight stems.

Mascotte '51. Exhibition blooms of soft yellow, heavily shaded and flushed cerise red.

Modern Times '56. Fragrant, red-striped pink blooms; sometimes reverts to red.

Mr Chips '70. Deep-gold, veined and margined deep-cerise, very large, high-pointed blooms.

Neue Revue '62. Striking, high-centred blooms of yellow white; picotee-red edge; large and very fragrant.

Typhoo Tea '74. Silver buds open to flowers of large classic form and lemon fragrance; it is a red and silver bicolour.

Floribundas

RED

Europeana '63 & CLG '68. Slightly fragrant, dark-crimson, rosette-shaped blooms. Hague Gold Medal '62.

Eye Paint '75. Single, open, bright scarlet with a showy white eye and fluffy golden stamens; slightly fragrant, abundant blooms.

Matangi '74. Large open blooms, slightly fragrant, red, base yellow shades.

Old Master '74. Semi-double, slightly fragrant, open blooms; red purple with white reverse.

Priscilla Burton '78. Semi-double, fragrant, deep carmine; very free bloomer.

PINK

Cherish '80. Sculptured shrimp-pink buds and blooms; slightly fragrant and high-centred. AARS '80.

Dearest '60. Well-formed buds opening to soft pink with salmon shading; blooms in clusters. NRS Gold Medal '61.

Elizabeth of Glamis '64. Large salmon-pink, flat blooms in clusters; very fragrant. NRS Gold Medal '63.

Fashion '49 & CLG '51. Open blooms of coral peach; fragrant large clusters. NRS Gold Medal '48; Bagatelle Gold Medal '49; Portland Gold Medal '49; AARS '50; ARS David Fuerstenberg Prize '50; ARS Gold Medal '54.

Honeyflow '57. Very large sprays of white-edged, apple-blossom-pink, single blooms; tall bush.

Pink Chiffon '56. Classic shade of La France pink (petticoat pink); large-cupped to flat blooms and very fragrant.

Pink Wonder (Kalinka) '70 & CLG '76. Porcelain pink with deeper shadings and delicately perfumed; large and fragrant.

BLUE

Angel Face '68. Pointed buds; deep-clear-lilac, ruffled blooms with showy golden stamens. AARS '69; ARS John Cook Medal '71.

Lavender Girl '58. Spicy fragrance, rosy purple with magenta reverse changing to lavender; large cupped blooms.

Lavender Pinocchio '48. Bud olive brown opening to fragrant, lavender pink; large clusters.

Lilac Charm '62. Pointed buds, large, flat, fragrant pastel-mauve clusters. NRS Gold Medal '61.

Shocking Blue '84. Large, long, pointed well-formed flowers of magenta mauve; very fragrant, abundant blooms.

BUFF AND BONE

Cafe '56. A most unusual coffee-with-cream colour on a dwarf bush; fragrant clusters.

Violet Carson '64. Peach and biscuit with silvery reverse; very fragrant large clusters.

YELLOW

Allgold '48 & CLG '61. Buttercup-yellow, semi-double, slightly fragrant blooms. NRS Gold Medal '65.

Bellona '76. Fragrant, well-formed, golden-yellow blooms on long stems.

Goldtopas '63. Rich amber-gold, cupped blooms, attractively ruffled in clusters.

Kerry Gold '67. Deep canary yellow, outer petals veined red; profuse blooms and fragrant.

ORANGE/APRICOT

Apricot Gem '77. Hybrid tea-type buds and large trusses of rich orange-apricot blooms.

Bagheera '76. Orange-red, well-formed, slightly fragrant blooms on long stems.

Bahia '74. Golden-orange, large-cupped blooms; spicy fragrance.

Gingersnap '78. Distinctively orange, bright cup-shaped, ruffled, slightly fragrant blooms.

Golden Slippers '61. Petite orange blooms, yellow-shaded centres. Portland Gold Medal '60; AARS '62.

Orangeade '59 & CLG '64. Semi-double pure-orange blooms, very brilliant and slightly fragrant. NRS Gold Medal '59.

Orange Silk '68. Shallow, cupped, slightly fragrant, vivid orange-vermilion semi-double blooms.

Trumpeter '77. Large, open, orange-red, slightly fragrant blooms.

MULTI-COLOUR

Brownie '59. Buds are tan shades edged pinkish; blooms are large, cupped and fragrant in the unusual combination of lavender, tan and brown.

Charleston '63. Chrome-yellow buds open to semi-double, slightly fragrant blooms of yellow flushed crimson, becoming all crimson with age.

Circus '56 & CLG '61. A colour spectacle of red, yellow, orange and pink blooms; spicily fragrant, large high-centred to open flowers in large clusters. Geneva Gold Medal '55; NRS Gold Medal '55; AARS '56.

Imp '70. Small, slightly fragrant, chartreuse-margined red; reverse silvery pink.

Masquerade '49 & CLG '58. Semi-double open, slightly fragrant blooms in bright yellow, turning salmon pink then shades of red. NRS Gold Medal '52.

Picasso '71. Light-red, semi-double blooms appear hand-painted with centre reverse and margins white and sometimes striped.

Woburn Abbey '62. A vivid rose with large clusters of red, tinted golden-orange, blooms 8.75 cm (3½ in) across. These are fragrant, cupped and borne in colourful masses. Both colour and bloom quantity make it a striking rose. It is prone to mildew in humid climates.

Miniature Bush Roses

RED

Honest Abe '78. Deep velvety red with high, pointed buds and full, slightly tea-fragrant blooms.

Minuetto '71. Mandarin red to vermilion with contrasting yellow base and stamens.

My Valentine '75. Full high-centred, crimson red; very free flowering.

Wee Lass '74. Clusters of semi-double, blood-red small flowers.

Zwergkonig (Dwarfking) '57. Small, cupped then flat, slightly fragrant, carmine-red blooms carried singly and in clusters.

PINK

Baby Pinocchio '67. Small fragrant blooms in lovely shades of salmon pink.

Carol-Jean '77. Clear pink, small full blooms in profusion; slightly fragrant.

Dresden Doll '75. Semi-double, cupped blooms in lovely soft shades of pink to cream; fragrant.

Fashion Flame '77. Light salmon-pink, pointed buds open to full, high-centred, deep-salmon blooms.

Gypsy Jewel '75. Small, high-centred full blooms of deep rose pink.

June Time '63. Masses of tight little light-pink blooms with a deeper reverse.

Pinwheel '77. Pink and gold blend; small, open, slightly fragrant blooms; pointed buds.

BLUE

Angel Darling '76. Slightly fragrant, single lavender flowers, wavy petals; continuous blooming.

Lavender Jewel '78. Deep lavender, beautifully formed, slightly fragrant blooms.

Lavender Lace '68 & CLG '71. High-centred, fragrant lavender blooms.

WHITE

Easter Morning '60. Small ivory-white clusters; tightly reflexing blooms.

Swany '78. Small flat-cupped, pure-white blooms on bushy plant; also suitable for ground cover and hanging baskets.

White Angel '71. Long buds of soft pink opening white; blooms small, reflexed and fragrant.

YELLOW

Colibri '58. Star-like blooms of sunset yellow; small and slightly fragrant.

Cream Gold '78. Well-formed buds open to full, high-centred, cream and gold, fragrant blooms.

Gold Coin '67. Pure buttercup-yellow, small, fragrant blooms.

Jackie '55 & CLG '57. High-centred, fragrant straw-yellow fading to white blooms.

Rise 'N Shine '77. Long, pointed buds; blooms small, high-centred, fragrant, clear deep yellow.

ORANGE

Baby Darling '64 & CLG '72. Pointed buds; flowers small, orange to orange pink.

Fashion Flame '77. Well-formed, full, slightly fragrant blooms of soft coral orange.

MULTI-COLOUR

Magic Carousel '72. Deep-pink buds opening white to cream, margined deep pink and with white reverse; full, high-centred, slightly fragrant blooms.

Over-The-Rainbow '72. A cheerful high-centred bi-colour which repeat flowers quickly and covers itself in masses of blooms. Fiery red petals are yellow on their reverse side and at the base. It is slightly fragrant.

Stars 'N Stripes '80. Petals irregularly striped red or pink on white; free flowering.

Strawberry Swirl '78. Small high-centred blooms of strawberry red and cream.

Top Gear A brilliant '83 introduction from Armstrong's of California, USA. Dark red with yellow base. One of the best miniatures to date.

Toy Clown '66. Creamy white with a red border, semi-double, open blooms.

Climbing, Rambler and Weeping Standard Roses

Sea Foam '64. WS. The many-petalled, slightly fragrant flowers are white to cream and soft pink and carried in generous clusters through spring, summer and autumn.

Aviateur Bleriot '10. R, WS. Aviateur Bleriot is a charming reminder of Edwardian days, but its colour, magnolia fragrance and full form have kept it a place in rose catalogues through subsequent decades. It is a cluster rose, pale yellow on a lemon base when first open, becoming light as the blooms age.

Excelsa '09. R. Massive clusters of dainty, cupped Tyrian-rose to light-crimson flowers weigh the pendulous canes down in a spring display.

Bloomfield Courage R, WS. The rich colouring is startling for the contrast between dark velvety red petals and their white centre surrounding a mass of deep-golden stamens.

Veilchenblau '09. R, WS. A vigorous, flower-laden, cluster rose bearing distinctive 3.5 cm (1¼ in) wide, white-centred, violet blooms. These are fragrant and borne recurrently in huge clusters on short stems.

Joseph's Coat CLG '64. Yellow and red, semi-double fragrant blooms in clusters.

Old Garden Roses

Many old garden roses are species roses — the original types of rose grown before hybridists increased their number and altered their characteristics. There are numerous others beside those listed. Interest in these roses is increasing.

THE GALLICAS

Rosa gallica — The 'French', 'Provins' or 'Red Rose'. Gallicas are small metre- (yard-) high shrubs which are very prickly and bristly and form a thicket of canes with many subterranean suckers. They stand severe frosts and are resistant to black spot. They bloom lavishly carrying many spring blooms on short stems. They have ruffled and quartered petals and some have a button-eye formation in the centre of the bloom. Where known the dates of introduction to European gardens are given. Height and width are shown, height first.

Assemblage des Beautés Prior to 1790. Button-eyed, ruffled, very full, crimson-scarlet blooms. 120 x 100 cm (4 x 3 ft).

Belle de Crécy Age unknown. At first cerise pink, this ages to mauve pink and has a button eye and strong scent. 120 x 100 cm (4 x 3 ft).

Camaieux 1830. Purple bloom, splashed and striped with blush white, gradually altering to mauve grey and white, and frequently with green centre. 100 x 60 cm (3 x 2 ft).

Cardinal de Richelieu Known since 1840. A gallica China hybrid known since 1840 and noted for its deep-purple, usually green-eyed, very double blooms. It has few thorns. 160 x 100 cm (5 x 3 ft).

Charles de Mills Age uncertain. The rounded, flat flowers have crinkled petals of crimson wine and purple. 150 x 120 cm (5 x 4 ft).

Duchesse de Montebello Age unknown. Clear, soft pink-cupped blooms against greyish foliage and loose growth. 150 x 120 cm (5 x 4 ft).

Gloire de France Known since 1819. Double purple, with mauve and lilac-white flowers. 100 x 100 cm (3 x 3 ft).

Jenny Duval Known since 1821. Blooms vary from dark lilac pink to purple Parma violet and grey violet, sometimes flushed with cerise. 120 x 100 cm (5 x 4 ft).

Officinalis (The Apothecary's Rose; Red Rose of Lancaster). Known since thirteenth century. Probably the oldest gallica still in cultivation. It is semi-double with wonderfully fragrant, crimson flowers, showing yellow anthers. It is a variegated sport, and has large, dark-red fruits.

Président de Seze Prior to 1836. Full, double, crimson blooms.

Sissinghurst Castle An ancient gallica rediscovered during the making of Sissinghurst Castle gardens, this is dark red and has a thicketing growth habit.

Tuscany Age unknown. Though this is one of the oldest gallicas, its deep, velvety, maroon blooms show yellow stamens. 120 x 100 cm (4 x 3 ft).

Versicolor (*Rosa Mundi*; *R. gallica* Variegata). Prior to sixteenth century. It is a variegated sport of, and similar to *R. gallica* Officinalis, except that the flowers are striped crimson with blush-pink background, though some revert to the non-variegated parent. It blooms very freely and needs support to carry the weight of the blooms. 200 x 120 cm (6½ x 4 ft).

DAMASK ROSES

R. x damascena (Bifera; the Autumn Damask Rose). Flowers in summer and repeat flowers in autumn. Damask roses are open, twiggy, somewhat prickly and straggly bushes, with long arching canes.

Celsiana Known since 1732. Produces small clusters of large, loose blooms, showing golden stamens at their cente. They are pink at first, changing to white.

Ispahan Known since 1832. This has scented, pink, tightly reflexed button-eyed blooms in clusters, flowering for a long period during mid summer. 150 x 120 cm (5 x 4 ft).

Mme Hardy 1832. Thought to be a damask-alba cross, the pure white, many-petalled, flat blooms, have a small green eye. 180 x 150 cm (6 x 5 ft).

Quatre Saisons (Four Seasons, Autumn Damask); *R. x damascena semperflorens*; *R. x damascena* Bifera. Known since fifth century BC and considered to be a hybrid between *R. gallica* and *R. moschata*. This is very sweetly scented, clear pink, and double with quartered summer and autumn blooms, showing an eye. 120 x 100 cm (4 x 3 ft).

Trigintipetala Also known as Kazanlik.
Introduced 1889. The highly scented blooms of this
pink rose are grown in Bulgaria for rose attar, used
in perfume making.

York and Lancaster Rose R. x *damascena*
Versicolor. Known before 1551. The medium to large
flowers are half blush white, or half pink, and some
are either white or pink, with an occasionally pink or
white petal. It is claimed to symbolise the end of the
Wars of the Roses.

THE ALBAS

These are mainly double roses, which bloom in late
spring or early summer, and are scented. The bushes
are tall and upright with grey-green leaves and hooked
prickles.

R. x alba Maxima Age unknown. The Jacobite,
Cheshire or Great Double White Rose, opens flat and
produces oval hips. Height 200 cm (6½ ft).

R. x alba Semi-plena (Alba, White Rose of
York). Age unknown. The rose has globular red hips
and white to blush, semi-double blooms. 180 x
150 cm (6 x 5 ft).

Celeste or Celestial Late eighteenth century. A
sweetly scented, very delicate-pink roses. 160 x 120 cm
(5¼ x 4 ft).

Felicité Parmentier 1834. Blush white with
reflexed petals. 130 x 100 cm (4¼ x 3 ft).

Königin von Dänemark 1826. At first cupped,
the large clusters of small, pale salmon-pink, double
blooms develop into reflexed, quartered flowers of
paler pink as they open. 150 x 120 cm (5 x 4 ft).

Maiden's Blush Before fifteenth century. Loose,
blush-pink flowers, like those of Great Maiden's
Blush. 180 x 150 cm (6 x 5 ft).

Mme Legras de St Germain Prior to 1848.
Camellia-like blooms, flushed yellow at their centres,
open flat and change to white. The shrub is nearly
thornless. 180 x 180 cm (6 x 6 ft).

Mme Plantier 1835. May be grown as a pillar
rose or as a large, spreading bush. It has double,
creamy flowers with green eyes. 150 x 180 cm (5 x
6 ft).

PROVENCE (CENTIFOLIAS)

Centifolias or Cabbage Roses appeared in Dutch
paintings towards the end of the sixteenth century.

Centifolias are open growers, with pendulous foliage and pendant, double, many-petalled spring
flowers.

Bullata Before 1815. Large, wrinkled (bullate)
leaves and large, globular, pink flowers. 120 x 120 cm
(4 x 4 ft).

R. x centifolia Sixteenth century. Sometimes
called the rose of the painters. Pink, with a strong
scent, full, globular many-petalled flowers. 150 x
120 cm (5 x 4 ft).

Chapeau de Napoléon R. x *centifolia cristata*.
1826. Also called the Crested Hat. A pink, many-
petalled rose which is not truly a moss despite the
mossy sepals. 150 x 120 cm (5 x 4 ft).

De Meaux Before 1800. Pink, small, pom-pom
flowers, are a deeper pink towards the centre. 120 x
100 cm (4 x 3 ft).

Fantin-Latour Age uncertain. The clusters of
pale pink, double flowers, open flat. A very free-
flowering rose, named after the French painter.

MOSS ROSES

These grow 1 to 1.5 metres (3 to 5 feet) high, flower
in spring, with very double, highly scented blooms,
like the centifolias, except that the calyx and flower
stems are covered in moss-like hairs. They prefer cool
winter climates.

Common Moss R. x *centifolia muscosa*. 1727.
The original moss has pink, globular blooms, with
button eyes. 120 x 120 cm (4 x 4 ft).

Comtesse de Murinais (White Moss). 1843.
The quartered flowers are blush pink and open flat,
then fade to white, the moss is brownish. 180 x
120 cm (6 x 4 ft).

General Kléber 1856. Fully double, pink flowers,
open flat to reveal a button eye, it has green moss.
150 x 120 cm (5 x 4 ft).

Mousseux du Japon Age uncertain. Magenta
rose-pink flowers, become greyish-lilac with age. The
purplish stems and leaves are mossed. 60 x 60 cm
(2 x 2 ft).

Nuits de Young (Old Black) 1851. Velvety
maroon flowers show yellow stamens, this is the
darkest moss rose. 150 x 100 cm (5 x 3 ft).

Shailer's White Moss (R. *centifolia muscosa
alba*). 1788. Cupped, white blooms are blush tinted
while young. 120 x 100 cm (4 x 3 ft).

William Lobb (Duchesse d'Istrie; Old Velvet Moss). 1855. Double, crimson-purple blooms are mauve lavender on the reverse as the flower ages. It has green moss. May be used as a pillar rose or small climber. 180 x 180 cm (6 x 6 ft).

THE RUGOSAS
Rugosas are old roses, native to Japan and parts of China, and were more or less neglected until the late nineteenth and early twentieth centuries when their hardiness in cold winters was one reason hybridisers became interested in them. Today the modern hybrids, rather than the species, are grown in gardens. Where known, the hybridiser's name and date of introduction are shown after the rose name and origin.

R. rugosa Alba Good-looking foliage is a background for the huge, scented, single white flowers and large, orange-red hips. 180 x 180 cm (6 x 6 ft).

Belle Poitevine Bruant, 1894. Bright-pink, scented, semi-double, flat flowers develop from long pointed buds. 150 x 150 cm (5 x 5 ft).

Blanc Double de Coubert Cochet-Cochet, 1892. The bush covers itself in semi-double, pure-white blooms, but has very few hips. 180 x 150 cm (6 x 5 ft).

Frau Dagmar Hastrup 1914. An *R. rugosa* seedling which is fragrant, single, pale pink and shows cream stamens. The crimson hips are large. 150 x 150 cm (5 x 5 ft).

Roseraie de l'Hay Cochet-Cochet, 1901. Produces clusters of wine-red, sweetly scented blooms very freely. There are no hips. 180 x 150 cm (6 x 5 ft).

Scabrosa Introduced by Harkness, prior to 1939. Very large, magenta-pink flowers are followed by the largest hips of any of the rugosas. 120 x 150 cm (4 x 5 ft).

Conrad Ferdinand Meyer F. Müller, 1899. A Gloire de Dijon hybrid, this has scented, silvery-pink blooms and outstanding thorns.

Max Graf *R. rugosa* x *R. wichuraiana*. Bowdich, 1919. Ground-covering, bright-pink, apple-scented rose which flowers throughout spring and occasionally in autumn.

Schneezwerg (Snow Dwarf). P. Lambert, 1912. The clusters of double, white flowers have conspicuous centres of golden stamens and small foliage. The hips are orange red. 180 x 150 cm (6 x 5 ft).

F. J. Grootendorst *R. rugosa rubra* x Mme Norbert Lavavasseur. Grootendorst, 1918. Dainty, small, crimson, scentless flowers have pink-edged petals.

Pink Grootendorst Grootendorst, 1923. Similar to the above, except that the colour is clear pink.

BOURBONS
China roses came to Europe via the Ile de Bourbon, now called the Island of Reunion, which was a stopping point for French ships sailing between the Far East and France. It was a chance hybrid between a China rose and *R.* x *damascena* that produced bourbon roses. Four hundred and twenty eight varieties of bourbons were raised by crossing them with gallica and damask hybrids. Bourbons had magnificent, many-petalled, richly fragrant blooms and a repeat-flowering habit, blooming during spring and autumn with some flowering in-between. The repeat flowering came from the China rose influence.

Boule de Neige Blanche Lafitte x Sappho. Lacharme, 1867. Beautifully formed, highly scented, snow-white flowers open from red-tinted buds. 150 x 120 cm (5 x 4 ft).

Commandant Beaurepaire (Panachée d'Angers). Moreau-Robert, 1874. Cupped, fragrant, mid summer blooms are splashed and striped with maroon, purple, mauve, scarlet and pink. 180 x 150 cm (6 x 5 ft).

Ferdinand Pichard Tanne, 1921. Cupped, scented, pink flowers fade to a lighter pink as they age and are striped with crimson. 180 x 150 cm (6 x 5 ft).

Honorine de Brabant Age unknown. Cupped and quartered, lilac-pink blooms are spotted and striped mauve and crimson. It may be a sport of Commandant Beaurepaire. 180 x 180 cm (6 x 6 ft).

La Reine Victoria J. Schwartz, 1872. Scented, cupped, pink flowers. 180 x 100 cm (6 x 3 ft).

Mme Ernest Calvat Vve Schwartz, 1888. Large, double, clear-pink blooms are darker on the reverse.

Mme Isaac Pereire Garçon, 1880. Similar to the above, with scented, cerise-pink, sumptuous blooms.

Mme Pierre Oger Oger, 1878. In warm conditions, the blooms may be pink overall. In cooler climates they are blushed pink at the edges. A sport of La Reine Victoria. 180 x 100 cm (6 x 3 ft).

Souvenir de la Malmaison (Queen of Beauty

and Fragrance). Beluze, 1843. Quartered, flat, scented, blush blooms are beautiful. A difficult rose to grow in warm climates. It has a climbing form. It is a cross between the bourbon Mme Desprez and an unknown tea rose. 120 x 120 cm (4 x 4 ft).

Variegata di Bologna Bonfiglioli, 1909. Globular, scented, white flowers are striped crimson purple. It needs a support. 250 x 150 cm (8 x 5 ft).

Zephirine Drouhin Bizot, 1868. Coppery young growth is a foil for the masses of scented, cerise-pink, loose, double blooms. It is a repeat-flowering climber. Height 460 cm (15 ft).

PORTLAND ROSES

The portland rose is assumed to be a chance cross between *R. x damascena* and *R. chinensis semperflorens*. One hundred and fifty varieties of roses were raised from the original cross. They were similar to bourbons but with shorter stems and the blooms were not held clear of the foliage. They were gallica-like, with more petals and smaller flowers. Few still exist, most disappearing in earlier breeding programmes.

Arthur de Sansal Cartier, 1855. Crimson-purple, double, quartered flowers open flat and the petals are lighter on the reverse. 120 x 100 cm (4 x 3 ft).

Comte de Chambord 1860. Double, pink flowers, become lilac towards the edges. 120 x 100 cm (4 x 3 ft).

The Portland Rose (Duchess of Portland) 1809. Semi-double, light-crimson flowers on an upright, suckering shrub. 60 x 60 cm (2 x 2 ft).

THE HYBRID PERPETUALS

These were summer-blooming roses that produced a second, rather smaller autumn flash of bloom. Those with longer flowering periods are still grown today. They were the result of crossing the China rose with the bourbon and portland roses. Blooms were large and globular, many of them larger than modern hybrid teas. Gradually they were merged with, and superseded by the hybrid teas, although at their height there were 2500 varieties. Long shoots in late summer could be pegged to the ground or tied to a wire frame to become ground covers or climbers.

Baron Girod de l'Ain A sport of Eugene Furst. Reverchon, 1897. Double, medium-sized, crimson-scarlet flowers have white-edged petals, capped at the centre, the outer ones reflexed. 150 x 120 cm (5 x 4 ft).

Baronne Prevost Desprez, 1842. Full, quartered, button-eyed flowers are rose pink, shaded a lighter pink.

Frau Karl Druschki (Snow Queen). Merveille de Lyon x Mme Caroline Testout. P. Lambert, 1901. Huge, pure-white, scentless blooms are formed from large, pink-tinted buds. 150 x 120 cm (5 x 4 ft).

General Jacqueminot (General Jack; Jack Rose). Roussel, 1853. Scarlet-crimson blooms are produced on long stems. It is the ancestor of most of today's red roses and may be a seedling of Glorie de Rosomanes. 120 x 100 cm (4 x 3 ft).

Mrs John Laing A seedling of Francois Michelon. Bennett, 1887. A fragrant, very long-stemmed rose, with large, soft-pink flowers.

Paul Neyron Victor Verdier x Anna de Diesbach. A. Levet, 1869. Peony form, rose-pink centres, outsized blooms, are produced on a bush with very few thorns. 150 x 100 cm (5 x 3 ft).

Reine des Violettes A seedling of Pius IX. Millet-Malet, 1860. Many-petalled, flat, cerise-purple blooms, change through violet and lilac to purple. 180 x 150 cm (6 x 5 ft).

Roger Lambelin Fisher Holmes sport. Vve Schwartz, 1890. Crimson blooms, with white-edged petals are fruity scented. 150 x 100 cm (5 x 3 ft).

Souvenir du Docteur Jamain Charles Lefebure seedling. Lacharme, 1865. Deep-purple, magnificently fragrant blooms. 180 x 100 cm (6 x 3 ft).

Vick's Caprice Sport of Archiduchesse Elisabeth d'Autriche. Vick, 1897. The double, pink and white-striped flowers may revert to plain pink. 180 x 120 cm (6 x 3 ft).

TEAS

The tea roses reached England in the early nineteenth century. The scent was similar to freshly packed tea. They had large leaves, long, pointed buds and beautiful flower form and colours, quite different from those of other roses; however they did not tolerate cold winters and had to be grown in conservatories, except in the warmer parts of the United States. Their high-centred form attracted the attention of hybridisers and soon many hybrid teas were available.

Catherine Mermet Guillot Fils, 1869. Flesh-pink blooms are large and shapely. 150 x 100 cm (5 x 3 ft).

Devoniensis (Magnolia Rose). Elinthii x an

unknown yellow China. T. Foster, 1838. Fragrant, creamy, double, white rose with a light blush at the centre. 150 x 100 cm (5 x 3 ft).

Duchesse de Brabant   Bernede, 1857. Very fragrant, cupped, clear, bright, rose-pink double blooms.

Hume's Blush Tea-scented China   R. x *odorata*. 1809. One of the original tea roses, this has pinkish white, double flowers produced singly or in twos or threes together.

Lady Hillingdon   Papa Gontier x Mme Hoste. Lowe and Shawyer, 1910. Fragrant, apricot-yellow flowers open from long, pointed buds. The foliage is bronze tinted. 120 x 100 cm (4 x 3 ft).

Maman Cochet   Marie van Houtte x Mme Lombard. S. Cochet, 1893. A scented, pale-pink rose with a deeper-pink centre, on a lemon-yellow base. 120 x 100 cm (4 x 3 ft).

Niphetos   Bougere, 1843. Fragrant, large, globular, white flowers are formed from pointed buds. 100 x 100 cm (3 x 3 ft).

Safrano   Park's Yellow Tea x Mme Desprez. Beauregard, 1839. Yellow buds form scented, single, white, star-shaped flowers, which with age become blushed and spotted with pink. 6 m (20 ft).

HYBRID MUSKS
These were the result of crossing a German rose, Trier, with hybrid teas and then with earlier varieties raised by Peter Lambert. They are very sweet-smelling, exceptionally free-flowering, recurrent-blooming bushes, producing large floribunda-like heads of spring roses with another wave of bloom in autumn on bushes that are broader than modern floribundas.

Ballerina   Parentage not available. Bentall, 1927. Scented, single, soft-pink, apple blossom-like flowers, with a white eye. 100 x 100 cm (3 x 3 ft).

Bishop Darlington   Aviateur Bleriot x Moonlight. 1926. Particularly fragrant, cupped, semi-double, creamy pink blooms with primrose overtones and bronze-tinted foliage. 150 x 150 cm (5 x 5 ft).

Buff Beauty   Raiser and parentage not registered. 1939. Produces clusters of double, buff to apricot-yellow, scented blooms, on arching canes against dark-green foliage.

Felicia   Trier x Ophelia. Pemberton, 1938. Clusters of scented, pink blooms are blended with salmon pink. 150 x 150 cm (5 x 5 ft).

Penelope   Ophelia x seedling. Pemberton, 1924. A scented rose producing large trusses of semi-double creamy apricot blooms. 180 x 120 cm (6 x 4 ft).

Prosperity   Marie-Jeanne x Perle des Jardins. Pemberton, 1919. Scented, creamy-blush, rosette flowers fade to white. There is another similar rose called Pink Prosperity which is bright pink.

Vanity   Chateau de Clos Vougeot x seedling. Pemberton, 1920. Trusses of bright pink, scented, single to semi-double blooms are produced on a tall open bush. 180 x 180 cm (6 x 6 ft).

MODERN SHRUB ROSES
These may be grown as shrubs, small climbers or pillar roses.

Clair Matin   Fashion x (Independence x Orange Triumph) x Phyllis Bide. M. L. Meilland, 1962. This produces clusters of scented, cupped, semi-double, pink flowers. The bush is recurrent blooming. 150 x 200 cm (5 x 6½ ft).

Cocktail   (Independence x Orange Triumph) x Phyllis Bide. M. L. Meilland, 1957. Single, crimson-primrose, scented blooms are produced on a recurrent-blooming bush with small, semi-glossy foliage. 120 x 120 cm (3 x 3 ft).

Golden Wings   Soeur Therese x (R. *spinosissima altaica* x Ormiston Roy). Shepherd, 1956. Large, single, pale-yellow blooms are deeper at their centre and show amber stamens. This is a continuous-blooming climber and is fragrant.

Nevada   Possibly R. *moyesii* x a hybrid tea but parentage not certain. P. Dot, 1927. This forms a large, mounding shrub covered in huge, creamy white, single flowers during spring with more later in the summer. 200 x 250 cm (6½ x 8 ft).

Sparrieshoop   (Baby Chateau x Else Poulsen) x Magnifica. Kordes, 1953. A shrub which can be used as a climber. The blooms are single, pink, large and fragrant. 180 x 180 cm (6 x 6 ft).

RAMBLERS AND CLIMBERS
These flower in summer only, late spring in some areas. The ramblers have small foliage and small flowers in clusters or trusses, during late spring or early summer. After flowering they produce new growth from the base of the plants. These growths flower in the following year while the older canes gradually die away. Well-known examples of the ramblers are the hybrids of R. *wichuraiana* (the Memorial rose) such as

Dorothy Perkins, Excelsa and Sanders White Rambler.

A second group of ramblers has larger flowers in smaller clusters, with occasional blooms after the first flowering. They flower earlier than the above, new growth occurs both at the base and as long canes higher up on the bush. They are hybrids from *R. luciae*. Examples are Alberic Barbier, Albertine and Emily Gray.

The scent in these roses emanates from the styles of the flowers which merge into a single column above the ovaries.

Many of these roses are grafted onto stems of different heights to be trained as weeping standard roses.

R. filipes Kiftsgate   E. Murrell, 1954. A huge rose with exceptional corymbs of creamy white, scented flowers followed by red hips. 9 m x 6 m (29 x 20 ft).

R. longicupsis   Introduced from China, 1915. Produces small, white blooms in very large corymbs late in the summer, followed by tiny red hips. 6 m (20 ft).

Alberic Barbier   *R. luciae* x Shirley Hibberd. Barbier, 1900. Yellow, pointed buds open to fragrant, pale-yellow, double flowers which fade to cream. 7.5 m (25 ft).

Albertine   *R. luciae* x Mrs Arthur Robert Waddell. Barbier, 1921. Coppery pink, strongly scented, double flowers are produced on a robust, branching grower. 6 m (20 ft).

Dorothy Perkins   *R. wichuraiana* x Mme Gabriel Luizet. Jackson and Perkins, 1901. A free-flowering rose, bearing masses of double, rose-pink blooms in large clusters. 4.5 m (15 ft).

Emily Gray   Jersey Beauty x Comtesse du Cayla. B. R. Cant, 1918. Produces double, buff-yellow flowers in clusters against bronze-tinted foliage. 4.5 m (15 ft).

Excelsa   Red Dorothy Perkins. Walsh, 1909. Like Dorothy Perkins, but with rose-red flowers. 5.5 m (18 ft).

Felicité et Perpétué   A sport of *R. sempervirens*. Jacques, 1827. Red-tinted buds, open to lightly fragrant, white pom-poms, produced either singly or in clusters. The foliage is almost evergreen. 4.5 m (15 ft).

Fortune's Double Yellow   (Beauty of Glazenwood, Gold of Ophir, San Rafael Rose). *R. x odorata pseudindica*. Introduced: Fortune, 1845. The

semi-double, orange-yellow blooms are shaded with salmon red and scented. 4.5 m (15 ft).

Ramona   (Red Cherokee). A sport of *R. amenonoides*. Dietrich and Turner, 1913. This has clematis-like, single, crimson blooms with a pink reverse. 4.5 m (15 ft).

Sanders White Rambler   Sanders and Sons, 1912. Generous clusters of rosette-shaped, fragrant, white flowers. 4.5 m (15 ft).

Seven Sisters   (*R. multiflora platyphylla*, *R. grevillei*). Introduced from China, 1817. The clusters of single flowers are in seven shades of lilac crimson, pink, and lilac white. A strong grower. 9 m (29 ft).

Veilchenblau   (Violet Blue). Crimson Rambler x unknown. J. C. Schmidt, 1909. Produces violet-blue, white-centred, small, semi-double, cupped blooms in generous trusses. An unusual colour. It has very few thorns. 4.5 m (15 ft).

Wedding Day   A hybrid of *R. sinowilsonii*. F. C. Stern, 1950. The yellow buds form star-shaped, single, white, scented flowers which in time, become blushed and spotted with pink.

NOISETTE CLIMBERS AND RAMBLERS
These are all recurrent-blooming roses.

Aimée Vibert   Champney's Pink Cluster x *R. sempervirens* hybrids. Vibert, 1828. Scented, medium-sized, pure-white, double flowers are produced in small clusters. 4.5 m (15 ft).

Alister Stella Gray   A. H. Gray, 1894. Yellow buds open to pale-yellow, fragrant flowers which fade to white and are produced in large heads. 4.5 m (15 ft).

Céline Forestier   Trouillard, 1842. Produces fragrant clusters of small, double, pale orange-yellow flowers with a deeper centre. 4.5 m (15 ft).

Crépuscule   Dubreuil, 1904. An adaptable rose useful as a pillar, ground cover, hedge, shrub or standard. The blooms are medium size in shades from palest orange to golden apricot.

Desprez à Fleurs Jaunes   Blush Noisette x *R. odorata ochroleuca*. Desprez, 1830. The flowers are scented, flat, double, button-eyed and yellow shaded with apricot. 5.5 m (18 ft).

Lamarque   Blush Noisette x Parks' Yellow Tea-scented China. Marechal, 1830. This produces clusters of small, double, white, fragrant blooms with pale-yellow centres. 4.5 m (15 ft).

Mme Alfred Carriere J. Schwartz, 1879. The double white, pink-tinted, cupped blooms are large and fragrant. It blooms throughout summer.

POLYANTHUS

These were the forerunners to modern floribundas and were mostly superseded when the latter developed large high-centred blooms. Polyanthus are almost continuously in flower.

Bloomfield Abundance Thomas, 1920. The difference between this and Cecile Brunner is that this has long, feathered extensions to each sepal. It is usually regarded as a sport of Cecile Brunner. 250 x 250 cm (8 x 8 ft).

Cameo A sport from Orleans Rose. De Ruiter, 1932. A dainty rose with clusters of semi-double, cupped, salmon-pink blooms which become orange pink. There is a climbing form.

Cecile Brunner (Mignon; Sweetheart Rose). *R. multiflora* x Mme de Tartas. Vve Ducher, 1881. Pink flowers have the high-centred form of a hybrid tea. It is a tea polyanthus. Height 100 to 200 cm (3 to 6½ ft).

Little White Pet P. Henderson, 1879. Red buds open to flat, pom-pom-like flowers, produced in clusters. 60 x 60 cm (2 x 2 ft).

Perle d'Or (Yellow Cecile Brunner). *R. multiflora* x Mme Falcot. Rambaud, 1883. Yellow flowers become lighter yellow when fully open. A vigorous tea polyanthus similar to Cecile Brunner in habit and flower form. 120 x 100 cm (4 x 3 ft).

The Fairy A sport of the rambler Lady Godiva. Bentall, 1932. Produces long arms of cupped, pink, semi-double blooms in large sprays. 75 cm (2½ ft).

Yvonne Rabier *R. wichuraiana* seedling x a polyanthus. Turbal, 1910. The white flowers are scented and have the suggestion of pale yellow at their centres. 120 x 100 cm (4 x 3 ft).

English or David Austin Roses

These modern shrub roses were hybridised by David Austin of the United Kingdom. His aim was to combine the characteristics of old garden roses — gallicas, damasks and others — with those of the repeat-flowering hybrid teas, floribundas, and climbers to produce repeat-flowering, fragrant blooms with old rose form. The blooms of David Austin roses may be deep or shallow, semi-double, single or full-petalled, cupped or rosette in form. There are pastel colours, rich pinks and yellows, crimsons and purples. Almost all these roses are scented and all are robust, vigorous plants — broader and taller than floribunda and hybrid tea roses. They may be treated as shrubs and many are also effective climbers. Tall varieties should be pruned lightly and continuously during spring and summer. Others are pruned by a third to half the length of their stems.

Abraham Darby Yellow Cushion x Aloha. 1985. Deeply cupped blooms are deep, peachy pink on the inner face and pale yellow on the reverse. Strong fragrance, robust with arching growth. 150 x 150 cm (5 x 5 ft) as a shrub; height 350 cm (11 ft) as a climber.

Canterbury (Monique x Constance Spry) x seedling. 1969. Fragrant, almost single, warm-pink blooms have boss of yellow stamens. 90 x 90 cm (3 x 3 ft).

Charles Austin Chaucer x Aloha. 1973. Large, double, apricot-tinged-pink, rosette blooms change to light pink with fruity fragrance. It is vigorous as a shrub or climber. 110–120 x 100 cm (3½–4 x 3¼ ft).

Cressida Conrad Ferdinand Meyer x Chaucer. 1983. Myrrh-scented, cupped, soft-pink blooms are apricot on the reverse. Use as climber or large shrub. 200 x 100 cm (6½ x 3 ft).

Cymbeline (Auslean). Unnamed seedling x Lilian Austin. 1982. Light-pink flowers are tinged brown. They are large and myrrh scented. 110 x 150 cm (3½ x 5 ft).

Gertrude Jekyll Wife of Bath x Comte de Chambord. 1986. This rose is so strongly damask scented it is grown commercially to manufacture perfume in Britain. Large rosette-shaped blooms are deep, warm pink or almost red in cool weather. 200 cm (6½ ft).

Graham Thomas (Ausmas). Charles Austin x (Iceberg x an unnamed English rose). 1983. Strongly tea-scented, cupped, pure-yellow blooms are overlaid apricot at first. Use as shrub or climber. Height over 200 cm (6½ ft).

Lilian Austin Aloha x The Yeoman. 1973. Salmon-pink, semi-double, scented blooms, shaded yellow at their centre. 110 x 110 cm (3½ x 3½ ft).

Mary Rose (Ausmary). Unnamed seedling x The Friar. 1983. Fragrant, cupped blooms of rose pink, are paler in autumn.

Moth Ash-pink, semi-double, almost single flowers open flat to reveal a central boss of stamens.

Yellow Button Wife of Bath x Chinatown. 1975. Blooms are light and deep yellow with yol-yellow centres. They are quartered, with a button-eye, and have a fruity fragrance. 90 x 90 cm (3 x 3 ft).

Yellow Charles Austin A sport of Charles Austin. 1981. Large-cupped, yellow flowers change to apricot, tinged with pink. May be used as a climber. Height 110–120 cm (3½–4 ft).

Cottage Roses

A modern class of continuous-blooming, almost-evergreen roses raised in Denmark by Poulsen Roser Aps, these are designed to suit small cottage gardens.

They are also strong, with disease-resistant foliage and are sufficiently vigorous to use on a large scale as ground covers, or to hold banks in place. They have a naturally rounded, mound-like form between 100 and 110 cm (3 and 3½ ft) square, and when planted at metre- (yard-) wide intervals make a charming low hedge or bed of colour. They are also lovely in the foreground of shrubbery or among perennials. Their small single and semi-double flowers have a distinctively Victorian character and they are easy to care for, since pruning amounts to a light overall shearing just prior to new growth commencing. They are named after their colours.

Apricot/Lemon Semi-double, 150 cm (5 ft).

Apricot Single, 100 cm (3 ft).

Soft Pale Pink Single (5 petals), 40 cm (16 in) high x 60 cm (24 in) wide ground cover.

Rose Pink Single, 100 cm (3 ft).

White Single, 100 cm (3 ft).

ROSES FOR SPECIAL PURPOSES

ABBREVIATIONS

HT	Hybrid Tea
Gr	Grandiflora
F	Floribunda
M	Miniature
CLG	Climbing

Standard

Hybrid tea and grandiflora varieties.

RED
Alexander
Avon
Chrysler Imperial
Fragrant Cloud
Mr Lincoln
Oklahoma
Olympiad
Papa Meilland
Precious Platinum
The Riverview Centenary Rose

PINK
Aotearoa
Aquarius
Carla
Chicago Peace
Eiffel Tower

Electron
Friendship
Maria Callas
Peter Frankenfeld
Pink Parfait
Portrait
Princess Margaret of England
Queen Elizabeth
Sheer Bliss
Showtime
Sonia
Tiffany
Touch of Class

MAUVE
Blue Moon
Fragrant Plum
Lagerfeld
Paradise

WHITE
Crystalline
Honor
Pascali
Pristine
Valerie Swane

**APRICOT/YELLOW/
ORANGE**
Amatsu-Otome
Anne Marie Trechslin
Apollo

Arizona
Beauté
Brandy
Broadway
Diamond Jubilee
Gold Medal
Kambala
Lolita
Mojave
Orana Gold
Peace
Royal Dane
Shining Hour
Sutter's Gold

FANCY AND BI-COLOUR
Brigadoon
Double Delight
Mon Cheri
Paradise
Perfect Moment

Weeping Standard

PINK
Dorothy Perkins
Renae

WHITE
Sea Foam

Climbing

RED
Altissimo
Avon
Black Boy
Chrysler Imperial
Mister Lincoln
Oklahoma
Olé
Papa Meilland

PINK
Blossomtime
Carla
Cecile Brunner
Chicago Peace
Handel
Maria Callas
Peter Frankenfeld
Princess Margaret of England
Queen Elizabeth
Sonia
Tiffany

WHITE
Iceberg
Pascali

APRICOT/YELLOW/ORANGE
Mojave
Peace
Rosa banksiae lutea
Sutter's Gold

FANCY AND BI-COLOUR
Red Gold

Pillar and Column

RED
Altissimo
Paul's Scarlet Climber

PINK
Titian

APRICOT/YELLOW/ORANGE
Golden Showers

Light or Filtered Shade Tolerant

Altissimo CLG
Amatsu-Otome HT
Amorette M
Anne Marie Trechslin HT
Aotearoa HT
Apollo HT
Aquarius HT
Arizona HT
Avon HT
Beauté HT
Big Purple HT
Black Boy CLG
Blossomtime CLG
Blue Moon HT
Brandy HT
Carla HT
Cecile Brunner CLG
Century Two HT
Charisma F
Class Act F
Confetti F
Cricket M
Crystalline HT
Double Delight HT
Eiffel Tower HT
Electron HT
Foster's Melbourne Cup F
Fragrant Cloud HT
Fragrant Plum HT
Friendship HT
Gay Princess F
Gold Medal HT
Golden Gloves F
Grande Amore HT
Handel CLG
Hans Christian Andersen F
Holy Toledo M
Honor HT
Iceberg F

Kaikoura M
Kambala HT
Kentucky Derby HT
Kirsten F
Ko's Yellow M
Lagerfeld HT
Lavender Lace M
Lilli Marlene F
Little Red Devil M
Lolita HT
Maria Callas HT
Marina F
Mary MacKillop F
Mary Marshall M
Michelle Joy HT
Mister Lincoln HT
Mon Cheri HT
Ocarina M
Oklahoma HT
Olé HT
Olympiad HT
Orana Gold HT
Otago M
Pascali HT
Paul's Scarlet Climber CLG
Petite Folie M
Perfect Moment HT
Pleasure F
Portrait HT
Precious Platinum HT
Pristine HT
Queen Elizabeth Gr
Red Devil HT
Rosa banksia lutea CLG
Roundelay HT
Royal Dane HT
Samantha F
Scarlet Queen Elizabeth Gr
Sheer Bliss HT
Shining Hour HT
Showtime HT
Simplicity F
Sonia Gr
Starina M
Sundowner Gr
Sutter's Gold HT
The Riverview Centenary Rose HT
Tiffany HT
Titian CLG
Touch of Class HT
Tournament of Roses Gr
White Simplicity F

Tropical

Anne Marie Trechslin HT
Aotearoa HT
Arizona Gr
Avon HT
Friendship HT
Gold Medal HT
Holy Toledo M
Kentucky Derby HT
Olé HT
Papa Meilland HT
Queen Elizabeth Gr
Roundelay HT
Scarlet Queen Elizabeth Gr
Showtime HT
Sundowner Gr
The Riverview Centenary Rose
  HT

Exhibition

Bing Crosby HT
Blue Moon HT
Brandy HT
Brigadoon HT
Carla HT
Century II HT
Chicago Peace HT
Crystalline HT
Double Delight HT
Fragrant Plum HT
Grande Amore HT
Honor HT
Lagerfeld HT
Lanvin HT
Lolita HT
Mister Lincoln HT
Misty HT
Mon Cheri HT
Papa Meilland HT
Perfect Moment HT
Precious Platinum HT
Pristine HT
Red Devil HT
Sheer Bliss HT
Shining Hour HT
Sunspray M
Touch of Class HT
Valerie Swane HT
Voodoo HT

Tubs

Amorette M
Apricot Nectar F
Confetti F
Cricket M
Foster's Melbourne Cup F
Foxy Lady M
Gay Princess F
Guletta M
Hans Christian Andersen F
Holy Toledo M
Iceberg F
Kaikoura M
Kirsten F
Ko's Yellow M
Lavender Lace M
Lilli Marlene F
Little Red Devil M
Magic Carousel M
Marlena F
Mary Marshall M
Otago M
Petite Folie M
Red Gold F
Regensberg F
Saratoga F
Sonoma F
Starina M

Hedges

Amatsu-Otome HT
Anne Marie Trechslin HT
Aotearoa HT
Apollo HT
Aquarius HT
Arizona HT
Avon HT
Carla HT
Charisma F
Chicago Peace HT
Chrysler Imperial HT
Class Act F
Double Delight HT
Eiffel Tower HT
Electron HT
Foster's Melbourne Cup F
Fragrant Cloud HT
Fragrant Plum HT
Friesia F

Gay Princess F
Grande Amore HT
Hans Christian Andersen F
Iceberg F
Ingrid Bergman HT
Kambala HT
Lilli Marlene F
Maria Callas HT
Marina F
Marmalade HT
Mary MacKillop F
Michelle Joy HT
Mister Lincoln HT
Oklahoma HT
Olé HT
Olympiad HT
Orana Gold HT
Papa Meilland HT
Pascali HT
Peace HT
Peter Frankenfeld HT
Pink Parfait Gr
Portrait HT
Princess Margaret of England HT
Queen Elizabeth Gr
Red Gold F
Roundelay HT
Royal Dane HT
Saratoga F
Satchmo F
Scarlet Queen Elizabeth Gr
Showtime HT
Simplicity F
Sonia Gr
Sutter's Gold HT
The Riverview Centenary Rose
  HT
Tiffany HT
Touch of Class HT
Tournament of Roses Gr
White Simplicity F

Borders

Apart from those listed here all
floribundas make lovely borders
depending on height required. All
the miniatures are excellent dwarf
borders.

Amorette M
Apricot Nectar F

Charisma F
Confetti F
Cricket M
Foster's Melbourne Cup F
Holy Toledo M
Kaikoura M
Ko's Yellow M
Lavender Lace M
Little Red Devil M
Magic Carousel M
Marlena F
Mary Marshall M
Otago M
Petite Folie M
Regensberg F
Simplicity F
Sonoma F
Starina M

Screen

Altissimo CLG
Anne Marie Trechslin HT
Aquarius HT
Blossomtime CLG
Blue Moon HT
Cecile Brunner CLG
Eiffel Tower HT
Friendship HT
Kentucky Derby HT
Misty HT
Olympiad HT
Papa Meilland HT
Pascali HT
Portrait HT
Queen Elizabeth Gr
Red Devil HT
Roundelay HT
Samantha HT
Scarlet Queen Elizabeth Gr
Sundowner Gr
Voodoo HT

Bedding

Miniatures are suitable for small
scale/low height bedding but
floribundas are more colourful
where taller budding is needed.

Amorette M
Anne Marie Trechslin HT
Apricot Nectar F
Brandy HT
Charisma F
Confetti F
Cricket M
Foster's Melbourne Cup F
Foxy Lady M
Friesia F
Gay Princess F
Holy Toledo M
Iceberg F
Kaikoura M
Ko's Yellow M
Lavender Lace M
Lilli Marlene F
Little Red Devil M
Magic Carousel M
Marina F
Marlena F
Mary Marshall M
Ocarina M
Otago M
Petite Folie M
Pink Parfait Gr
Red Gold F
Regensberg F
Saratoga F
Satchmo F
Simplicity F
Sonoma F
Starina M

Mass Planting

Amatsu-Otome HT
Arizona HT
Avon HT
Beauté HT
Blue Moon HT
Candy Stripe HT
Carla HT
Century II HT
Chicago Peace HT
Chrysler Imperial HT
Crystalline HT
Diamond Jubilee HT
Double Delight HT

Eiffel Tower HT
Electron HT
Fragrant Cloud HT
Fragrant Plum HT
Friendship HT
Grande Amore HT
Ingrid Bergman HT
Kentucky Derby HT
Kirsten F
Lagerfeld HT
Lanvin HT
Lolita HT
Maria Callas HT
Marmalade HT
Mary MacKillop F
Michelle Joy HT
Mister Lincoln HT
Misty HT
Mojave HT
Mon Cheri HT
Oklahoma HT
Olé HT
Olympiad HT
Orana Gold HT
Papa Meilland HT
Paradise HT
Pascali HT
Peace HT
Perfect Moment HT
Peter Frankenfeld HT
Portrait HT
Precious Platinum HT
Princess Margaret HT
Pristine HT
Queen Elizabeth Gr
Red Devil HT
Roundelay HT
Royal Dane HT
Samantha HT
Scarlet Queen Elizabeth Gr
Sheer Bliss HT
Shining Hour HT
Showtime HT
Sonia Gr
Sutter's Gold HT
The Riverview Centenary Rose
    HT
Tiffany HT
Valerie Swane HT
Voodoo HT
White Simplicity F

APPENDIX 4

ROSE PRODUCERS AND SUPPLIERS

Australia

Swane's Nursery, Dural, New South Wales 2158
Ross Roses, Willunga, South Australia 5172
Walter Duncan Roses, Watervale, South Australia 5452
Rainbow Roses, Ferntree Gully, Victoria 3156
Treloar Roses Pty Ltd, Portland, Victoria 3305

New Zealand

Avenue Roses, Levin
Bell Roses, Whenuapai, Auckland
D & S Nurseries, Ongaonga, Napier
Egmont Roses, New Plymouth
Frank Mason & Sons Ltd, Feilding
South Pacific Rose Nurseries Ltd, Christchurch
Tasman Bay Roses, Motueka, near Nelson
Trevor Griffith Nurseries, Timaru

United States

The Antique Rose Emporium, Brenham, Texas 77833
Armstrong's Roses, Somis, California 93066
Carroll Gardens, Westminster, Maryland 21157
Conard-Pyle Co, West Grove, Pennsylvania 19390-0904
Donovan's Roses, Shreveport, Louisiana 71133-7800

Farmer Seed and Nursery Co, Fairbault, Minnesota 55021
Fred Edmunds Inc, Wilsonville, Oregon 97070
Gloria Dee Nursery, High Falls, New York 12440
Hastings, Atlanta, Georgia 30302-4274
Heritage Rose Gardens, Branscomb, California 95417
High Country Rosarium, Denver, Colorado 80218
Historical Roses Inc, Painsville, Ohio 44077
Interstate Nursery, Hamburg, Iowa 51640-0208
Jackson & Perkins, Medford, Oregon 9751
Justice Miniature Roses, Wilsonville, Oregon 97070
Kelly Brothers Nurseries Inc, Dansville, Kentucky 14437
Lamb Nurseries, Spokane, Washington 99202
Liggett's Rose Nursery, San Jose, California 95125
Limberlost Roses, Van Nuys, California 91406
Lowe's Own Root Roses, Nashua, New Hampshire 03062
McDaniel's Miniature Roses, Lemon Grove, California 92045
Mellinger's, North Lima, Ohio 44452-9731
Miller Nurseries, Cananadaigua, New York 14424
Nor-East Miniature Roses, Rowley, Massachusetts 10969
Richard Owen Nurseries, Bloomington, Illinois
Roseway Nurseries Inc, Woodland, Washington Wa 98674
Sequoia Nurseries, Visalia, California 93277
Stocking Rose Nurseries, San José, California 95133
P. O. Tate Nursery, Tyler, Texas 75708
Thomasville Nurseries, Thomasville, Georgia 31799
Roses of Yesterday and Today, Watsonville, California 95076

United Kingdom

Anderson's Rose Nurseries, Aberdeen AB1 9QT

David Austin Roses, Albrighton, Wolverhampton WV7 3HB

Peter Beales Roses, Attleborough, Norfolk NR17 1AY

Cants Roses, Colchester, Essex CO4 5FB

James Cocker & Sons, Whitemyres, Aberdeen AB9 2XH

Dickson Nurseries Ltd, Newtownards, Northern Ireland BT23 4SS

English Cottage Roses Ltd, Stapleford Lane, Toton, Beeston, Nottinghamshire NG9 5FD

Fryer's Nurseries Ltd, Knutsford, Cheshire WA16 0SX

Gandys Roses, Lutterworth, Leicestershire AL3 7PS

Hillier's Nurseries (Winchester) Ltd, Winchester, Hampshire SO51 9PA

R. Harkness and C., Hitchin, Hertfordshire SG4 0JT

C. & K. Jones, Tarvin, Chester CH3 8JF

LeGrice Roses, North Walsham, Norfolk NR28 0DR

John Mattock Ltd, Nuneham Courtney, Oxfordshire OX9 9PY

Rearsby Roses Ltd, Rearsby, Leicestershire LE7 8YP

Roses du Temps Passé, Stafford ST19 9LG

John Sandy (Roses) Ltd, Almondsbury, Bristol BS12 4DA

Wheatcroft Ltd, Edwalton, Nottingham NG12 4DE

Warley Rose Gardens, Brentwood, Essex CM13 3JH

Canada

Aubin Nurseries Ltd, PO Box 1089, Carman, Manitoba R0G 090, phone (204) 745 6703

Carl Pallek & Son Nursery, PO Box 137, Virgil, Ontario L0S 1T0, phone (416) 468 7262

Hortico Inc, 723 Robson Road, Waterdown, Ontario L0R 2H1, phone (416) 689 6984; fax (416) 689 6566, $3 for catalogue.

Morden Nurseries, PO Box 1270, Morden, Manitoba R0G 1J0, phone (204) 822 3311, limited listing of roses, $2 for catalogue

Pickering Nurseries Inc, 670 Kingston Road, Hwy 2, Pickering, Ontario L1V 1A6, phone (416) 839 2111

Rose Farm, 26746 13th Avenue, Aldergrove, BC V0X 1A0, phone (604) 856 2631

Select Roses, 22771 38th Avenue, RR 9, Langley, BC V3A 6H5, phone (604) 530 5786

Walter le Mire Roses, Highway 3, Oldcastle, Ontario N0R 1L0, phone (519) 737 6788

Wilson's Nursery, 6227 Hopedale Road, Sardis, BC V2R 1B3, phone (604) 823 6359

INDEX

(Page numbers in **bold type** indicate main references. Page numbers in *italics* indicate illustrations.)

2. General Index